EDMUND WILSON

EUROPE WITHOUT BAEDEKER

SKETCHES, AMONG THE RUINS
OF ITALY, GREECE & ENGLAND

LONDON
SECKER AND WARBURG
1948

FIRST PUBLISHED IN ENGLAND 1948 BY
MARTIN SECKER AND WARBURG LTD.
7, JOHN STREET, LONDON, W.C.1

PRINTED IN GREAT BRITAIN BY
BARNICOTTS LIMITED
THE WESSEX PRESS . TAUNTON
AND
BOUND BY KEY & WHITING LTD.
LONDON

NOTE

THIS book is the result of a trip undertaken for the *New Yorker* magazine in the spring and summer of 1945. Chapters 1, 2, 4, 10, 11, 12, 13 and 14 were printed first in the *New Yorker*, but here appear in a revised and expanded form. An abridged version of Chapter 3 was printed in *Town & Country*, and parts of Chapters 3 and 9 have been printed in *Horizon*.

The reporting of the things that I heard and saw is as faithful as I could make it, except in the cases of the third and fourth sections of the chapter on British officials, in which I have used fictitious names and shuffled personalities a little, and of the chapter on U.N.R.R.A in the Abruzzi, which, though derived from fact, is fiction. Since my experience of the Abruzzi is too limited for me to work up imaginary localities which would seem satisfactorily representative, I have resorted to the perhaps questionable device of planting an invented story in real places that are called by their names and are for the most part accurately described. The people are not, however, the real ones, and I must apologise to the U.N.R.R.A. workers at Aquila, to the officer in command of the Aquila hotel and to the *sindaco* of the town of Orsogna for the roles that my characters are made to play. I have no reason to believe that the relations between British and Americans in Aquila were such as I have shown in this story; but the things that I have here made happen are the kind of things that often happened, and I have tried to create a typical situation.

CONTENTS

NOTES ON LONDON AT THE END OF THE WAR

THE English way of getting things done is quite distinct from the American way. It is quieter, more orderly, politer. When our ship was about to dock at London, a British pilot came aboard to take us up the Thames. The deckhands had been cleaning the deck and draining the water out of a hole next to the ladder up which he was to climb, and one of the sailors now closed the hole. The pilot, as he appeared over the side, said to the Norwegian sailor, "Good morning, thanks for stopping the water," and went immediately about his business on the bridge. I was somehow impressed by this and tried to think what an American would have said. He would probably have said nothing at all or would have made some kind of wisecrack. And so, when the officials of the port came aboard, it seemed to me that one's dealings with officials in England were pleasanter and more expeditious than with those of any other country. Even when they are holding you up, there is no strain and no friction. The officials of other countries tend to behave as if they assumed you were a crook, but the British officials look up at you with a candid and friendly eye which seems to assume that you are honest. I had the impression later, in London, when I saw people getting their ration books and complying with other wartime regulations, that the whole organisation of life for the war had been handled in this same calm and careful way. Compared to England after nearly five years of food rationing, fuel restrictions and the rest, the United States, in its first pangs of privation, seemed hysterical, uncertain and confused.

I stayed with a friend in London, who had been in the Ministry of Information. There arrived among his mail, the first morning, a pamphlet with the following title: *Address of the Honorable Archibald MacLeish, Assistant Secretary of State, Before the Annual Meeting of the Association of American Colleges, Atlantic City, New Jersey, January 10, 1945.* He amused himself by reading me passages and demanding, "Now, what does that mean?": "If the direct relations of peoples to peoples which modern communications permit are relations of understanding and confidence, so that the men and women of the world feel each other's presence and trust each other's

purposes and believe that the common cause of all the people everywhere is peace, then any reasonably intelligent organisation of the
world for peace will work. If, however, the direct relations of the
peoples with each other are relations of doubt and suspicion and
misunderstanding then no international organisation the genius of
man can contrive can possibly succeed. . . . What is unfortunate
about the current designation (of culture) is its suggestion to certain
minds that a programme of cultural relations is a decoration, a frill,
an ornament added to the serious business of the foreign relations of
the United States. You gentlemen, who know that a nation's culture
is a nation's character, would not so interpret it but others do. And
when they do, they endanger the best hope this country now possesses
of preparing the climate of understanding in which peace can breathe.
The people of the five continents and the innumerable islands can
only live together peacefully in the close and urgent contact of
modern intercommunication, if they feel behind the jangle and
vibration of the constant words the living men and women. It is our
principal duty, because it is our principal opportunity, to make that
sense of living men and women real. Our country, with its great
institutions of education and of culture, is prepared as are few others,
to undertake the work that must be done. If we will undertake it,
believing in it with our hearts as well as with our heads, we can
create, not only peace, but the common understanding which is the
only guarantee that peace will last."

What MacLeish was trying to say was that radio and aviation
could help bring the nations together as well as enable them to make
war more effectively; but this idea, already vague, had been expanded to nine pages of sheer verbalising nonsense. It is like one of
those great wads of spun sugar that are impaled upon little sticks
and sold to children at Coney Island. It is embarrassing for a
American to arrive in Europe and find that this is what we have been
sending them. The Atlantic Charter is not much better.

*   *   *

There is about London to-day a certain flavour of Soviet Moscow.
It surprises the Londoners if you remark on this and does not
particularly please them. But people told me at the American
Embassy that several other visitors who had been in Russia had said
the same sort of thing. The regimentation and the tension imposed by
the resistance to Germany have produced certain results very
similar to those of the effort, during the twenties and thirties, to

make the Soviet Union self-dependent. The people look rather shabby, but almost everybody looks equally shabby. A great number are working for the government, and everyone has a definite task. There is the atmosphere of emergency and transition to which everybody has settled down; many things are left undone or unfinished— in London the repair of buildings, in Moscow the carrying out of civic projects—leaving what would in normal times be regarded as intolerable eyesores. There is a great deal of getting oneself registered and of having to have passes in order to do things, and people are always lining up and waiting for hours in queues. There is also the relative democracy of manners—one of the striking changes in London—of people in the same boat who cannot afford to be too rude to one another, all threatened by a common danger and obliged to work together.

The English, since the war, have, also, been somewhat shut in from the rest of the world, as the Soviet Russians were. Their newspapers to-day are as meagre, though not so misleading, as the Russian ones; their sense of what the other countries are like and of what is going on outside England seems to have become rather dim. People who have been living in London through all or most of the years of the war—unable even to go to the seaside: a great hardship, apparently, for Londoners—all complain of a kind of claustrophobia; and young people in government offices who have had to give up to the war five years of that part of their lives which is usually more pleasantly employed, show the same mixture of boredom with devotion as the young workers for the Soviet economy toward the end of the second Five-Year Plan. And, as in Moscow, there are women in pants and the problem of neglected children. There is also the quietness of everybody, the submissiveness, the patience, the acceptance. The parks seem muted, like Russian parks. In the evening people lie on the grass or stroll along the paths or go boating on the Serpentine or play a primitive form of baseball called rounders, and are almost as soundless as the rabbits that munch grass in an enclosure. Even the American soldiers playing the American form of baseball are much less noisy than they would be at home.

*　　　*　　　*

I had forgotten what a pleasant city London was. No doubt it comes to seem more attractive as New York becomes consistently less so. From the moment a New Yorker is confronted with almost any large city of Europe, it is impossible for him to pretend to him-

self that his own city is anything other than an unscrupulous real-
estate speculation—whereas a capital like London is a place in
which people are supposed to live and enjoy some recreation and
comfort rather than merely to feed the bank accounts of landlords.
The green parks and the open squares that interlace the whole West
End seem enchanting after the windowed expressionless walls, the
narrow crowded streets, of New York. The best that Mr. Moses has
been able to do, admirable though it is, seems pathetic beside, say,
Kensington Gardens, which provide a real escape into the country,
not a mere space for benches and asphalt walks. The moist air, which
softens form and deepens colour, gives all these parks a special
charm, as one sees them under pearly clouds in the pale-blue sky of
an early April evening or, later, fringed with purple lilacs and studded
with white-blossoming chestnuts, amid turf soft and dense like the
air. And though a good deal of fun, at one time or another, has been
made of the London statues by people like Osbert Sitwell and Max
Beerbohm, it is cheering to a New Yorker with a depressed recollec-
tion of the figure of Fitz-Greene Halleck in Central Park, to find,
within a short walk in London, monuments to four English poets—
Chaucer, Milton, Shakespeare and Byron—and even allegorical
statues of the conventional public kind which give a certain effect of
vitality: the bronze Victory on one of the big arches driving her
horses into the sky and the Saint George of World War I killing a
dragon with the Kaiser's moustaches. You realise that the English,
through such symbols, almost as much as the French, have managed
to keep in the air an admiration for human excellence and an
imaginative vision of history. There is, however, one mechanical
monument which stands out among these human ones as a bleak
unassimilable block—a statue to the Royal Artillery in the shape of a
huge howitzer gun. This suggests that the war just ending may
eventually bring, for its memorials, bronze bombing planes, marble
tanks and granite anti-aircraft batteries. You have already, in fact,
something of the kind in the great war monument in Edinburgh
Castle—which I saw on a trip to the North—where there are yards
and yards of bas-reliefs of men with trench helmets, machine-guns
and gas masks, all the complicated unsightly accoutrements in use
in the last war. You feel here a definite break in the tradition of
human heroism: the armoured knights with their plumes and beaked
helmets were still caricatures of the human animal; but the big age
of engineering has reached the point, in England as elsewhere, of
getting this animal quite out of sight. An appropriate monument for
the next world war might be simply an enormous rocket which

would never have been touched by human hands from the moment it had been shot from its stand.

*   *   *

The effect of being attacked from the air by rockets and flying bombs must be something quite new in sensations. While our ship was lying in the Thames on a mild and quiet April day, a rocket went off somewhere not far away among the streets of little London houses on which we were looking out; and the pilot mentioned to someone the next morning that another had just passed overhead. When we got off the boat, we were told that the tram-line was now blocked, due to the blowing-up two days before of the bridge at the end of the street. It would hardly be correct to use, in connection with these automatic explosives, the word "nightmarish" which is so often called in to convey the idea of horror. A nightmare involves apprehension: the terror must always be expected. The Londoners say that, in the case of the Blitz, you were dealing with other human beings, could see them coming and could at least try to do something: a relationship between com-batants was established, so that a strategy could be evolved. But the "doodle-bugs" or flying bombs, and, even more, the rockets, came as a disruption completely irrelevant, completely unpredict-able, in even an emergency pattern of life. With the rockets there was nothing you could do: you could not either hear them or see them, and you might just as well not think of them at all. Though when you walked through one of those pleasant parks or squares that you were in the habit of passing every day, it might be a shock to find there a sudden great gaping ulcer, the crater of a V-2. Or you might, on some other occasion, be knocked flat in the street and stunned and have to be carried away, or you might be sitting at home and have all your clothes blown off and your skin peppered with masonry and plaster, or you might be annihilated. There were no crises of danger, it was constant; and people had to learn to live with it as a strain from which there was no escape. Nothing, of course, could have been further from the attitude of London during the days of the V-2 rockets than the atmosphere of abject panic described by German propaganda. At the time the V-2's were falling, there was an exhibi-tion in Oxford Street which showed a diagram and model of the rocket and photographs of some of the damage; and curious people were dropping in, very much as they did on the waxworks and the fortune-telling machines.

But those who know what the Germans were preparing say that, if they had gone on with their programme, London would have been rendered uninhabitable. A commission which visited the Pas-de-Calais, after that part of the coast had been cleared, found a whole hillside studded with giant guns, fixed in their positions and aimed at London and capable of firing five or six projectiles a minute; and, in another place, a hilltop that had been scooped out and equipped with rocket sites for some larger type of weapon than V-2's.

*   *   *

The London theatre, to a New Yorker, is amazing. It used to be very much less interesting than ours, but it is at present incomparably better. Our stage has been demoralised by Hollywood: no one really, any more, takes it seriously. We have very few producers or directors who would even like to do a good job, and these rarely get to the point of trying. But in London the theatre still exists, and the war has had the effect of stimulating it to special excellence. With so much of tight routine in their lives, so little margin for vacation or luxury, and feeling somewhat helpless in their hemmed-in world, the Londoners—again like the Russians—have needed the theatre for gaiety, for colour, and also—what is very important and what, for educated people, the American films can't supply—for the vicarious participation in the drama of personal emotions which is possible only in peacetime, when men and women are relatively free.

In the first place, they put on in London plays that are really first-rate. During the month that I spent there, it was possible to see three plays of Shakespeare's (as well as a film of *Henry V*), John Webster's *The Duchess of Malfi*, two plays of Ibsen, two of Bernard Shaw, one of Chekhov, one of Strindberg and, on a lower but still respectable level, two plays by Noel Coward, Somerset Maugham's *The Circle*, and a dramatisation of Jane Austen's *Emma*. Some of these were brilliantly done, and all that I saw were produced with a kind of theatrical competence that is almost obsolete on Broadway. Not only have the Londoners at the present time an appetite for serious plays, they are also intelligently interested in acting. I found everywhere discussion of actors in their roles, of a kind that has not been heard at home since the early years of the twenties. I saw half a dozen of London's top actors: Ralph Richardson, Laurence Olivier, John Gielgud, Cecil Trouncer, Sybil Thorndike, and Peggy Ashcroft—performing in repertory companies in which they were as likely to play small parts as big ones and had none of the fantastic billing which has done so much to spoil our theatre. *Richard III* and *The Duchess of Malfi* were astonishing to me who had just come from New York and who had not for years—if ever—heard Elizabethan blank verse read without losing the rhythm of poetry and yet with every line comprehensible and effective as human speech. With us this tradition has been lost from the time, I suppose, when John Barrymore was persuaded to play *Hamlet* as if it were all in prose. And to-day a Shakespearean production usually combines a variety of accents, American, British and ham, and a variety of metrical or non-metrical conceptions of the rhythm of Shakespeare's lines in a way that does the poet little justice. But Shakespeare in England is all of a piece and quite natural on the stage, as it never is with us. It is strange to find that the speeches sound more personal and forcible and practical, more alive at the present time, than the people of contemporary London, who beside them seem thin and dim.

Unlikely though it may appear, the Elizabethan *Duchess of Malfi*, not professionally performed in many years, is probably the most fascinating show to be seen on the stage in London. It seems to me, in fact, one of the best productions that I have ever seen of anything anywhere. You would think that this old tragedy of blood, with its grotesque horrors and highly wrought poetry, is the kind of thing of which a revival would be sure to turn out boring or comic; but this production by the poet George Rylands is so immensely imaginative and skilful and the acting at the same time so dynamic and so disciplined that it holds you from beginning to end. You might have thought that Webster's style was too precious for the stage, but every speech has its force and its point. And they somehow get the emotions of wartime into both *Richard III* and the *Duchess*: the speeding-up of crime and horror, the cumulative obsession with grievance and revenge. No: *The Duchess of Malfi* is not funny. You understand what Gertrude Stein means when she says that she reread, during the war, in France, Shakespeare's tragedies and historical plays and realised for the first time that human life could be like that. One sees the fall of *Richard III* just as Hitler is staggering to defeat; and, in *The Duchess of Malfi*, the scene where her doom is announced to the Duchess amidst the drivellings of the liberated madmen, at the moment of the exposé of the German concentration camps.

Thus the theatre, like everything else, gives the impression of being breathless and strained, of being ridden by fatigue and fear. One can gauge in a different way how desperate the pressure must be when one goes to a contemporary play which is intended to be

consoling. The *Wind of Heaven*, by Emlyn Williams, well done
though it, too, was, depressed me by attempting to exploit the need
of the people for something to believe in, something to assure them
that, after all, there is a merciful God behind the world. Mr. Williams
makes a Messiah appear in Wales at the time of the Crimean War:
a saintly child who can cure the cholera and about whom is heard in
the air the sound of celestial music. But you remember, when you
go out of the theatre into the blacked-out London streets, that there
is no Messiah there.

*   *   *

In general, what I have seen of the artistic and literary world,
dwindled and starved though it is, is impressive through its good
faith and sobriety. These people have been living on the threshold of
death, and they have had to pursue their work under the threat of
defeat by the Germans and the suppression of their free press, and
with, in any event, no prospect of immediate reward in either money
or fame. There is, however, as in the case of the theatre, a real need
that they may take pride in serving.

Here the training of so many of them at Oxford and Cambridge
has stood them in good stead. If they are not, so far as I know,
turning out anything quite first-rate, they are not letting their
standards down—whereas, with us, even the people of talent who have
escaped Henry Luce and Hollywood have sometimes inebriated themselves with a frenzy of war propaganda. There are several good
English writers who do literary articles for the newspapers, but they
do them so extremely badly that one can hardly recognise their
hands, and this does not seem to affect their other work. What is
fatal to the American writer is to be brilliant at disgraceful or
second-rate jobs. A man who has been to Oxford is always likely to
keep a certain residuum that is not much affected by change or by a
different intellectual climate. It is a learning that involves some
wisdom: a detachment toward geography and history and a steady
appreciation of those products of the human mind that outlast
societies and periods. You can talk to him, more or less, no matter
what is happening at the moment and whether or not you share his
opinions. But with the kind of American writer who has had no
education to speak of, you are unable to talk at all once Hollywood
or Luce has got him.

It was also reassuring and pleasant to hear Elizabeth Bowen say
that, except for some disagreeable moments when "one of those

humming things" had landed near her, she had enjoyed London during the war, "Everything is very quiet, the streets are never crowded, and the people one dislikes are out of town."

*　　　*　　　*

I listened, at a literary party, to a conversation between two writers who were comparing notes about their experiences in the volunteer fire brigades. They had both been to public schools, and they agreed that it was quite different from "school." I gathered that what was lacking was the spirit of the school team: the cockneys who were sometimes in command merely counted on people to do the right thing in a more matter-of-fact way. Such a conversation could hardly have taken place between graduates of American prep schools, in their late thirties as these men were, because even an expensive education does not usually unfit Americans to work with other kinds of Americans and also because at that age Americans would not still be looking back to their school days.

This reversion to public school memories is a conspicuous and curious feature of the recent writing of the English. I cannot remember that the public school background played any important role in the literature of the earlier period that I was nourished on in my teens. That was the generation of Wells and Bennett, Shaw and Chesterton, Kipling and Masefield. None of these men had been to Oxford or Cambridge; none, with the exception of Kipling, had been to a public school—and the brutal and raucous version of the second-rate Army and Navy school that we get in *Stalky & Co.* is as different as possible from the Winchester and Eton that we read about in the later writers. In the first decades of the twentieth century, the British middle classes had something to say for themselves: they did not feel any need to identify themselves with the official governing class. But—what, at first sight, seems queer to an American—these writers have had no successors unless you count someone like J. B. Priestley, who does not particularly interest the people who found some profit in the earlier crop of writers. Instead, you had Strachey and Virginia Woolf, Forster and Harold Nicolson, Aldous Huxley and T. E. Lawrence, all of them—except Mrs. Woolf, who had however, her university connections—educated at Oxford or Cambridge, and in most cases deriving from the official class or actively engaged in its work. All these have a tone in common, a common social-intellectual atmosphere, which are not at all the tone and atmosphere of the Bennett-Wells-Shaw generation. And the following generations of Connolly, Orwell and Auden grew up in that atmosphere, too, and have never quite lost that tone. The more vigorous ones, in their various ways, broke away from the Bloomsbury circle; but, confronted by the coming catastrophe, they tended at first to creep back into the womb of the public schools—see the memories of Isherwood and Connolly and the earlier poems of Auden—of which they gave rather an equivocal account, inspired partly by a childlike nostalgia and partly by an impulse, perhaps childish, too—one noticed it first in Strachey's essay on Arnold— to blame the schools for their own inadequacies and for everything that was wrong with England. On the way over, I read a book by a young man named Denton Welch, a good deal of which is occupied with his school days and which presents an extreme case in point. Denton Welch was desperately dissatisfied with school and kept trying to get away, yet he loves to remember his boyhood and seems to want to remain a baby. When I inquired about him in London, I learned that he lived in the country and had continued to write about his teens. There was a certain amount of dispute as to what his age really was, some insisting that he has always pretended to be very much younger than he is. At any rate, he seems to represent the final stage of this regression toward childhood. He is not at all a bad writer, but he has been able to find no other theme than that of his own attractive youth and its quarrel with the horrid people who broke in on its bemused self-consciousness by rudeness or admiration.

It is thus as if the code and the glamour of the traditional upper-class world were the last things to survive in English letters. You find them in a different form in the later work of Evelyn Waugh. Beginning, in *Decline and Fall*, with the comic misadventures of a naive young man who has set out to study for holy orders but is first seduced and then destroyed by aristocratic friends, he has ended, in *Brideshead Revisited*, with a bedazzlement by great houses and noble names that would probably embarrass Ouida. The middle classes here occur only as overbearing *nouveaux riches* or as ill-bred and boring upstarts. And what, indeed, has become of that old middle class of which the writers mentioned above were the spokesmen? Even in the Bloomsbury phase that came between these generations, the only first-rate non-upper-class figure was D. H. Lawrence, the coal-miner's son, who had almost as little in common with the Bennett and Shaw point of view as he did with Virginia Woolf's. Must we conclude that that articulate middle class that thought it was working for democracy and freedom is now almost completely dead, having failed, in the time of its prosperity, to create a lasting civilisation, so that there is nothing to-day left but a labouring and shopkeeping people, more and more equalised by the pressure of the war services and of wartime restrictions, over whom hangs a fading phantom of the England of the public school?

*　　　　*　　　　*

Certainly this new lower middle class, which may be destined to absorb the others, supplies an eager and growing market for the worst—in movies, radio and journalism—that the United States has to send them. Our Hollywood stars are already their stars, our best-sellers their best-sellers. To an American, these signs of Americanisation seem mostly stale and depressing. The British feed themselves on our banality without catching our excitement and gusto. Many of them now chew gum.

*　　　　*　　　　*

The influence of America on England had already gone pretty far when I was here in 1935, and a reaction against it was evident in the humour of the London revues, which were ridiculing the United States at the same time that they were borrowing American jokes and exploiting American methods. To-day the influence is more pervasive and, though criticism on the stage and in the press is restrained by our relations as allies, the rebellion against it also seems stronger. Everybody goes to the American films, and everybody under forty-five of whatever social class seems to say *O.K.* and *That's right*, and the American use of *fix* in the sense of *mend* or *arrange* has also become very common. People, I believe, more often begin statements with *Look* than with the old *I say*; and an American is sometimes startled at hearing a phrase like *het-up* pronounced by an English voice. But the English, as a result of all this and of their recently having been swamped by the American Army and Navy, seem to have become rather neurotic about Americans. They look back on the descent of our troops as an ordeal of almost the same horror as the Blitz or the robot bombs. It must, of course, be a dreadful nuisance to have the people of some other country dumped suddenly upon one's own, and the English have had cause for complaint in the uniformed hillbillies and hoodlums who took advantage of the blackout in London to snatch purses and attack women. In the case of the American officers, whose sometimes obnoxious behaviour has astonished as well as outraged them, they cannot understand that in a country like ours, without permanent class-stratifications,

there is no section of the population from which officers may be
drawn who can be counted on to play the same role as the officers in
European countries. A man who gets a commission in wartime may
be a well-conducted person or he may be a rough diamond. If he is a
blackguard, he will be less trained to conceal it than would be the
case in England. This is one of the results of our system which must
be faced and accepted for better or worse.

But now that the Army is mostly gone, I had assumed that this
resentment had subsided, and was therefore surprised, in London,
to hear a good deal of bitter criticism of practically everything
connected with America. I had begun by being deprecatory about
those products of the United States—*Time* magazine, movies, etc.—
to which I objected as much as they did. But I soon found that this
was not understood: it is a part of the Englishman's code, probably
derived from school games, never to criticise his country to outsiders,
and he thinks that if you criticise yours, it is an admission of inferiority. I first became aware of this attitude some years ago at
home, in meeting a visiting English scientist who told me that he
hesitated to say that he had enjoyed Sinclair Lewis's *Babbitt* because
he feared that we might not like it. This seemed to me odd at the
time, but I realised, when I came to England, how different in such
matters the English point of view is to ours. They do not publicly
engage in self-criticism; they are too intent on keeping up face. And
I felt that, in comparison with England—or, in fact, with any
European country—we were not a *nation* at all—that is, we were not
an entity which perpetuated its local breed and had to compete with
and protect itself among entities of other breeds; but a *society* in
course of construction, composed of the most diverse elements,
in which it was the way of living and not the national existence and
essence which people considered important. Thus the admission of a
weakness to a foreigner is, for an Englishman, an act of treason,
whereas a satire on Babbitt, for us, is merely a comment on a social
tendency.

But I eventually became rather irritated. If the people I met in
London did not, as they often did, attack America and Americans
directly, they would resort to the old offhand methods which one
reads of in books of the last century and for which it seemed to me,
in 1945, a little late in the day. One man who had been in the United
States pretended to think that Vermont was a town in Florida and
that it was pronounced as if it had the same root as "vermiform,"
and another, an Oxford don who had lectured for a year or so at
Harvard, a scholar of enormous reading who quoted lyrics in

Portuguese and had the Russian poets all at his fingertips, remarked that he had never read Walt Whitman, who was considered, he understood, a great writer in South America. When I said that *Leaves of Grass* was probably the greatest American book, he asked me whether I thought it even more important than the writings of Whyte-Melville. I did not actually talk with people who believed— though I heard that the legend was current—that the long legs of the American women were due to the prevalence of Negro blood; but I met several well-educated persons who had ideas that were almost as fantastic. George Orwell, for example, had the notion that the language was being improverished in America: that we had, for example, few separate names for the different kinds of insects, but called everything "some sort of bug."

With the more offensive people I presently took a tougher line. I would retort that the American soldiers who had committed misdemeanours in England were our revenge for the obnoxious British propagandists who, from the moment the English had realised that they needed us against the Germans, had been sent over to put pressure on us, and I cited examples, in this line, of British atrocities in the United States. The first rebuttal I got was an unper- turbed retort that in general the diplomatists and agents who were sent to New York and Washington were not out of the top drawer: when a man did not come up to scratch, he was usually assigned to the States. But my new tactic was not ineffective. The British, though impassive, are pugnacious: they have always stood four-square in their own little country with their fists clenched against the world. They understand giving blow for blow—again, the school games idea. When the challenge of rudeness was offered, I would take it up in conversations that went more or less like this: "The English," I would declare, "are fantastically incurious and ignorant about the United States. A friend of mine in Scotland who knows America well was saying that they see North America on the single page of an atlas so that it looks about the same size as England, and so assume that it is a small homogeneous place." "One of the things," my English friend will reply, "that make it difficult for us to learn about America is the inferiority of American books, which are usually so badly written that it is impossible for an Englishman to read them." Or: "The social classes in England are quite different races of beings, who even speak different languages. Perhaps the jargon of the American movies may prove to have this use in England: that it will give them a common medium by which they can communicate." "What about the American Negroes? They seem to be excluded from privilege as no group in England is. And, though I am used to talking to Americans, I often find it very hard to understand what a Negro is saying."

This attitude of the English toward America is, of course, partly a wartime phenomenon: a symptom of exasperation, of the peculiar state of mind produced by being penned up at home for five years, and in uncertainty, since 1940, about England's surviving at all. I provoked an immediate resistance whenever I expressed the opinion that Europe, after the war, would have to be governed by somebody or something; but it took me a little time to realise that the English at once assumed that I meant that we ought to run it. When I had done so, I would explain that the difficulty would be rather, once the Germans were defeated, to induce the United States to take any further interest in Europe. Yet the British, though they shudder at the notion of any other power's dominating Europe, shrink also from the idea of co-operating, for purposes of international control, with the other great Western countries. They used to reproach us, with reason, for creating the League of Nations and then refusing to take our place in it, but, during my visit, I have got the impression that the average educated Englishman is still thinking of the future of the world in terms of old-fashioned balance-of-power, for which nations are irreducible units that can associate in pacts and alliances like the combinations of molecules in chemistry but cannot cohere to produce a new structure by a process of crystallization.

The great difference that one finds between England and the other English-speaking countries is due perhaps mainly, I have come to see, to the fact—of which, obvious though it is, I had not fully appreciated the importance—that the English inhabit an island, whereas the rest of us are spread across whole continents and, with wide spaces of sea around us, unconstrained by menacing neighbours, have acquired a certain nonchalance, a readiness to get on with people, that makes the non-English Anglo-Saxon something distinct from the native of England. The Englishman sits tight on his island and makes forays into the outside world which are adventurous or predatory but do not establish friendly relations.

*   *   *

I had never before fully grasped what was meant by "British rudeness." The point about it is that what we consider rudeness is their form of good manners. In other countries, manners are intended to diminish social friction, to show people consideration and to make them feel at ease. In England it is the other way: good breeding is something you exhibit by snubbing and scoring off people. This is of course closely connected with their class system, and it is partly a question of accent, vocabulary and general style, which your inferior cannot acquire. I have been told that, when a way of talking begins to pass into common use, the higher people evolve something new which will again fence them off from the lower. Certainly I heard interchanges in London of which I could hardly understand a word. But their competitiveness is also involved: it is a game to put your opponent at a disadvantage, and if you succeed in saying something blighting in a way which makes it impossible for him to retaliate without a loss of dignity more serious than that which he incurs by accepting it, you are considered to have won the encounter. You have the status of King of the Castle till somebody else comes to pull you down. Nothing in this respect seems to have changed from the days of which Henry Adams wrote in his *Education*, when what he had heard described as "the perfection of human society" required that a man should be able to "enter a drawing-room where he was a total stranger, and place himself on the hearth-rug, his back to the fire, with an air of expectant benevolence, without curiosity, much as though he had dropped in at a charity concert, kindly disposed to applaud the performers and to overlook mistakes."

For all that with other peoples is understood by politeness or courtesy they have a special word, *civility*, which is spoken of as something exceptional and rather unimportant. To say that a person is *civil* is usually patronising; to complain of someone's *incivility* usually means that a vulgar person has made himself offensive by breaking the rules of the game and not accepting the inferior position to which you have tried to assign him. They have also as a part of their rudeness what may be called mock considerateness, which may well be described in the words of a distinguished Russian artist with whom I once had a talk about the English. "They're at their worst," he said, "when they're being kind! They scratch you and scratch you and scratch you—and then they take out a little bandage and graciously bind you up—and then they begin to scratch again." You find it all in the *Alice* books, those wonderful studies of English life and character. Alice is a little lady; she is supposed to have been very well brought up; and it is a part of her good breeding to have learned how to make other people uncomfortable without ever losing the pretension of being a thoroughly tender-hearted person: " '*Où est ma chatte?*,' " she addresses the Mouse,—"which was the first

sentence in her French lesson-book. The Mouse gave a sudden leap
out of the water, and seemed to, quiver all over with fright. 'Oh, I
beg your pardon!' cried Alice hastily, afraid that she had hurt the
poor animal's feelings. 'I quite forgot you didn't like cats. . . . Don't
be angry about it. And yet I wish I could show you our cat Dinah.
I think you'd take a fancy to cats, if you could only see her. She is
such a dear, quiet thing,' Alice went on, half to herself, as she swam
lazily about in the pool, 'and she sits purring so nicely by the fire,
licking her paws and washing her face—and she is such a nice soft
thing to nurse—and she's such a capital one for catching mice—oh,
I beg your pardon!' cried Alice again, for this time the Mouse was
bristling all over, and she felt certain it must be really offended.
'We won't talk about her any more, if you'd rather not.' . . . 'Are
you—are you fond—of—of dogs? . . . There is such a nice little dog,
near our house. . . . A little bright-eyed terrier, you know . . . and it
belongs to a farmer, you know, and he says it's so useful. . . . He
says it kills all the rats and—oh dear!' cried Alice in a sorrowful
tone. 'I'm afraid I've offended it again!' For the Mouse was swimming away from her as hard as it could go, and making quite a
commotion in the pool as it went." Lewis Carroll meant this to be
funny, and he knew that the nice little English girls to whom the
book would be read would love to hear about the Mouse being
frightened and finally making an unseemly commotion while Alice
remained perfectly cool. Yet Alice, with her brutal good manners,
was of course constantly jostled and crowded by creatures that were
brutal in a more overt way. They were not by any means all mice:
she had to stand up for herself among Mad Hatters and Ugly
Duchesses, and any English child who read the book would have
thought her a little fool if she had not given as good as she got.

*   *   *

Yet they usually seemed rather shocked when I said that the
Soviet Union, England and the United States were three very
different social systems that had little, among the three, in common,
and that were only united at the moment by the accident that they
were all afraid of Germany.

*   *   *

The President died April 12; and I went to the House of Commons
to hear Churchill pay his tribute to Roosevelt. His speech was,
however, held up by a curious and unexpected incident which turned

out to be more interesting to an American visitor than the little
oration itself. A new M.P., a Dr. Robert McIntyre, who represented
the Scottish Nationalist Party, presented himself to be seated without the customary Parliamentary sponsors. Now it seems that a
Member of Parliament, when he first takes his place in the House,
is supposed to be sponsored by two other members, who escort him
on either side, as, stopping three times to bow to the Speaker, he
walks down between the benches. Dr. McIntyre, the spokesman for
an intransigent group, had decided to appear alone, in order, as he
said, to dissociate himself from "the London party game"; but the
result was that the Speaker, in his very high chair and wearing his
shoulder-length wig, immediately challenged the Doctor's procedure
and, when he began to explain his position, cut him short with,
"You have no place to speak from. You cannot make a speech." He
was sent to sit behind the bar—that is, to a kind of limbo consisting
of a "cross-bench" at the back of the room; and he retired, walking
backwards and making the Speaker two more bows. A spirited
debate now took place. A Scottish member, Mr. Buchanan, with a
strong Scottish accent urged, that the old rule be suspended for a day.
Dr. McIntyre, he said, had been "duly elected after fighting both
party machines," and was certainly entitled to his seat. Other
members objected that the rule had a very important purpose:
if sponsors were not required, there would be nothing to prevent
any vagabond of the streets from walking into the House of Commons and taking his seat as a member. It turned out that this
regulation, in force since 1688, had come in question only once
before—in 1875, when a certain Dr. Kenealy had been personally
so unpopular that he could not get anyone to sponsor him—on
which occasion the requirement had apparently been waived. The
supporters of Dr. McIntyre were unable to make any headway. A
Conservative member, Earl Winterton, even inquired indignantly
whether the House were obliged to tolerate Dr. McIntyre's remaining in the room at all, and provoked from Mr. Buchanan a counter-
question addressed to the Speaker: "Could you not order Dr.
McIntyre's execution just to satisfy Lord Winterton?" The question
of whether or not Dr. McIntyre was to be seated had to be put to a
vote. "I could not," said Mr. Churchill, "advise the House on this
occasion to depart from tradition and custom. On the contrary when
the British House of Commons is under the gaze of the whole world,
and the admiring gaze of a large part of it, we should not in the least
shrink from upholding the ancient traditions and customs which
have added to our dignity and power."

I had that afternoon been very much impressed, amidst the
carvings and the gilt of Westminster, by the spectacle of the opening
of Parliament: the huge gold mace, the Speaker framed in his wig,
the attendants with their necks rigid and their chins stuck out,
all proceeding through the solemn portals while the crowd was made
to stand at attention. I had never quite felt before—since we have
nothing in the least like this—how dramatic and how compelling
these anachronistic rites could be, how much that power and
dignity of England of which the Prime Minister spoke still resided in
a mystic core of which such things as crown and mace and wool-
sack were the most conspicuous symbols but which lived and
provided an orientation for almost every British subject. As our
ship was docking at London, I had been struck when the British
stewardess, born in India and married in the States, who had been
but once in England, had observed, looking out at the grassy shores:
"There's something *worthy* about it, don't you think so?" And yet,
now that the Prime Minister was appealing thus for the continuance
of an obsolete custom on the ground that it would be a good thing for
British prestige abroad—in a word, that it was better publicity—
I felt that the power and the glory were perhaps ebbing out of these
symbols, that the old virtue was no longer quite there.

I later read in a paper the programme of the Scottish Nationalist
Party, which included the following points: "The break-up of large
landlord states among farmer-owners responsible to the Nation;
Government ownership responsible to the Scottish people alone;
a central bank and control of private and municipal banks, customs
and excise; the curbing of combines by immediate legislation making
it illegal for a Scottish firm to sell a majority of its capital to non-
Scots and by a differential tax on chain-stores; national ownership of the coal reserves of Scotland"; and, as "war aims," "national
freedom for Scotland and all other nations." To an American, these
demands of the Scotsman had a certain familiar ring. I do not know
how important this party may be or how legitimate its grievances are.
The Englishmen I asked about it smilingly brushed it off, conceding
sometimes that it might be a good thing if the Scotch had a parliament of their own, which would prove to be merely, they said, a sort
of "glorified borough council." But the more open-minded kind of
Englishmen, toward the end of the eighteenth century, must have
smiled in very much the same way about the demands of the
American colonies. At any rate, the oration for Roosevelt was held
up while a division took place. The members went out to vote;
Mr. Churchill had to withdraw with his speech in his hand. The

decision was overwhelmingly for the government, against the seating of the Scottish member: 273 to 74.

*   *   *

This quiet laughing-off of the Scottish M.P. and the derouting of his challenge by Parliament led me to reflect on the methods which the English have invented and perfected for warding off inconvenient questions. A favourite device is the False Issue. This is best handled in the tone of light ridicule. They acquire the technique so early that I think they must be trained in it at Oxford.   If you do not want to stand by the Poles, you make fun of them for their effervescence, thus implying that they are quite irresponsible; if Gandhi is becoming too powerful, you are amusing about his loin-cloth and goat. Only in more aggravated cases do you resort to moral indignation. If the Americans expect loans to be repaid you denounce them as "Uncle Shylock"; if the Irish are becoming importunate, you raise a hue and cry against Parnell on the ground that he has committed adultery. When the outrage has not merely to be defended, but to be perpetrated in the presence of the victim, a special skill and address are required. This demands that the thing be presented either—on the ground of gentlemanliness—in such a way that, if the victim objects, he will appear to be behaving badly; or—on the ground of a manly idealism—in such a way that, if he does not subscribe, he will seem to confess sordid self-interest. I saw later, in Italy and Greece, this game worked again and again on inexperienced and unsuspicious Americans. The point is that, unless you are used to it, you are unable to imagine that a person so correct in appearance and tone as the well-trained British official is can be up to anything really outrageous. In America, external crudeness usually goes with a lowness of motive. But in England it is mostly with the humble that the straightforwardness and decency reside. The Norwegian captain of our ship told us that when he was making his first voyages, he was warned by other Norwegians that everybody would try to cheat him, with the single exception of the English. I am sure that this was quite true of the English with whom the captain came into contact; but it is certainly not true of the people who make and carry out British policy or in the higher reaches of British business.

I may mention here, also, a device much in vogue among British intellectuals for the purpose of taking down a rival without sacrificing outward dignity or the semblance of generosity. I forbear from quoting actual examples, but the kind of thing I mean is as if Fletcher were to have said to Shakespeare: "You know, I don't think you

ever did anything better than *Love's Labour's Lost*. You had a real
lyric gift," etc.

*   *   *

Thus an American of English stock, coming to England at a time
when we are supposed to be working in close alliance, finds himself
estranged from the English more than ever before. We have always,
I suppose, an instinct to make connections with the English past
from which we have been cut off; and this instinct, at the present
moment, finds itself up against a blank wall. It has been brought
home to me, certainly, more sharply than it has ever been before,
that the real English social revolution occurred, not in England, but
in America; and that the United States stands to England in the
relation of England's own modern history, as if the first French
Republic had been detached and set up in another country, where it
was able to prosper in a material way far more than it could have
done at home, while the old regime in France continued fighting the
old kind of wars with its neighbours and adapting itself as it had to,
to a moderate industrial development.

But the English will not recognise this: they go on pretending
that it never happened, and the more the success of the United States
is forced upon their attention, the more determined they are to ignore
it. It is difficult for an American to grasp the persistence and completeness of this British refusal. We take a friendly interest in England
and we remember the past without rancour; we cannot understand
to what lengths they go in order not to know about us. It is a shock
for the American visitor to read in Westminster Abbey the inscription to Major André, and to realise what his monument implies:
"Sacred," the legend reads, "to the memory of Major John André,
who was raised by his Merit at an early period of Life to the rank of
Adjutant General of the British Forces in America, and, employed
in an important but hazardous Enterprise, fell a Sacrifice to his zeal
for his King and Country on the 2 of October A.D. 1780, aged 29,
universally loved and esteemed by the Army in which he served, and
lamented even by his Foes. His Gracious Sovereign KING GEORGE
the Third has caused this monument to be erected." You would
never get the impression from this that André was hanged as a
spy, and that his name, in America, was indissolubly associated with
the betrayal of Benedict Arnold. The man who had died at our hands
and been buried at Tarrytown had been dug up and brought to the
Abbey, and one could not even get a glimpse through his epitaph at
the violent page of history on which he figured. I was not surprised

afterwards to notice, in a review of a book by an Englishman who had visited the United States, that he had gone there quite ignorant of the defeat of the British in the War of 1812 and had not known that the British Army had at that time burned the Capitol and the White House—quite unnecessarily and simply, as Henry Adams wrote, "because they thought it proper, as they would have burned a Negro kraal or a den of pirates." Naturally one does not want to keep sore a feud based on ancient injuries; but an American is forced to the feeling that it is the British themselves who nurse it. We are the only one of the British colonies which has completely got away from the system. We have escaped being exploited like Canada by having our raw materials all taken by England and being prevented from building up our own industries; we were not left disunited like Ireland (though the British hoped to see our disruption at the time of the Civil War). We broke away from the English and beat them and sent them back to their island; and they have never forgiven this.

*   *   *

Altogether this visit to England has been for me almost as much of a revelation of an alien and little known world as my trip to the Soviet Union in 1935. Though I have five times before been in England, it has been usually just to pass through. I have never before stayed here for any length of time except in the summer of 1914, when, with American college friends, I took a bicycle trip from Scotland to Cornwall, mostly making the rounds of the cathedral towns and consuming large teas in country inns. We saw nothing, except casually, of the people, and the English I had since got to know I had seen mainly in the United States. Now I am having some first-hand experience of that tough-rooted and densely-branched English life which I had learned about principally from books and which seems so unexpectedly different from our looser and shallower growth. I see now that those appalling novels which we read for amusement in America and which seem to us half fairy-tales like Homer, the myths of a remote and an archaic world—*Vanity Fair, Bleak House, The Way of All Flesh*—are true pictures of English society. They do not represent, as we tend to think, merely the cynical worldliness of Thackeray, the grotesque imagination of Dickens, the grievances against his family of Butler: they portray basic English qualities, with which, after nearly two hundred years, Americans have to reckon again: the passion for social privilege, the rapacious appetite for property, the egoism that damns one's

neighbour, the dependence on inherited advantages, and the almost
equally deep-fibred instinct, often not deliberate or conscious, to
make all these appear forms of virtue. I have lately often thought
of these books. When you know that they deal with realities, they
become so much more powerful and terrible than the criticism
of irreverent outsiders. Beside them, Bernard Shaw seems a popular
Irish entertainer and his satire mere persiflage. A more deadly
description by a foreigner is that by Henry James in *The Wings of the
Dove*, which has also been much in my mind where the relations
between Americans and English are concerned. Here the American
disinterested idealism, indiscriminate amiability and carelessness
about money, along with the aimlessness and petering-out of
Americans who have made themselves rich and their helplessness
outside of America, are contrasted with the desperate materialism
that is implied by position in England. *We* find making money
exhilarating, but we also find it exhilarating to spend it. Money for
us is a medium, a condition of life, like air. But with the English it
means always property. A dollar is something that you multiply—
something that causes an expansion of your house and your mechanical equipment, something that accelerates like speed; and that may
be also slowed up or deflated. It is a value that may be totally
imaginary, yet can for a time provide half-realised dreams. But
pounds, shillings and pence are tangible, solid, heavy; they are
objects one gains and possesses. And every good in England is
bound up with the things one can handle and hold.

*   *   *

I stayed for a time at the Hyde Park Hotel, which still managed to
keep up the appearances of a Victorian comfort and grandeur. The
waiter asked me what I wanted to order for breakfast in my room the
next morning. When, in reciting the meagre menu, he mentioned
scrambled eggs and sausages, I said, "That's fine!—bring me that."
"That's not what they usually say when they see it, sir," he dampen-
ingly replied. I should have done well to take his warning, for when
my breakfast came, the eggs turned out to be concoctions of egg-
powder, and I saw what someone had meant when he told me that
sausages in England were now a form of bread.

*   *   *

The strain of the war has made the English irritable, and it may be
that these notes are affected by the atmosphere of general resentment
in which Americans too, are involved.

I had dinner one evening with a Labour man who had a job in the
Air Ministry and with a journalist who had fought for the Loyalists
in Spain and was now an anti-Stalinist radical. It was the moment,
near the end of April, when the Americans and the English had
nearly completed their hideous work of ploughing Germany under,
and the conversation, over the coffee, was becoming quietly ghoulish.
The official archly remarked that, when the Germans went home after
the war, they would find their country "rather changed." The
radical, in reminding us that Warsaw had been "completely wiped
out," gave a kind of involuntary grin—but presently caught himself
up: "Who could have imagined," he said, " six years ago, that we
would soon be talking in this frivolous way about the destruction of
whole populations?" I had often thought of this myself. Through the
whole of the previous war humanitarian feeling survived and
continued to assert itself: it was assumed that the misery and
slaughter were abnormal and undesirable. There had been Harden,
Rolland, Barbusse, Bertrand Russell and Bernard Shaw, Upton
Sinclair and John Dos Passos—to say nothing of Lenin and the
Socialists of the Zimmerwald Conference—to protest against the
war as a bad thing in itself. But to-day it is perfectly plain that
human life is no longer an issue. No one pretends to give a damn
any more—unless they are one's close friends or relatives—whether
people are killed or not. After the first shock of the German bombings, we in America followed the contest between the Royal Air
Force and the Luftwaffe as if they were football teams. After we
ourselves became involved, nobody but an occasional old liberal like
Oswald Garrison Villard, to whom nobody paid attention, seemed to
feel any scruples whatever. The newspaper reports of our bombings
were designed to make them sound quite jolly. "Smiling skies," one
would read in the dispatches, "sent out flying squadrons"; when our
planes destroyed the monastry at Monte Cassino, the building
"blew apart like a house of cards," and the Germans ran out "like
rats"—as if they had not been human beings. When we began to
mash up Berlin, people said that it was an ugly city and that its
buildings were no great loss. We have, to be sure, had to be treated,
like the Germans, with a certain amount of indoctrination to arrive
at this point of indifference. We have had to be convinced, as they
are, that the enemy are not really people. Just after the official
reports of the Japanese atrocities had been published, I went to a
movie newsreel which had been made to arouse the public. First you
were given a dose of the dead or still writhing bodies of Chinamen
slaughtered by the Japs; then you heard one of the American officers

who had suffered at the hands of the enemy and who declared that,
on the basis of his experience, he considered the Japs to be "animals"
—at which point the announcer took it up and pounded it home with
ferocity: "You hear what Captain So-and-So says. He thinks that the
Japs are animals. And now we must fight these *animals!* We must buy
bonds to defeat these *animals!*" Goebbels hardly used a different
technique in working up the Germans to the point at which it seemed
to them quite natural to exterminate the Poles; and our efforts have
been equally successful. We can contemplate now with equanimity,
with a cheerful self-satisfaction, a kind of warfare that crushes whole
cities and that brings down agony and death on thousands of
women and children.

Yet the long-continued concentration on killing people whom we
rarely confront, the suppression of the natural bonds between ourselves and these unseen human creatures, is paid for by repercussions,
the spitefulness of fear and stifled guilt, in our immediate personal
relations. Our whole world is poisoned now, and we must recognise
that outlawing the enemy makes it easy to dislike one's allies.

*   *   *

When I was finally leaving England, the officials were equally
polite, but it turned out that, from the British point of view, my
papers were not in order. By that time I was a war correspondent
and I had not been provided by the American bureau with a permit
from the Allied Forces office, so I was not allowed to fly that morning but made to go back to London to equip myself with the necessary document. The American authorities, when I returned to them,
insisted that I did not need this passport, that my papers *had* been in
order, and a certain amount of animated argument was carried on
over the telephone. I had a glimpse, in the course of all this and of
some future complications, of the conflicting tendencies, in Europe,
of the British and the American methods. The British handle their
formalities entirely without fuss, but they are very exact about them.
They were quite correct, I found, in telling me that the permit they
insisted on my having would be asked for when I arrived in Italy.
On the other hand, if I had not had it, the Americans would certainly
have let me through. The point was that a new kind of credential had
just gone into use with the Americans without the British having had
notification. But the American officials thought that the fact that they
sent a man to an airport provided with American credentials ought
to be enough for the British.

The Americans like to act for themselves and to do things with freer hand. They do not always take the routine of their paperwork quite so seriously as the British do. To the latter, they doubtless seem hit-or-miss, and they probably make annoying mistakes of a kind that is rare with the British. It is the result of having more space to move in, more margin of resources to dispose of. With the British every penny counts and every link in the chain must be tight. They do not understand our looser methods—the methods of a big gang of men working together with a minimum of formality to get something quickly accomplished, so that they can sit down and eat a good dinner.

2

ROMAN DIARY : ARRIVAL—A VISIT TO SANTAYANA

From the air, the green and deep-chocolate fields make intarsia like the floors of Herculaneum. Then a countryside that has lost its rural pattern to the scrawlings of attack and defence and been left notched with boomerang-shaped trenches and perforated with the craters of shells. Some of the houses still keep their pink roofs, but many are stove-in or broken barnacles. The cattle look as small as lice. Even after you have landed, it is hard to grasp that you have really come to Rome. You are still in the world of the air, as, from the airfield, you watch sturgeon-snouted planes taking off like fish surprised in shallows.

The man who drove me into Rome turned out to come from Massachusetts, and we talked about the cranberry crop on Cape Cod. They had written him that the warm spell in March had brought the cranberries out prematurely, and he was worried for fear a frost would kill them. The freshness of the campagna in the morning, with the donkey-carts going to town, excluded any idea of its antiquity. I asked the driver about some old stumps of Roman ruins—fragments of brown brick masonry, with weeds growing out of them like hairs on warts—and he answered, "I guess that's the old water line." They seemed sordid and completely irrelevant to the beautiful clear spring morning and the familiar-looking American gas station where we stopped to fill up our tank.

*   *   *

Rome astonished me by its brilliance and cleanliness. I had not been here since 1909, when I was fourteen years old, and what I remembered was rather an ignoble modern city, dirty, commonplace and somewhat provincial, with enormous ancient monuments embedded among hotels and shops. What I found, at this bright end of April— as we ripped into the Piazza Venezia and caught a view of the Colosseum behind the dazzling and dripping white frosting of the immense Victor Emmanuel Memorial—seemed, amazingly, as smart and as sparkling as any city of pre-war Europe. Mussolini *had* evidently done something for Rome in policing it and building it up. Flimsy and rather chichi though so much Fascist architecture is,

the solarium-like modernist buildings of light-tinted plaster and glass
give the city a kind of *élan*; they are much more cheerful and perhaps
no more jerry-built than the same sort of thing in Moscow.

One feels in the air, after London, the freedom and exhilaration of
a people who, earlier than the rest, have escaped from the repressions
of the war; and, after Naples, it is reassuring to find Italians who
seem self-respecting, well-washed and well-dressed. There are many
people riding bicycles, which have gleaming handle-bars and spokes
and all of which seem to be more or less new. The women are remarkably handsome, and it is wonderful how they have managed,
with materials so poor and scant, to get themselves up so effectively.
Their short skirts always seem well hung, and their raised wooden
pattens with straps at the heels, in which they walk with bare feet,
are the only attractive footwear that I have seen since I came to
Europe. They also know how to do their black hair so that they
always look tempting from behind even when their faces, as one
passes them, turn out to be long-featured or coarse. One feels that
these Roman women have a natural ineradicable chic that is common to all sections and classes. And the bookstores and newsstands are fizzing and frothing with the covers of new books and
reviews, of which the white or pink or green paper backs have kept
that lavish Italian touch—in ample spaces and ornamental typo-
graphy—that is so different from the sober prose elegance of the
yellow-backs of Garnier or Calmann-Lévy. I have never seen so
many bookstores, news kiosks and wandering book-carts in any
city, even Paris, and the quantity and variety of translations, as well
as the modern French classics reprinted in French, would give, if
nothing else did, a cosmopolitan tone to the streets. American and
English novels that one knows in their original native boards get a
flavour of Asti Spumante from their lively Italian titles: *La Via del
Tabacco*, *L'amante di Lady Chatterley*, and (James M. Cain's) *In
Due Si Canta Meglio*. I am surprised to see the vogue of Herman
Melville, all of whose novels they seem to be translating. The walls
are covered with posters, remarkably well designed, exhorting the
public to buy war bonds; declarations in fine black-and-white, full
of rhetoric against the Fascists; and—gashing the surface of the city,
keeping open the recent wounds—the systematic outcry of the
Communists: a hanged man on a gallows, with the slogan "*Vendi-
chiamoli.*"

The little cakes in the *pasticcerie* looked appetising and perfectly
normal—I had tried some in Naples, which had been gritty and
gooey and depressingly deficient in sugar; but when I went into one

of the most tempting of these places and sat down at an outside
table, it proved to be embarrassing and uncomfortable. You found
yourself not far from a group of pallid and ragged people who were
waiting to get into a door where the Americans were giving them a
handout; and you were buzzed about by little dirty kids with an eye
on the sweets you were eating, whom the waiters shooed away like
flies but who were always back the moment after.

*   *   *

Just before I had left New York, I had received with surprise and
pleasure, a copy of *Persons and Places*, inscribed to me by George
Santayana, so I thought it might be in order for me to look him up in
Rome.

The Colosseum was terrific as I came upon it, or rather as it came
upon me, out of antiquity and out of my childhood. I had forgotten
how big it was. On the first day, when I had merely had a glimpse of
it behind the Victor Emmanuel Monument, I had seen it, at the end
of a vista, arranged by Mussolini, that took it down from its full
stature and made it look, as someone said, like a man on his knees.
But now that it rose to its imperial height, it seemed gigantic even
by modern standards, and I felt dazed and almost incredulous at
finding myself suddenly dropped down in Rome and going to see
Santayana behind the Colosseum. I walked around the old Madison
Square Garden, which, so unlike the American building, embodied,
in its grimness and grandeur, a human attitude that made it an official
mask; between it and the Arch of Titus; and along the cobbled Via
Claudia, with, on the one hand, a scratched yellow wall and, on the
other, a dense texture of purplish-pink brick, the rubbed and eroded
remains of some long-demolished ancient building, that showed holes
like a crumbled sand castle and looked dishevelled with dry dusty
shrubbery bristling down from the top. Then a tunnel of low acacias
that overarched a quiet street; another old wall that screened off
what?—there were so many kinds of things in Rome, all mixed up
yet with walls between them. Then a street out of the eighteenth
century, with high pediments over the windows and brown shutters
spread wide on the gamboge walls. Then the Via di Santo Stefano
Rotondo. Here, among the dead relics of the Caesars' Rome, there
had grown, through the Christian centuries, convents and churches
that are still intact and evidently more or less living. The street, with
no footpath, all cobbles, that slopes toward undulating old gutters,
follows the curve of another wall, grass-grown and of irregular

height, with, here and there deep, gouged-out scars and the arches of
bricked-up doors. Below an antique iron lamp on a black iron arm
that contained an electric bulb, a man and a girl were silently
kissing.

There was an entrance through this ancient wall to the Hospital of
the Blue Nuns, to which, after the outbreak of the war, Santayana
had come to live. The order was Irish, and their convent enjoyed
some sort of extraterritoriality: an English-speaking non-citizen like
Santayana was presumably safer here than elsewhere. Inside all was
snug and decent in rather a non-Roman suburban way: the straight
cypresses, the well-trimmed lawn, the green-shuttered orange
building, the little tinny dome that looked as if it belonged to a small
college observatory. I inquired at the gatekeeper's house and was told
by a little girl that there was *un dottore, un professore*, who must be
the person I asked for. The Blue Nuns were decorative and fantastic,
for they actually wore great starched head-dresses that had been dyed
with some deep bluing. They were English and said at once that the
professor was always glad to see people. They wanted to take me
right in, but I thought they had better announce me and make sure
that he wanted to receive me, so I waited in the dark little parlour,
very British and middle-class with its sentimental modern Catholic
pictures, till the nun appeared again and led me out and down a long
corridor.

He came to the door in a plain brown dressing-gown, with a cord
like a Franciscan friar's. I had not expected to find him so slight.
Never tall, he must have shrunk with age, and the smoothness and
blandness of the face that one sees in the photographs has faded and
lost its mould; but his round black Latin eyes have remained alive and
attentive. His complexion is more swarthy than I expected and his
nose, seen in profile, more pointed. He received me with simplicity
and courtesy and excused himself for reclining on a little chaise-
longue with a blanket over his legs. He occupied a single room, in
which he both worked and slept. There was a table at his right, with
papers and books, and, at his left, a small bed, concealed by a screen.
There was almost nothing else in the room.

I thanked him for sending me his book. "Did I send you a book?"
he asked. "I don't think I sent it to you," he said gently when I
replied that he had and told him my name. "You wrote in it," I
tried to remind him. "The publishers sent out copies," he suggested.
"*They* must have written in it." "No," I insisted. "It seemed to be
your writing and it was dated Rome." "I have a poor memory for
names," he murmured. He seemed to want to slip away from the

subject, but I was nonplussed and embarrassed at coming to see him
when he did not know who I was. I said something more in an
attempt to establish with him the right connection, and in a moment
the explanation had occurred to him. "An American soldier came
here," he said, "and asked me to autograph some copies. Perhaps you
got one of those."

With a freedom that surprised me, however, he at once began
talking about his recent books: *Persons and Places* and *The Middle
Span*; and so about his career and his family. He was evidently
rather dissatisfied with the form in which his memoirs had had to
appear. He had wanted to include illustrations, but the conditions
of war had made it impossible to collect or transmit the photographs
(the manuscript itself had had to be smuggled out of Italy); and there
had been things in the second volume about certain of his American
friends which, against his own inclination, another friend had
induced him to omit. The third volume, though already completed,
couldn't, for personal reasons, be published till after his death. As
he spoke of the people he had known in connection with his portraits
of them in these memoirs and in *The Last Puritan*, his small mouth
would occasionally twist in a mischievous little smile, as if he had
been still a clever boy at Harvard. Except physically, he seemed
hardly to have aged: he had none of the pomp of authority, none of
the arrogance of reputation, but merely an old-fashioned politeness
that was cool and yet quite informal. All he felt he had to know about
me in order to talk of himself was that I was one of his readers.

His position—between two civilisations—had been, he went on,
unusual, and he had dealt with it in an unusual way. His mother and
father, both Spaniards, had been more or less identified with the
Philippines, and he had never been sympathetic with the idea of
Anglo-Saxon domination. Yet he had lived in the United States
through the period—the nineties and the early nineteen-hundreds—
when this ideal had been in the ascendant and, in associating himself
with American institutions, had in a sense been "taking the side of
the enemy." He had never been willing to "co-operate," to prop-
agandise in any form for the Spanish, any more than for the
American, side. It seemed to me, indeed, as I talked to him, as it had
in reading his books, that he was perhaps the most international—
or, better, the most super-national—personality I had ever met. I
told him that the United States was less predominantly Anglo-Saxon
now, and he said that he knew that was true: he could see by the
literature they sent him from Harvard that the University was
"reaching out tentacles" in a way that was very unlike the old

narrow Anglo-Saxon conception of Harvard. And now the United States *had* been called upon to play a great role. America and Russia had emerged as the principal powers in the world. People had used to talk, when we were annexing the Philippines and Cuba, of the "Manifest Destiny" of the United States. It wasn't Manifest Destiny now, but a demand that had been made upon America in the natural course of things, and he had always believed that when it happened that such demands were made upon one, one had to accept the responsibility: not to do so was to make "*il gran rifiuto*." And the situation of South America was thus, also, now to be changed. We, and not Spain any longer, were to become the chief influence there. Well, he had always been against the idea of Spain's influencing South America, just as he had been against the idea of England's influencing the United States.

I said that I had just been in England and started to speak of the exacerbated antagonism of the English towards the Americans. "You don't have to tell me!" he stopped me. He had talked often with an English colonel who had escaped from an Italian prison and had been hidden by the nuns—"it was courageous of them"—for months in the hospital there. He had seen that this colonel was troubled about England's losing her place in the world. He had himself lived in England and he liked the English; they had taken him in in a friendly way, and, if he had been given a chair at Oxford, which had seemed possible at one time, he might have spent the rest of his life there. But eventually, as usually happens, he had, I gathered been rebuffed or frozen. He had delivered, he said, two public lectures. At the first one—a reading of a chapter from *Character and Opinion in the United States*—the people had responded: they had laughed (at the expense of the Americans, no doubt). But at the second one certain things had happened—he touched on them rather gently: something about the bad lighting and the way he had been introduced—and he had known, when he sailed for the Continent, that he would never go to England again. The English were like the French, he explained. He liked France very much in some ways, and, if the French had not been so narrow, he might perhaps have lived in France. But they were occupied with their own interests to a degree that made real intercourse with them difficult—everything else was only politeness. "And the English are not polite," I suggested. "The English are not polite," he confirmed. I was struck both by his sensitive feeling in his relations with other people and by the contrasting or compensating detachment with which he seemed to have passed the cities in review and chosen the one that fitted him best.

It was somehow a little uncanny to hear him talk about the outside world and show a grasp of what was happening there. I had
felt, when I had first come in, that the atmosphere of the convent was
spooky, and, while we were talking, it had begun to rain, so that the
room had become rather dark. It was at the same time respect-
inspiring and disturbing to one's wartime preoccupations to find this
little husk of a man, at once so ascetic and so cheerful, sustaining
at eighty-one so steady an intellectual energy, inhabiting a convent
cell, among the layers of historical debris that composed the substance of Rome, intact and unmoved by the tides of invasion and
revolution that had been brawling back and forth around him; and
when he talked about these outside occurrences, it was as if he attached them to history: the war was an event like another which would
presently belong to the past.

I think that he fancied himself in his role of monastic sage, and that
his drab Franciscan dressing-gown was not perhaps altogether an
accident. He told me, as if it interested and pleased him, that he had
lived there for two years without money. He had not been able to get
any from America and the nuns had given him credit—though he
now paid like any other inmate. He believed that the war had pro-
longed his life by forcing him to come to the convent. Before that,
he had been growing fat, and his friends had been rather disapprov-
ing of what they considered his too comfortable life, which they felt
was doing damage to his spiritual side—they thought his condition
was becoming "quite vicious." But now the diet had made him thin-
ner. He had little to eat but the vegetables that were raised by the
nuns in their garden—with, usually, an egg for dinner. Even the colds
he had used to have had disappeared since he had been eating less.
And if it hadn't been for the war, he would certainly have travelled
and worn himself out sooner—"not that it matters now," he added.
He had had something like a stroke last winter. He had used to walk
all over Rome, but he was forced to be careful now. He had intended
to go to Avila, because he had friends and near-relatives there, but
if he had done so, he would have had certain duties, have had to
occupy himself with family affairs, and it had been rather a relief,
after all, to be obliged to stay in Rome. And then he would have had
to speak Spanish, and he did not really speak it well. The Spanish
they had spoken at home had always been rather mechanical—his
mother had never spoken any language really well. (It seemed to me
extremely characteristic that he should thus have felt the necessity of
speaking Spanish as an objection to visiting Avila. It was not merely,
I thought, the shrinking of age from the trouble of doing something

not habitual but partly a reluctance, towards the end of his life, when he had shown himself a master of English, to try to express himself in a medium which he was not able to handle brilliantly. He had remarked that it was a great advantage to be able to speak English in the hospital though, of course, he spoke Italian, too.) He would also like to go to America, but he wouldn't, because he would have to be entertained, and he knew that he could never survive it. I thought that he was proud of his reputation in America and of his American career and connections. In his earlier days, he said, his work had not been known at all, but now they were reading even his earlier books. Yet his point of view, he added, was unfashionable, since he dealt with things not in the modern way but rather in terms of the medieval categories.

He had evidently, during his stay in the convent, accomplished an immense amount of work—though he spoke of having written, or of wanting to write, "something," as if it were merely a method of passing the time. I felt, as I had done already in reading his later books, that he was a writer of passionate vocation; that this writer had been marking time during the years of his academic service, when he had had to play the specialised philosopher, but had been fledged on his emergence from Harvard and had triumphed in the solitude of his later life, when, even more than through his early verse, he had revelled in a poet's power. He had just done a small book about Jesus, which was a result of his seclusion in the hospital, where, failing other reading matter, he had had to fall back on the books of the nuns. He had been through the whole of the Bible, a good deal of St. Thomas Aquinas and a number of Catholic novels, which he had found of a certain interest. Besides his memoirs and this book on the New Testament, he had been writing a long treatise on politics, of which he showed me the high stack of manuscript on the table beside his chair. He had not dealt with the two world wars in his memoirs because he had been discussing them there. He had been much concerned, he said, with the first one, and written books that had been inspired by it directly; but he had only been aware of the second as he was of the Battle of Cannae.

He touched on a number of subjects with the blend that one finds in his books of sympathetic appreciation with a scepticism that was slightly mocking. When I spoke of the relative freedom that I had felt in the atmosphere of Rome, as if it had really picked up the people to get rid of the Fascist machine, he said that the regime, at its best, had had certain very admirable features. For one thing, they had done a lot for the young people. And they had been helpful—to

him, I gathered—in a way that was characteristic of Americans, but
completely unknown in Europe. And then his irony began to creep
in. He had received a letter one day inviting him to become a Roman
citizen. He had gone to the bureau indicated and explained that he
was a Spanish subject and that that was what he preferred to remain. They told him that being a Roman citizen would not interfere
with this. What were the obligations involved? he asked. Very
simple: you paid so many lire. So, he said, he had declined the
honour and had not availed himself of this chance "to become
civis Romanus."

He thought that it had probably been thanks to the Pope that
Rome had not been bombed, and he went on to discuss with much
interest the Church's internal politics. No new cardinals had lately
been appointed: there were only forty now where there should be
sixty-nine (the seventieth is never appointed). The Pope was waiting
till after the war so as to get them from both sides: some from
Germany; the Archbishop of Westminster, undoubtedly; some from
the United States. I said that the Catholic Church at home was playing, as a pressure group, a new and rather sinister role. It also
worked the other way, he answered: America was a pressure on the
Vatican. They depended on American money, as everybody in the
world now did. Then the irony set in again. "A very great man," he
said—with a pleasantry which deftly diminished this man's inflated
reputation—"is coming to see me here," He named a celebrated
Catholic convert on an official mission to Rome. " I think there's
something of the Calvinist about him," he said when I asked him his
opinion of this man. "He's unforgiving with his enemies. I like the
Catholics better when they're charitable." Someone had said about
him, Santayana, he remarked in the conversation that followed, that
he himself was a Catholic in everything but faith. I remembered that
a friend of his had told me of his once having said: "There is no God
and Mary is his mother."

I thought that I was staying too long and made a move to go; but
"Don't go unless you want to," he said, and I saw that he was really
glad to talk. I had gotten, from people who had known him, the
impression that he was rather inaccessible, but I had found that the
opposite was true and that what they had meant was something else,
which I shall try to explain in a moment. One of the wonderful things
about him was, on the contrary, the readiness and grace with which
he played a classical role: that of the sage who has made it his
business to meet and to reflect on all kinds of men and who will talk
about the purpose and practice of life with anyone who likes to

discuss them—as with me, whom he didn't know from Adam—since these are matters which concern us all. On his dignity and his distinction he did not need to insist: he let them take care of themselves; and his attitude toward a visitor—an attitude rather rare with the literary and the learned—was simply that of a man in the world who was trying to make some sense of it as you were. He now developed, at some length and with a vividness which I cannot reproduce, a theory that Western philosophy had made three crucial false steps in its history. The first had occurred when Socrates had "put the physical world under the heel of the moral." Socrates himself, in the beginning, had limited himself strictly to the moral, but his followers had made things worse by bringing in the metaphysical. The second "*faux pas*," as he called it, had been the mistake of the Reformation when it had taken and perpetuated all that had been bad in paganism instead of reviving, like the Renaissance, the elements that had been good. The third had been the mistake of the German idealistic philosophers like Kant (and not merely of the Germans, but also of Locke, Hume and Berkeley) in adopting the impossible position that the order of discovery of objects comes before the order of their genesis—as if (he laughed) the idea of our grandfather came before the fact of our grandfather! He talked about the German philosophers—as in his witty and deadly book, *Egotism in German Philosophy*—with an instinctive antagonism, which he tried, not entirely successfully, to temper with detachment and humility. Schopenhauer and Nietzsche, he said, he had never had any difficulty in following, but the others he could not follow. Not that he criticised them on that account: he felt that it was his fault and wished he could. But the point of view of the idealistic philosophers was completely inacceptable to him. "For me," he said, "our conception of the flaming sun is a sensation of the same order—an essence (in the special sense that he has assigned to this word in his system)—as the older conception of Apollo with his golden rays. Neither is an object that we know, as the idealistic philosophers believe."

When at last I arose to go, I made another attempt to get to the bottom of the mystery of the autographed book that had been sent me. I asked him how he had come to know my name. "Oh, *I* didn't know it," he said mildly. "The man who brought the books had a list of names of people that he thought would like to have them." I felt, as I left, that the philosopher derived a certain satisfaction from treating me with amiability but not knowing or caring who or what I was. I remembered Gilbert Seldes' telling me that he had

taken a course with Santayana at Harvard and that, at the end of the
final lecture, when they had given him a great ovation, Santayana
had dropped his eyes and seemed for a moment on the point of
acknowledging it, but then had apparently thought better of this
and allowed the class to leave without a word; and it came back
to me, also, that Logan Pearsall Smith had written of Santayana:
"How he gives himself to you, pours out the rich stores of his mind,
and forgets all about you the moment you leave the room! He
doesn't dislike you, and doesn't like you or anyone else." I had
mentioned in our conversation having recently met two persons of
whom he had once seen a good deal, and had been struck by his
total failure to show even a conventional interest in how they were or
what they were doing. In Rome, I discovered, he was personally not
known, had never even been met, by American and Italian residents
who seemed to know everybody else in the intellectual world. The
only time I ever heard of his having been seen by anyone but me was
when he came to the Embassy one day to attend to some necessary
formality. Yet I do not think that Pearsall Smith is right in declaring
that he "doesn't like anyone." On the evidence of his memoirs, it is
obvious that some of his friendships have been deep and lasting.
He spoke to me of certain complaints on the part of the reviewers of
these books to the effect that he had written at too great length about
people of little importance; but "I wrote about them," he protested,
"not because they were public figures but because they were important to *me!*"

It would not be precisely true to say that Santayana is narcissistic,
but he is interested in his own thought as a personal self-contained
system, and in his life as a work of art which owes its integrity and
harmony partly to a rigorous avoidance of indiscriminate human
relationships. The objective materials with which his mind works
have been the systems of other thinkers and the assumptions under-
lying civilisations. It is easy to see, when one meets him, how his
attitude toward the world has derived from his personal characteristics and from the circumstances of his life. A pure Latin of small
stature, with fastidious taste and a subtle mind, it was his fate to
spend most of his formative years living among Anglo-Saxons. In
another man this position might have produced an alternation of the
defiant with the propitiatory; but Santayana has subjected himself to
a self-discipline which has kept him both firm and, as he said to me
of his relations with the English, "discreet." The discretion is self-
protective, the mockery a tempering of insolence. I felt occasionally,
in his tone about other people, a suggestion of something feline

which was perhaps not quite congruous with the true Socratic irony; and he seems always to have found it difficult to resist a display of virility. Unsympathetic with the Germans, he yet admired the officers in uniform that he saw in his student days; and his weakness for Mussolini may partly have been due to a similar reaction.

But to say this is merely to say that the books of George Santayana have been written by a human being; and one is, if anything, even more impressed by him after meeting him than one had been in reading these books. The image of him came back to me afterward in the course of the solitary evenings that I spent when I was first in Rome: alone, with his plain table and his narrow bed, so far from Spain and from Harvard, yet with all the philosophies, the religions, and the poetry through which he had passed making about him an iridescent integument, the manners of all the societies in which he had sojourned awhile supplying him with pictures and phrases; a shell of faded skin and frail bone, in which the power of intellect, the colours of imagination, still burned and gave out, through his books and his gentle-voiced conversation, their steady pulsations and rays, of which the intensity seems even to increase as the generator is more worn by use. I don't imagine he is troubled by the thought of death or that it even impinges as a shadow: his present so triumphant functioning appears to absorb and enchant him. Nor is he really alone in the sense that the ordinary person would be. He is still in the world of men, conversing with them through reading and writing, a section of the human plasm that, insulated by convent walls and by exceptional resistances of character, still registers the remotest tremors. He has grown, it seems, almost immune to physical or emotional shock. While others, in these years of the war, have been shaken by the downfall of moralities or have shuddered under the impact of disaster while they have been following the conflict with excitement, his glass has scarcely clouded or brightened; but the intelligence that has persisted in him has been that of the civilised human race—so how can he be lonely or old? He still loves to share in its thoughts, to try on its points of view. He has made it his business to extend himself into every kind of human consciousness with which he can establish contact, and he reposes on his shabby chaise-longue like a monad in the universal mind.

3

ROMAN DIARY : SKETCHES FOR A NEW PIRANESI

SET down suddenly in Rome to-day by an American army plane
and still feeling yourself a part of the American war-machine that has
clamped itself on Europe, your first involuntary reaction to the
Forum is likely to be that all that irrelevant old rubbish—the broken
stones and the chunks of brick—ought to be cleaned up and carted
away and the place turned into a nice public park. The columns,
single prongs or small clusters, that have lost their companions or
mates, give the impression of useless old teeth that ought to be pulled
to make room for the bridgework of a modern colonnade. A play-
ground for the Roman poor is what the Forum just now mainly
serves for. Little children with gray clothes and dusty legs climb up on
the loosely piled marble or play trains, astride a fallen length of
column, while their mothers sit around on scattered fragments. It is
difficult to focus your mind to the consciousness that these rounded
flags—with enormous lacunae among them, like the gaps in an
ancient text—are actually the Via Sacra, where Horace met the bore.
But the Temple of Faustina wrenches you up to confront that giant
world, as it lifts out of the dirt and debris its tremendous steep
brick steps and its facade of stupefying grandeur, a huge intact block
of antique Rome. Below it, the Allied Commission has put up, for
the instruction of the troops, a large sign in dubious English, which
mixes Latin and Italian names:

Temple of Antonio and Faustina
Begun 141 AD following the death of Faustina, wife of Antonio
Pius and who was declared a goddess by the Roman Senate. When
the Emperor died he was made a Joint Patron Deity of the Temple.

Beyond, on the Palatine Hill, stretches the shapeless agglomeration
of the Palaces of the Caesars, with empty eyeholes in their grass-
sprouted brick and, at the top, a fringe of pine and cypress that seems
to have grown like the weeds, with no tending. Faceless though they
have mostly become, the old sallow arches and fractured walls have
the look of faded old men with tufts of hair growing out of their
noses and ears. When you explore the stripped carcases of these
structures, with their entrails laid open and their naked ribs, you

ind them ugly and rather repellent: it is hard to make head or tail of
what was once organisation and splendour. Descending into the dark
vaulted chambers, you find nothing but human excrement. And the
elegances and luxuries of later times first gladden and then depress,
as you find them defiled and neglected. You climb to a still thriving
garden, enclosed by a low box hedge, which has roses hanging
garlanded on stakes and plantings of red gladioli, yellow lilies and
magenta dahlias, and think at first sight that this part has been kept
up; but, entering the maze behind it—box paths with a palm in the
middle—you discover that it is now a latrine and that the little walls
of hedge have been broken down, where people have forced their
way out. A grotto that must once have been charming, matted with a
great growth of vines from which water continually drips, enshrines a
green and limpid pool, the clearness of which, however, reveals only a
pulp of old papers. The Renaissance stone lion that guards it has
one front paw broken off and is scribbled all over with initials.

The Palatine Hill is a favourite resort for the black British
Basutoland troops. The Italians are afraid of these Africans, and they
herd away here by themselves, sauntering along the paths or milling
quietly among the ruins. One finds groups of them, mingled with
Sikhs, with whom they do not, however, associate, on a summit
where a big arc of masonry opens to the empty sky, and where an
unprotected gap in the walk discloses, in the bowels of a vanished
palace, a great underground length of gallery: some cellar for stores
and slaves, which, laid open, after a thousand years of darkness, by a
recent falling-through of the roofing, inspires, for the history-read
visitor, a certain dread and awe. But, for the Africans—who have
been recruited by being told that the White Father was in danger and
who have been surprised to find other Negroes who say they live in
the United States—the splendours of the Caesars, Italy, Europe itself, cannot mean very much more than they did to Attila's Huns.
The only consolation they find in Rome seems to be the low class of
prostitutes who meet them toward nightfall in this part of the
Forum. The girls take them to a part of the ruins that has a row of
little compartments: just the thing for an informal brothel.

*   *   *

I found in the Allied Commission, in the department of food
distribution, L.M., whom I knew from college, and I had from him a
very realistic and highly entertaining account of the day-by-day
workings of his organisation.

He had been trained, when he first came over, at a place called
Tizzi-Ouzou near Algiers, where there was "a so-called school of
military government." Here American and British officers were for
the first time quartered together and confronted with the problem
of getting on. The tone as well as the routine were, however, set by
the British. Instead of American reville or roll call, they had British
morning parade. They would line up in a huge courtyard, and the
British commandant would appear on a balcony, look at his wrist
watch and announce: "Gentlemen, the time is now eight forty-five.
Parade dismissed!" The Americans and British were mixed in the
ranks and at the moment when they broke formation, the American
would walk straight away, but the British had to execute a "right
turn," salute, bringing their hands down smartly, and march forward with a military step. They would thus run right into the
Americans and a scene of confusion would result. The same thing
took place morning after morning. And they were out of tune in
other ways. The movements of British drill are usually calculated to
make a sound in order to keep the men in unison: the British wore
hob-nailed shoes and were always snapping their heels, whereas our
men wore rubber heels and sometimes felt like ineffectual phantoms.
Then there was the issue of tea: where Americans and British had to
mess together (we had the same situation at our correspondents'
hotel), it always annoyed the former to be forced to wait till seven-
thirty for dinner because the latter liked tea at five. Both sides, in this
phase, however, were making efforts to be amiable together; but
"the cleavage began from the moment when they got on the ship for
Naples—and they've been cleaving ever since. The A.C. is a shot-
gun wedding. There was a certain amount of fellowship at mess when
we first arrived in Rome and we were all mixed up together, but later
the Americans and the British separated out from one another
completely." (This, too, was true at our hotel, where, eating three
meals a day in the same dining-room with the British, I never but
once heard of an English correspondent sitting at the same table with
Americans.) The two armies, in the Allied Commission, were supposed to be represented equally, but they were equal, he said, only in
the sense of the story about the wartime rabbit stew, in which it was
discovered that "one part horse, one part rabbit" mean one horse to
one rabbit. The proportion of British to Americans was actually
something like sixty to forty, but the former, through various devices,
had acquired the real control. Our army promotion system played
into the hands of the British because it worked on a rationing basis:
we could have only so many colonels, so many majors, and so forth.

but with the British, the rank went with the job, so that, though any given department might be organised with equal numbers of equal ranks, the British could and did soon promote as many of their own men as they liked, and now outranked the American element. The real power behind Colonel Clark, the nominal head of the Commission, was an Englishman who told him what to do. We had become civil servants for the British, who treated us like colonials, "playing Santa Claus with our food, oil and man power. As Sumner Welles says, we're the tail to the British kite!"

He had some amusing stories of Naples. The Neapolitans would take paving-stones out of the streets in order to slow up the American trucks and get a chance to steal the bags of flour. They would also slit the sacks in the trucks, and then later, when these had been taken out, the little boys would come around and scrape the flour off the floor. In the station at Naples there were two little boys who worked together in the following way. When they saw an American carrying bags, one would stick a hatpin into him while the other grabbed the bags, as he dropped them. At Civitavecchia, he said, a considerable amount of salt had been stolen with the connivance of the carabinieri —salt is a government monopoly—who, as their price, took a cut of the shipments. Someone had told him that the same thing was mentioned in one of the classical Roman historians.

But these were merely the pettier peculations. He knew of an American officer who had been offered a handsome villa to live in after the war if he would agree to let a load of supplies be diverted to an improper destination. In Sicily, a British officer had been living in a castle with a local countess and levying a personal tax on every cargo of wine that went north. He was now in Italy proper and the authorities were supposed to have the goods on him; "but did you ever hear of an officer—especially a British officer—being convicted by a court martial?" L. himself had had one experience which had struck rather a sour note. He had got to know an Italian family whom he had liked and to whose house he had sometimes gone. It was a kind of palace made of white soap. The father was a splendid old figure, with a pair of enormous *baffoni* and a great shock of thick white hair. He had the concession for making records of all the music that was played in the Vatican—the big organ, the Sistine Choir; but at the present time none could be made and the family were rather hard-up. One evening he had proposed to L., in the blandest and most natural way in the world, that L. should supply him with the flints that the Americans were shipping in for cigarette-lighters for the soldiers. He would sell them, and they would split

D

the price. L. has decided, he tells me, that he can't go to the house
any more.

*   *   *

The Borghese Gardens—into which you pass, at the top of the
broad Via Veneto, through the old chipped reddish weedy Roman
wall and the stone gates with the modern eagles. Here one always
finds an atmosphere of gaiety, of leafage, of light bright colour—
everything both larger and more casual than in a park in London or
Paris, and enchanting with a freedom and felicity that are characteristic only of Rome—all a little not precisely tinselly, not precisely
flimsy, but slightly both tempting and teasing the foreigner by a
careless disregard of plan, a cheerful indifference to purpose, that,
nevertheless, acquire a certain insolence from blooming among the
monuments of so much solid civic building, so much noble and
luxurious beauty. With all this behind them, these immense rambling
grounds can afford to lack foundation, be perishable—like D'Annunzio's *Elegie Romane* and Respighi's *Fontane di Roma*.

I found myself almost every afternoon, when I had been to call for
my mail, wandering up into the Borghese Gardens to read it and the
Italian papers in a little out-of-doors cafe called La Casina del Lago.
You went inside a special enclosure, shut off from the rest of the park
by a little black iron fence, behind which were posted at intervals,
whitish and dim in the shadow, a set of small antique statues, and
walked along a gravelled alley vaulted with fine straight green oaks,
which seemed marvellously cool and reposeful after the dirty main
drive and the meridian heat. The strange blend of informality and
grandeur that is so much the quality of Rome! Outside, one would
have passed a wall, loaded down with midsummer vines, which
just revealed sculptured griffins and the flank of an embedded
sarcophagus; and now one met a gray ducal stone lion grasping a
sheaf of stone arrows in his paw but pedestalled on some make-
shift brickwork which on one side it overlapped. The *casina*
resembled a temple: a small portico with classical columns. In front
of it were little round tables sheltered by ample umbrellas and
surrounded by wicker chairs, and wide-branching pink rhododen-
drons growing out of large clay jars. A radio, concealed over the
portico, was always warbling romantic opera or concert renditions of
Mozart, often, curiously enough, announced as emanating, I suppose
by way of records, from the Metropolitan Opera House in New
York or the Boston Symphony Orchestra. The waiters were unobtrusive, sympathetic: they soon appeared, brought you apricot

ice and little pink *paste* in frilled paper cups, then drifted into the
background and let you alone.

I read letters from G. when I got them, and wished she were with
me to go around with. Rome—even for Italians, apparently: the
lovers in D'Annunzio's *Il Piacere*—ought to be seen as an historical
pageant and in company with someone else. I haven't gone to many
churches or museums. My idea has been that, sometime later on, I
shall bring my children over to see them, as I was brought in my
teens; and in the meantime, I have felt this spring as if the whole past
of Rome has been pushed by the war into a history that is now
finished. My attention is always on other things: on the phenomena
of Anglo-Saxon, Germanic, Russian Soviet civilisation that is taking
over the world. The old routine of the tourist, reading up the earlier
chapters of the story which is to culminate in his grandfather, his
father and himself, seems relegated to the archives now, like the
final instalment of a serial bound up in the completed volume of a
suspended magazine.

*   *   *

One Sunday I was asked for lunch to a place in the country some
distance from Rome, and was driven there, in an official limousine,
by one of the other guests, a rather important man from the British
Foreign Office. There was also a uniformed English girl, whose father
was a well-known diplomat, then at the San Francisco Conference.
They engaged in a conversation so low-voiced, laconic and private as
to become almost telepathic. The first part of this peculiar interchange was more or less intelligible to a stranger—we were all sitting
together in the back seat: Captain D. told Sir S. what she had done
during the war with masterly matter-of-factness: she had apparently,
in some capacity, been connected with the firing of anti-aircraft
guns; and they talked about the effects of quinine—she had just
come "out" to Italy—which you were supposed to take to ward off
malaria, but which, the girl said, would turn you yellow, so that she
felt she'd rather risk malaria. But then their voices sank still lower,
and there was nothing but Christian names and nicknames, mono-
syllabic questions and answers in a kind of private code. The only
name that I recognised was "Winnie," who, Captain D. explained,
lay in bed in the afternoon—"which nobody else is able to do"—
and so came out "full of beans" at night, when the cabinet ministers
were tired. And there leaked through to me rather dimly one of those
inevitable British stories about someone who had snubbed someone

else in a sharp and satisfactory manner. Sir S. would occasionally
raise his voice and address a remark to me, as if I were sitting in
another room.

All this time we were passing through a region that had been
absolutely laid waste by the fighting. Of whole villages there was
nothing left but rubble and empty walls—though the women still
went back and forth, balancing jars on their heads, and the children
played by the roadside, climbing on the old rusty guns that had been
camouflaged with green dappling and now lay about, sometimes
belly up. Spattered and speckled walls, balconies hanging in shreds.
The pink, white or yellow houses looked almost too soft for real
buildings: a railroad station presented the aspect of a partially
gnawed graham cracker, and one was reminded by other ruins of
loaves of bread with the crusts rather clumsily sliced off or of
dilapidated cardboard boxes from which most of the paper coat had
been ripped and the gray underneath partly torn. One house, with
its staircase exposed, looked like a broken conch-shell which shows
the interior spiral. Another, with the staircase destroyed, had been
equipped with a long ladder which gave access to some still usable
upstairs rooms. In another, on an upper story, a family of little
children were sitting around in their Sunday clothes—black suits,
green and red dresses—in a room of which only two corners were
left: below them dropped a precipice of ruin; but they had brightened what remained of the room with little pots of flowers, and seemed
to have got used to living in the open and in the danger of breaking
their necks. In the main square of a fairly large town stood a headless
unidentifiable white statue, with one arm still pathetically upraised in
a gesture that had no longer any meaning, perching on what looked
like a rockery but was really a blasted pedestal.

Sir S. pointed out to his companion that the women were "very
well-dressed compared to the women at home." His tone about the
Italians was invidious, but his opinion was not borne out by my own
observation in England. The women in these roadside towns *did*
look better than English women, but only because they had more
chic. The bright little short dresses which they were wearing with
bare legs were more vivid but less substantial than the clothes one
saw in England. This was Sir S.'s only comment on the scenes
through which we were passing till we came to a badly shelled
cemetery which had once had a wall around it and which still bore,
over its battered gate, the legend "IN CHRISTO QUIESCENTES."
"Sad to see that shattered!" he murmured.

*   *   *

But the longer you live in Rome—and as the charming and chilly spring gives way to the smothering summer—the more you feel the stagnation and the squalor that are the abject human realities left by the ebb of power and splendour. You notice, in a little side street such as the Via dei Cappuccini, the stopped-up urinal that overflows the cobbles and the melancholy old sprawling black sandals that lie in shreds in the road; and you become unpleasantly aware of the long accumulation of excrement in the corners of the great grass-grown back-stairs of the Church of Santa Maria Maggiore. The beggars begin to get on your nerves. Corrado Alvaro, the novelist, who has done a series of articles on them, tells me that they have a bus of their own, which brings them into town in the morning. The supposedly crippled paupers jump briskly out of the bus, make water against the wall, then go into their professional act, becoming paralysed, bent and pathetic. Not all are fakes, however, he says; and this soon becomes all too obvious. The streets are full of people who are wasted with malnutrition or suffering from various infections, some of them not even begging, but lying on curbs or in doorways in fevered stupors or with bloated feet. There are women with tiny ugly children whom they expose all day to the sun. Near the entrance to our hotel in the Via Sistina is a woman with a limp shut-eyed baby that always seems doped or dead: we try to think it is a fake made of rubber. One of the most ambitious begging efforts is a remarkable family orchestra which is absolutely indefatigable and always to be found in some public place. The father, with an accordion, is the principal performer, and around him cluster seven children, tooting and piping on instruments that look like miniature saxophones. One of the boys doubles with cymbals. The mother stands keeping time, holding a pale heavy-lidded baby. Sometimes they play *Lili Marlene*, sometimes the *International*.

The street boys, the "*ragazzini*," are all intent on illicit business. They are the visible communications of the network of the Black Market. If you so much as glance at one, he slides up to propose to you a women and a room or to offer to buy your cigarettes. Cigarettes are the great medium of exchange, and their price goes up or down in proportion to the number of Americans who happen to be in Rome that week. The normal price of a package seems to be two hundred and fifty lire, that is, two dollars and a half, but it once sank to one hundred and twenty-five, when there were a lot of soldiers here on leave. The kids buy from the American soldiers cigarettes, clothes, and food, and take them home to their parents, who sell them at central exchanges. On one occasion, a white G.I.,

who found himself with a dead-drunk Negro, asked a band of
ragazzini whether they wanted "to buy a black man." They paid him
twelve hundred lire, and the boys took the Negro off, stripped him
and sold everything he had on at a profit of several thousand lire.

The nights in Rome are unlike nights that I remember in any other
city. It seems queer, in the midst of a town that is populated as
densely as this, to hear roosters crowing at dawn and the persistant
moan of a screech-owl. It came back to me that the Latin word for
screech-owl was *strix*, and that there must always have been screech-
owls in Rome since the Romans had first called them that. I couldn't
at first imagine where these chickens and owls made their homes but,
came to the conclusion later that they must be in the Villa Medici.
The absence of nocturnal traffic, due to the lack of oil and light, make
the city unexpectedly quiet, so that the noises seem terribly loud: a
shopkeeper pulling down his tin shutter startles you with a shattering
crash, the exploding exhaust of a truck gives the effect of a ten-inch
gun, the yowling of starved and exacerbated cats seems to emanate
from souls in Hell, and the songs howled by drunken G.I.'s are not
very much more cheerful or pleasant. There is no way of missing a
note of the depressing and interminable pounding of somebody
playing the piano in the British Other Ranks hotel a few doors down
the Via Sistina: he knows only two or three tunes, but he occasionally
attempts to vary them by starting on something new, always, however, giving it up, after groping out the first few bars, and returning to
the same old melodies.

And there is the desultory whistling of trains that do not sound as
if they were really going anywhere. One seems to see them just
standing in the station and peep-peeping at the sight of a brakeman,
as a dog will start suddenly yapping at the sound of a passerby—but
futilely, annoyingly, pathetically. They make you feel as nothing else
does that there are no more communications in Italy and that you
lie there imprisoned in this pit of the past, where the flimsy construc-
tions of the Fascist regime—which was supposed to have made the
trains run on time—have collapsed and joined the rest.

*   *   *

Under the clear pale-blue innocent dome of the sky, the swallows
at certain times of day, go flickering and twittering in swarms. There
is a revue called *Ma le Rondini Non Sanno*, and, according to its
eponymous song, what the swallows are fortunate not to know is
"what's going on down there." As June turns into summer, the

atmosphere of Rome seems to become more corrupt and turbid. The mess in our correspondents' hotel, the rations assigned to which are obviously being sold to the Black Market, has recently been getting so bad as to be sometimes completely inedible. The correspondents take it out on the waiters, who have been shifting from servility to surliness; and one day an American officer, who has something to do with the management, threw an unappetising dish on the floor, provoking, by this overdemonstration, the suspicion that he himself is responsible for our not getting the proper food. In order to escape these meals, we have been going to the Fagiano in the Piazza Colonna, once one of the best restaurants in Rome and now a dining place for Allied personnel; but Fagiano itself is deteriorating. As one drifts out, after a hot afternoon, into the tepid air of evening, down gray avenues where the slow apathetic people are spreading all over the pavements or through the dark cobbled pavementless side-streets where brawlers are shouting at the top of their lungs, one feels that there is nothing left of the bright and varied surface of Rome but a brackish iridescent scum. At the Fagiano, with its old Roman columns embedded in a modern facade, one has a fancy that the respectable dinners which were still being served there this spring, have been actually dematerialising, vaporising, into the murk of the summer dusk, which is itself the foul emanation of a humanity decaying and crawling, like slugs in a fisherman's jar that has been left too long in the sun. The space around the Marcus Aurelius column is the Bourse of the Black Market. You cannot sit down in one of the cafes of the square without someone's sitting down beside you and making you some sort of proposition. Now, you note, we have put up a barbed-wire barrier in front of the Fagiano to protect the army cars and keep the bickering and haggling crowd at bay. The little boys get in, however, and stand at the open windows, and sometimes people hand them out bread.

*   *   *

With the stultifying atmosphere of Rome in June has come to be associated a book that I have been reading through these summer days: *Roma 1943* by Paolo Monelli. This is a political and social history of the demise of the Fascist regime, and so full of the jokes, the slogans, and the jargon of the streets and the papers, with which I was unfamiliar, as well as so complicated in its chronicle of duplicity and confusion, that it took me rather long to get through it. I would apply myself to it after lunch and usually fall into a dead and perspiring sleep—so that the book, with its gray wartime paper and the queer stale flavour of its prose, seemed saturated with exhalations from the Roman streets in summer, as the *popolo romano* of these streets is given a character for me by Monelli's account of their behaviour in the last days of Mussolini's reign.

Paolo Monelli is an able journalist, and *Roma 1943* is an historical document of value (it ought to be translated into English). Monelli worked, during the Fascist regime, on such papers as the *Gazzetta del Popolo* and the *Corriere della Sera*—journals which had some tradition of independent political thinking, though they eventually succumbed to the official line. Monelli, in any case, is anxious to let us know that he was not always uncritical of the authorities and sometimes tried to take a line of his own, and his book has obviously been prompted by a feeling of political guilt which makes the reader too, rather uncomfortable. In order to write such a book, as he says, in order to perform an autopsy on Fascism, one has to conduct an examination of conscience. But, to a foreigner, this is a little repellent. He shows the abject servility of the Fascist press, which he saw from the inside, with a detail which we cannot think funny because it is so disgusting, and he exposes the faults of his countrymen with something almost like complacency, declaiming and waving his hands over the national humiliation, yet snatches with an embarrassing eagerness—wherever it is possible to do so—at the courage of an Italian regiment or the industry of an Italian colony.

What is most curious to the foreign reader is the style in which the book is written. Giovanni Papini once said that the trouble with Italian prose was that it had never gotten away from the ornamental periods of Boccaccio; but if one has been reading Silone or Moravia, one has come to expect a style that has escaped from mandarin requirements and come closer to the colloquial language. Now Monelli, for all his slang of the moment, is still enmeshed in the ancient rhetoric of festooned sentences that go on for pages, show-pieces of literary vocabulary that accumulate adjectives and nouns with a minimum of "functional" effectiveness, convolutions of statements that grow up inside statements, like the whorls of a navel orange, and that give the impression at once of exasperating deliberation and of eyebrow-heaving vehemence (there is, in a single sentence, one parenthesis two pages long that contains a subordinate parenthesis of over a hundred words). This is a style which one associates most readily with the intrigues of a Renaissance court or the manoeuvers of the Council of Trent, and which it seems at first queer and absurd to find used for a critical analysis of the

backstage of Fascist politics and for the history of military movements that one has read of in press despatches.

But then one has to accept the fact, reading on, that modern
Italy is still partly like this. It is precisely Monelli's style which
explains why he was able to live through Fascism and more than half
swallow its grandiose pretentions. While Mussolini was spoiling and
wobbling, while his associates were conspiring against him, dis-
trusting and double-crossing one another, while the generals were
slipping away, evading their responsibilities and leaving Rome open
to the Germans, they still talked a language of literature, still fell
back on heroic poses. Among the consequences, writes Signor
Monelli, of the "intellectual laziness" of Italians are "the habit of
making everything into literature—ideas, theories, feelings, and
social and moral behaviour, so that we want our action to be literary
as well as our writing. And since love is one of the favourite themes
of our literature, we import an amorous point of view into our
opinions and our activities in the field of international politics."
Of the first of these tendencies there are many examples among the
events recorded in *Roma 1943*. When, in the summer of 1943, the
opposition to the war was mounting and it was plain that Italy had to
withdraw, the King is supposed to have said to Badoglio of the old
anti-Fascists like Bonomi and Orlando, who had been proposed to
form a new government: "But they are all ghosts!"—to which
Badoglio is said to have replied: "Your Majesty and I are also
ghosts." And in the second of these tendencies Monelli himself
indulges in a later passage: "It was not all at once that tryanny
revealed itself at the beginning of the dictatorship; it only matured
slowly, in the course of a series of arbitrary acts on the dictator's
part and a series of concessions and abdications on the part of the
people, who, as happens in the case of the concessions that the man
in love makes to the woman he loves, believed itself to be perfectly
free while it was allowing itself to be robbed of its freedom and its
privileges."

The book ends with the account of an incident which, to the
friendly American visitor, cannot fail to be moving as he reads it.
Monelli tells how, after horrible weeks of futile fighting and general
demoralisation, the Allies arrive in Rome. The Piazza Barberini is
empty and bright in the moonlight. "An enormous armoured car
has stopped at the corner of the Quattro Fontane; when we get there,
we see a line of other cars which have also stopped further up the
street. A curious and eager little crowd is making a hum of voices
about them, but does not shout or acclaim them. A lean and very

tall soldier is standing in front of the first car and chewing something. The people stare at him but do not speak. I call out (in English): 'Where do you come from?' 'From Texas,' he replies. I feel myself suddenly giddy amidst limitless open spaces which receive and dissolve the pain, the anguish of nine months, and in which relief itself is lost. Two little girls come up with a tricolour flag in their hands and give it to the soldier. He turns and looks up seriously at his comrades, who are sitting on top of the car and dangling their legs: 'Here's a flag,' he says. One of them stretches out his hand, and takes the flag, and hoists it on the turret."

But even this proves depressing when one has finished the book and reflects how little freedom our "tricolour" has brought them.

*   *   *

The young Italians who have come to manhood just before or during the war and who have fought in the resistance movement do seem to make a race quite distinct from any of the older people who have had in one way or another to adapt themselves to the Fascist regime. A young man of this kind, whose acquaintance I have made, a poet and teacher of literature, strikes, by his spirit and candour, a note that is at least hopeful. He points out that there have been always in Italy the same sharp and startling contrasts of character. The people of a city like Rome are predominantly distrustful and cynical; the men lend themselves to all kinds of servilities and frauds, the women all too easily become prostitutes. It is difficult to make them believe in ideas; but their indifference is always redeemed by the emergence of heroic individuals who are willing to die for ideas. Even in the sixteenth century, when Italy was ruled by Spain and under the heel of the Inquisition, when the self-respect of Italians was at one of its lowest ebbs and Italy mainly a field for the battles of alien armies, you had a man like Giordano Bruno; and then later, Garibaldi and Mazzini. (I had realised, since coming to Italy, that my friend Carlo Tresca had been made in this mould. I remembered how the coldness and rigour with which he had talked about politics had contrasted with the bombastic language of the articles in his paper, *Il Martello*, through which he had harangued his followers. Such men were incorruptible, and, except by execution as in Bruno's case, or by assassination, as in Carlo's, absolutely indestructible. They revived the antique virtue which had never quite died in Rome.) And now, my friend went on, it was not altogether impossible that Italy, having sloughed off Fascism earlier than the

est of the world and finding herself in ruins again, as she had done
o many times before, might produce, as she had done before, some
ew movement that would lead the world. But the Mazzinis and
Jaribaldis of the future would have to think, not as Italians, but as
Europeans.

*   *   *

At that time, thought I did not know it, the Italian moving
picture, *Città Aperta*, based on the resistance movement, had just
been finished in Rome; and, as I put these notes in order, it has just
been shown in New York. This picture is very much to the point in
the connection of which I have been speaking. How could we
correspondents, drowsing and grumbling about Rome in our
antiquated tourist hotel, have imagined that a work of such power, at
the same time intense and restrained, had been produced in the Via
del Tritone, where the prostitutes thronged every evening and
through which we walked to reach the Fagiano, out of a patchwork
of old lengths of film bought in the Black Market and with no kind
of studio light, so that everything had to be shot during the day-
time; or that the Roman Anna Magnani, that brilliant and intelligent
actress, whom we saw in the review *Cantachiaro*, impersonating a
D'Annunzio duchess in the manner of Beatrice Lillie and satirizing
the Allied occupation, had just given her marvellous performance as
the mistress of an underground worker. It is the antique virtue again,
and you can see it come to life in this film.

4

TWO SURVIVORS : MALRAUX AND SILONE

DURING the decade before the war, when the tradition of
Lenin was still alive and Marxism had still its prestige as a moral and
intellectual force, there appeared in Europe two first-rate novelists
who, though quite different in other ways both presented the
contemporary world in terms of the Marxist class conflict: the
Frenchman André Malraux and the Italian Ignazio Silone.

Malraux and Silone belong to the same European generation: there
is only a year between them, Malraux having been born in Paris in
1900 and Silone in a little town of the Abruzzi in 1901. Malraux, who
studied Oriental languages and went to the East as an archeologist,
became interested in the Chinese revolution, in which, from 1925 to
1927, he played an active role. He worked with the Communist
Kuomintang and was a member of the Committee of Twelve
which organised the Canton uprising. He wrote, out of this experience, his two novels *Les Conquérants* and *La Condition Humaine*,
and the first of them brought him to the attention of Trotsky, whose
acquaintance he made in the years when Trotsky was living in
France and who tried to correct what he regarded as Malraux's out-
of-date French romanticism and reconstruct him as an unambiguous
Marxist. Later, in the Spanish Civil War of 1936-39, Malraux took
part on the Loyalist side as chief of an escadrille and accepted the
direction of Moscow in its strategy and policy for Spain. Otherwise
he has remained, however, quite independent both of Trotskyist and
of Stalinist influence.

Silone, on the other hand, had been an active revolutionary worker
from 1917, when, at the age of seventeen, he became secretary of the
peasant movement, syndicalist in its political complexion, which had
been launched in his native Abruzzi. Soon thereafter, he went to
Rome, where he was first editor of a Socialist paper and then one of
the founders, under the inspiration of Moscow, of the Communist
Youth International, and where he took part, in 1921, in organising
the Italian Communist Party. In the years between 1925 and 1929, he
was a member of the Central Committee of the Party, doing underground work in Italy under the Mussolini regime and representing
the Party in Moscow during a period when its leader was in jail and
at such times as Silone himself did not happen to be in jail. When in

became evident, at the end of the twenties, that the Russians in the Communist International were beginning to dictate policy from the point of view of Russian interests at the expense of the freedom of the Communists of the parties of other nations to determine their own lines of action, Silone resigned, with a group which included about half the Italians; nor did he afterwards associate himself with the followers of either Bukharin or Trotsky, who had set up split-off Communist groups, for he felt, as he says, that these groups had all the defects of the Stalinist parties without the power of Moscow behind them. He left Italy at the end of the twenties and went into retirement in Switzerland, where for the first time he began to write novels and where he remained until 1944, when, after the fall of the Fascists, he returned to live in Rome.

The temperaments of Malraux and Silone present in certain respects a very sharp contrast. Malraux, though he served in Spain in the army of international Communism, has had, especially in his earlier career, an element of the international adventurer—part explorer of the ancient Oriental world, whose most exciting sensation it was to find there the twentieth-century class struggle; part Byronic egoist and actor, driven by an obscure compulsion to assert his will for its own sake—whereas Silone, since he has broken with Moscow, has been assuming a personality which combines in a peculiar way the traditional severity of the Communist with the compassion of a parish priest. For Malraux, the conception of the class struggle gave him a vision of the drama of history, in which he could play a role, fierce, courageous, perhaps noble; for Silone, it drew clear moral issues which showed him how to direct his energies toward ends that would benefit his fellows. Malraux is largely preoccupied with the tactics and significance of action, Silone with ethical problems. But both, during the critical years of their youth, accepted the Marxist assumptions as a guide to the contemporary world and worked for the Communist objectives, and this phase of their lives has supplied the themes of their most important books.

Now, for the sincere Marxist revolutionary who was able to think for himself and not afraid to follow his judgement, further belief in the Soviet Union as a power working for international socialism—if it had not become impossible already—became definitely so with the signing in August, 1939, of the Hitler-Stalin pact. There is an observation in Malraux's new novel which, though there applied to something else, sounds as if it had been inspired by the illusions of foreign Communists and Communist sympathisers about the conditions of life in the Soviet Union: "It is as impossible," he makes one of his characters say, "to see a country which embodies a myth in which one believes as it is to see a woman with whom one is in love." And the horror of the destruction of Europe and the degradation of human values, protracted through the five and a half years of this war, made the realisation of the socialist hope seem more and more remote and doubtful. For writers like Malraux and Silone, their natural line of development was broken; but, confronted with the scene of wreckage—living in the debris of defeated France under the German domination or isolated in Switzerland in an exile which must at moments have seemed likely to be permanent—they had to lay hold on the new situation and find some way of making something of it for the honour of their old ideals; and what they have made is of exceptional interest.

Malraux's novel, *La Lutte avec l'Ange* (evidently referring to the ordeal of Jacob in Genesis XXXII), which was published in Switzerland in 1943 in an edition of but fifteen hundred copies, is offered as the first section of a larger work—a work which could hardly have been finished, given the historical immediacy of the subject, before the war had come to an end, and which Malraux, who after the expulsion of the Germans was on active duty as colonel of a regiment could hardly have had a chance to finish. It is impossible, thus, to judge this instalment in any conclusive way, since it is concerned with presenting situations of which we are not yet able to see the upshot and propounding far-reaching questions to which the answers have not yet been found. The book develops a double story of two generations of an Alsatian family: the career of the German father a diplomat in the German service, who has seen something of World War I, and the adventures of the half-French son, who, in World War II, fights for the French. It is this son who is supposed to put together the whole rather complicated chronicle. Taken prisoner at the fall of France and sent to a concentration camp at Chartres, he goes back over his own experience and reflects on his father's exploit as he has learned of them through a set of notes which has come into his hands after the latter's death. The father, a capable and clever man, has that insatiable love of adventure, half-quixotic and half-perverse, which is characteristic of Malraux's heroes. Malraux brilliantly analyses his motives in a passage which explains his interest, passionate though apparently gratuitous, in the Young Turk movement of the beginning of the century: "His need to get away from Europe, the solicitation of history, the fanatical desire to leave a scar on the earth, the fascination of a project which he had ontributed not a little to shape, the fellowship of combat, and iendship." (It is worth noting that the protagonist of an earlier ook, *La Voie Royale*, a superman explorer with very little interest in olitics, says, in explaining the impulse that drives him: "I want to ave a scar on this map.") In Turkey, this accomplished Alsatian omes under the influence of the propaganda of the Pan-Turanian ovement, which aimed at uniting in a great Turkish empire all iose peoples who were assumed to be of Turkish stock; but as he avels in Afghanistan and finds only a "people of sleepwalkers" uite unconscious of their Turanianism, the whole myth suddenly des away. He returns and gives up his mission and presently lapses ack into working for the Germans, with whom he is always a little estive. Just before the first World War he is present at a cross-xamination, by the head of the Secret Service, of a supposed ussian woman spy, when they bring in her little son to try to make er betray herself, and later, when the war has begun, he assists at a oneering experiment with the use of poison gas. On this occasion, ie German soldiers, finding the Russians asphyxiated and choking, eld to a primitive human instinct and, instead of taking the ussian position, try to rescue the dying men. The Alsatian, him-lf half-intoxicated with gas, is soon irresistibly impelled to behave the others are doing: he picks up a gasping Russian and starts to rry him back toward the field hospital. In him, as in the soldiers, ere is something which revolts and balks against the cruel methods warfare that the German general staff is developing. But the scene w shifts back to his son, and, following immediately after the isode of the gas attack, we get an episode out of World War II— tank advance by the French, in which the young man had figured fore he was captured by the Germans. We are taken inside the nk; it is lumbering and groping at night through a heavy barrage of iellfire, and it slumps into an unseen trench, where it seems to lie avily helpless. Modern warfare has gone on getting worse, more ushing and more abasing. Nothing has been done to curb it, and e human race itself seems to have fallen, like the men in the tank, the bottom of a dark ditch, imprisoned and overwhelmed by a eat mass of anti-human machinery. Nor does there appear in the cond of these episodes, as there did in the gas attack, any sign of a aternal solidarity between the soldiers of the hostile armies.

Here the volume ends, but a larger vista of interest has been opened for the reader than this bare outline of the action would indicate. he narrator has a remarkable great-uncle, an intellectual, rather a lettante but in a serious German way. He has been a correspondent

of Nietzsche's and sometimes entertains Freud. At his house he hold
periodical conferences, to which he invites a varied company of
savants and at which set subjects are systematically discussed. Th
father of the narrator, returned from his travels, arrives in time for
one of these conferences, at which a great German anthropologi
who has been working for fifteen years on a book, is expected t
explain his views in a revelation of special importance. But it turn
out that he has just decided not to publish the book. This had bee
an Hegelian affair which led up to the proposition that the civilisa
tion of the Germans was the supreme end-product of history; but
the author has now ceased to believe this because he has ceased t
believe that what he calls "the human adventure" has any consisten
significance. The more he has come to examine the various kinds of
society which the human race has produced, the more he has bee
driven to question the continuity of human history and the logic of
human effort. He tells the company about the people who were fo
centuries firmly convinced that the person of their ruler was th
moon, that his power waxed and waned with it and that when
went into eclipse the king had to be strangled by his subjects; an
those natives of the Melanesian Islands who have never made an
connection between childbearing and sexual intercourse, refutin
attempts to enlighten them by pointing out that it is by no mean
true that the former always results from the latter. Just as th
narrator's father has lost the racial conception of Turanianism in th
presence of the Afghan tribes, so the German anthropologist ha
been losing the sense of the unity of human ideals and purpo
among the mutually exclusive delusions on which human civilisa
tions have been based. And are we not still, Western man, he ask
enveloped in some such delusion, which we are no more capable of
perceiving then the goldfish is of imagining its aquarium, which to
must seem to comprise the whole world when it is in reality a sma
glass box? And if this is our true situation, what, then, *is* our bas
delusion? Nationalism, someone suggests. No, not merely nationa
ism—our all pervading and inescapable false notion may well b
our idea of history and the conception of Time that goes with i
"Has the notion of man a meaning? In other words: under th
beliefs, the myths, especially under the multiplicity of ment
structures, is it possible to distinguish a permanent idea or directic
(Malraux uses the characteristically French and essentially inte
lectual word *donnée*), which retains its validity through history an
upon which a concept of man can be based?"

The question is never answered. These perplexities, one suppose

are the struggle with the angel, which left Jacob, it will be remembered, a prince who had "power with God and with men"; and the
whole discussion, though not very typical of the time at which it is
made to take place, the early years of the century, when the nations
seemed to be prospering under capitalism and few doubted the
inevitability of progress, serves to bring to a clear formulation the
kind of misgivings which has been tugging at our minds during these
years which have upset our assumptions. Malraux has here sidestepped completely all the obvious melodrama of the triumphs and
the defeats of the Fascist regimes, which our novelists in the United
States, comfortably far from the battle, have been exploiting with so
much fervour and cashing in on with so much success. Malraux's
hero is half-French and half-German, and his theme is not the
struggle with the Nazis, or even any longer the Marxist struggle of
classes, which gave the confrontation of forces in his earlier books,
but the justification of man himself.

La Lutte avec l'Ange is not, from the point of view of architecture
and writing, one of the most satisfactory of Malraux's books. It
seems rather to show the marks of having been written, against
pressures and under difficulties, only by dint of determined applica-
tion. Both the style and the mode of presentation give sometimes
—through overwriting or congestion—a certain effect of effort. An
admiration for English literature has apparently been responsible
here for some results that seem awkward in French. Malraux has
been praised by Gide, in deploring the feminity of French fiction, for
writing books which, by their masculine qualities, come closer to
such Anglo-Saxon novels as *Tom Jones* and *Moby Dick*, and he is
said, during the last years of the war, to have become a strong
Anglophile. Certainly, in *La Lutte avec l'Ange*, he has managed to
reproduce—though usually with bad effect—some of the most
flagrantly non-French traits of his favourite English authors:
Kipling's knowing international allusiveness, Meredith's elliptical
expression, and Conrad's mixed-up narrative method. Malraux, who
is said at one point to have escaped getting shot by the Germans by
impersonating an English officer, thus almost appears, in a literary
way, as one of those "displaced persons" whom a department of the
Allied Commission is now making efforts to repatriate.

But any effort to get outside the formulas which, in preserving the
French classical elegance, have tended lately to keep French literature
stereotyped and thereby rather provincial is undoubtedly an excellent
thing, and one finds in *La Lutte avec l'Ange* passages of sinewy and
searching thought, strokes of dramatic imagination, of which only a

E

man of genius would have been capable. Above all, there is a seriousness, an undulled perspicuity, about the large problems of human
destiny, that has become the rarest thing in the world. This novel is
both the most impressive and the most exciting piece of literature
that I have yet seen inspired by the war.

The typical heroes of the novels of both Malraux and Silone have
been workers for Marxist revolution, but the two writers have
strikingly differed in their attitudes toward what the Communists
used to call "the masses." Certainly, Malraux himself did not reach
the revolution primarily through sympathy for the underdog, but
rather, like his protagonist in *Les Conquérants*, through disgust with
the bourgeoisie—to which, in the author's case, must be added the
motivation of a very strong sense of what non-Communists call
"human decency." All the main characters in Malraux's novels are
more or less extraordinary or exceptional men, and the Communist's self-identification with the hardships and interests of the
working class has been the aspect of the social struggle which was
least adequately rendered in his novels. Now, however, in *La Lutte
avec l'Ange*, he has taken some special pains to try to make the
common man sympathetic; yet these scenes are not his most successful. The conversations between the soldiers just before the gas attack
seem a little gotten-up and laboured, the reflections to which they
give rise on the narrator's part a little self-conscious and sententious;
the whole thing has a suggestion, at moments, of a pastiche of the
Barbusse of *Le Feu*. The gas attack in which the German soldiers
show their human solidarity with the Russians is not so effectively
done as the tank battle in which the man of intellect loses control of
his monstrous machine.

Silone, on the other hand, has tended to be mainly preoccupied in
his fiction with the relation of the dedicated revolutionist to the
people whom he is supposed to be serving. When the Communist
line loses touch with the people, he comes to the conclusion that there
is something wrong, and though his protagonist, Pietro Spina, in his
novel *Pane e Vino*, never wearies of renewing his efforts to make
connections between the peasantry and the Communist Party, his
failures bring him constantly closer, at the expense of the Marxist
doctrine, to the point of view of the peasants. Pietro Spina, impatient
of the exile into which he has been driven by the Fascists, returns,
disguised as a priest, to his native Abruzzi mountains in an attempt
to rouse the people against Fascism and to build a revolutionary
movement, but he finds himself baffled at every turn by the primitive

mentality of the Italians, who see the world in terms of sins and pardons, saints and miracles, prayers and rites. He finds that, in spite of his efforts, he can make his only contact with them, not through his appeal to their class-consciousness, but through his natural sympathy for them, the sobriety of his life in their midst, a moral rectitude and a spiritual candour which they recognise and to which they respond.

And just as the false priest of *Pane e Vino* is, in the course of his relations with these peasants, half transformed into a real priest, to whom they look for forgiveness and guidance, whom they believe to possess powers of healing, while he, on his side, is coming to preach to them less as a mere political agitator than as a militant disciple of Christ, so Silone himself has drawn closer to the conceptions of primitive Christianity and has been trying to make a kind of merger between the ideals of modern socialism and these. "In the modern drama," he writes in the foreword to his new book, "a new element has appeared as a protagonist: the proletarian. Not new in the sense of not already having existed in antiquity, but because his ordeal and his destiny were not then considered suitable subjects for history, thought and art. If to us moderns the situation of this character seems the nearest to the human truth, it is because, in the last analysis, between the ancients and us there has been Jesus." This new book, first published in Switzerland in 1944 and now just brought out in Rome as the first of Silone's productions to be published in his native country, is a long play called *Ed Egli Si Nascose—And He Did Hide Himself*, a quotation from John XII (it is interesting that both Malraux and Silone should have gone to the Bible for titles), in which it is recorded that Jesus withdrew and disappeared from among his followers, after preaching:"Walk while ye have the light, lest darkness come upon you: for he that walketh in darkness knoweth not whither he goeth. While ye have the light, believe in the light, that ye may be the children of light." *Ed Egli Si Nascose* develops, on a larger scale and with a different implication, one of the incidents in *Pane e Vino*. In that novel there was a young man from the country who had gone to study in Rome and who, falling in love with an anti-Fascist girl, had associated himself with a revolutionary group. When his small supply of funds gave out, he resorted, in order to finish his courses, to taking money from the Fascist police for information against his companions. But he has been horribly tormented by conscience and, when he is caught in the country by the local police, he allows them to kill him on the spot on the assumption that he is a genuine revolutionary. His death is thus

an expiation and, in the account of it and the scene of his funeral
there are echoes of the Last Supper, the Passion and the Crucifixion
Now, in *Ed Egli Si Nascose*, Silone has made this episode his central
theme. The young man is here driven to redeem himself by the much
more positive gesture of actually printing and distributing a proletarian manifesto, and his murder at the hands of the Fascist
police proves the stimulus—where Spina has failed—that rouses the
people against the regime and leads them to organise a united
opposition. His death brings the play to a climax with a kind of
liturgical drama, which has its Joseph and Mary, its Magdalen, its
John the Baptist and its Holy Communion, all worked out in a
systematic parallel. Silone has explained in his foreword his belief
that "the revolution of our epoch, which has been promoted by
politicians and economists," presents "the appearance of a 'sacred
mystery,' in which the very fate of man is at stake." "In the sacred
history of man on earth, we are as yet, alas, only at Good Friday
The men who 'hunger and thirst after righteousness' are still being
derided and persecuted and put to death. The spirit is still forced to
hide in order to save itself."

In *Pane e Vino*, Silone had already had Pietro Spina ask the same
question as Malraux's anthropologist: "What is man? What is this
human life?" "Every revolution," he tells young Murica, the
informer who is to expiate his treason, "always turns on this
elementary question." And, "in this horrible society," where man is
"mutilated, disgraced, deformed, insulted," the problem is to become "a new man," or, rather, to become for the first time "a man
in the true sense of the word." Silone's way of finding a continuity in
the vicissitudes of human history is to conceive it as a vast enactment
of a drama to which the life of Jesus has given the symbolic clue.

Ed Egli Si Nascose, as a work of art, is less successful than *Pane e
Vino*. The novel, in its chronicle of the adventures of Spina and its
procession of Italian characters, had something in common with the
great panoramas like *Huckleberry Finn* and *Dead Souls*, and Silone
has not shown in this play a dramatic sense comparable to his
narrative one. The emergence, furthermore, of the mystery play
from the milieu of the modern Abruzzi may be found distasteful by
readers who are remote from the Catholic religion; certainly it will
be found dismaying by the old secularist type of Socialist. But the
piece is full of excellent things: particularly the post-mortem discus-
sions of the psychology of Communist activity in the period before
the war. "The underground character of the movement," the young
renegade is made to explain, " offers to the weak man the important

and deceptive advantage of secrecy. He lives in sacrilege and shudders at it, but this is all concealed from the world. He is outside the hateful and terrifying law, but the guardians of the law do not know it. His denial of the established order remains an intimate and secret thing, as if it took place in a dream, and precisely on that account is likely to run to ideas that are drastic, catastrophic and bloody; but his external behaviour remains unchanged. In his habitual relations this kind of weak man remains as timid, silly and nervous as before. He conspires against the government in the same way that he may be in the habit of dreaming that he is strangling his father, with whom he will sit down to breakfast in the morning." And there is an equally merciless passage on revolutionary work as a drug. The Communist's life is so dangerous and hard, one of the underground workers explains, that the only way to accomplish anything is to eliminate the strain on your nerves, and to do this is to induce a narcosis. "But," one of the women characters objects, "excuse me if I ask a stupid question. How can we be true and brave fighters for the revolution and be drugged at the same time? Shall we turn into a movement of sleepwalkers? . . . If we come to the revolutionary cause precisely through our sensibility—because our sensibility has been wounded by the savagery, the injustice, the brutality which we have found in present-day society? If we neutralise our sensibility, aren't we destroying in ourselves the very feelings that have brought us to the revolution?" The narcotised revolutionist may become unscrupulous and cruel and lose sight of the ends that he set out to serve, and the weak man who loves concealment may find it easy, under pressure of terrorism, to betray the underground movement and to keep this betrayal concealed. When young Murica has turned stool pigeon for the Fascists, he begins to be tortured by the notion that, if no one ever finds him out, he will never be punished for his treason, and it is a horror of this idea that good and bad may be mere matters of practical expediency which drives him, in moral protest, to do something that will get him into trouble. For Silone is here grappling with a problem that is one aspect of the problem of Malraux: the justification of a human morality at this moment when the religions are losing their force and man, finding himself alone on the earth, has to recognise that it is he who decides what should and what should not be done. The situation of the German Nazis was precisely that of young Murica: why worry about moral principles if you are never to be called to account?—and, unlike Silone's young student, they could not see that they did have to worry.

Silone, confronting this question, has reverted to the Christian

religion in a special non-ecclesiastical form, a version which one may
find it easier to sympathise with than the formal and official versions
of some of the recent Protestant converts to Catholicism. His point
of view is a curious one. He makes one of his characters speak of
"the new idea of good and evil" of "those who do not believe in the
death and resurrection of Jesus but do believe in His agony," and he
has explained to the present writer that he does not accept what he
calls "the mythology of Christianity," that the liturgical form of his
play and the analogies with the Gospel in his novels have come to
him, in the most natural way, as a result of having known in his
childhood no literature except the Bible and of never, till he was
seventeen, having seen any drama except the Mass. Yet certainly
the life of Jesus has still for him a mystical meaning, and, in a paper
read recently in Rome before the Associazione per il Progresso degli
Studi Morali e Religiosi—I quote from the newspaper account—he dis-
associated his present position from that of the Russian ex-Socialist
"God-seekers" after the defeat of the 1905 revolution, but asserted
that he belonged among "those of whom St. Bernard speaks, those
whom God pursues, and whom, when He overtakes them, He
tears to pieces and chews and swallows." All this does not, however, prevent him from taking a very active part in the work of the
Socialist Party as a member of its Central Committee.

Malraux and Silone thus seem to stand to-day almost alone in
Europe as writers of first-rate talent who have continued to take
imaginative literature with the utmost seriousness and who have
never lost their hold on the social developments, larger and more
fundamental, that lie behind national conflicts. They have survived
the intellectual starvation, the spiritual panic of the war, and they are
among the most valuable forces still alive on their devastated
continent. Still they are trying to perform through their writing what
Malraux makes one of his characters describe as the function of art
"a rectification of the world. . . . It seems to me that the cardinal
confusion has arisen from our having assumed—in our conception of
Greek tragedy it's striking—that to represent a doom is to suffer it.
But that's not true: rather, it's almost to possess it. The very power
of being able to represent it, to conceive it, allows it to escape from
its real fate, from the implacable divine scale; brings it down to the
human scale. In what is essential, our art is a humanisation of the
world." This is a much humbler point of view than that of the
defiant Romantics of the first half of the nineteenth-century or of the
professional Titans of the second half, but it trusts in human strength

and vindicates human pride as the writers of our day have not always done. "The greatest mystery," says Malraux in another fine passage of his novel, "is not that we should have been thrown up by chance between the profusion of matter and the profusion of the stars, but that, in that prison, we should produce from ourselves images sufficiently powerful to deny our insignificance."

5

THROUGH THE ABRUZZI WITH MATTIE AND HARRIET

WHEN Mattie Nugent went out to the Abruzzi, she expected something pretty rugged and brought along a blanket-roll and rations. She was amazed to be put up at Aquila, her headquarters as an U.N.R.R.A. worker, in a magnificent new hotel, which had been built under the Fascists as a ski-ing resort and had been lately commandeered by the Allied Commission.

She was received by a good-looking young major, with a small smartly-clipped dark moustache, who, though he wore an American uniform, gave her the impression of being British. "I'd love one!" she declared enthusiastically, when he suggested she might like a cocktail even before she washed off the dust; and he guided her through high-ceilinged chambers that, palatially cool though they were, had a little that pasteboardy appearance which she had noted in the big office buildings put up by the Fascists in Rome: a lobby, where a woman—an Italian, she thought—very quiet but rather chic—looked up from the book she was reading; a spacious lounge with yellowish marble walls that opened pleasantly out on a garden, full of sun but devoid of flowers, in the centre of which, on a pedestal stood a black bronze of a naked young girl clasping behind her an enormous fish that seemed to Mattie, like so many things in Italy, not sensual merely but almost obscene; and, beyond, a soft-carpeted soft-lighted bar that reminded her of the latest thing in the "intimate" and the "modern" in the Statler hotels at home, but which was lined with a series of murals of English and Scottish soldiers amusing themselves in night-clubs or active at outdoor sports. "These decorations must be new," Mattie remarked, as they waited for drinks. "Yes, it was crawling with young Fascists on skis when the A.C. took the place over. But there's a very clever chap here who paints and he dashed off these muriels for us." The "muriels," which was meant as a joke, rather amused Mattie. She wondered whether the Major were Canadian.

"This is a rest-home, you know," he went on. "It's the first big attempt that's been made to get the Americans and the British together. Churchill's watching it, and so is F.D.R." "How is it working out?" "Oh, swell. The first one, in Sicily, was not a success; but this time we're going to swing it! We've actually got the Americans playing cricket and the British playing soft-ball." "Those soldiers in the picture are all British," said Mattie, when she had studied the panels. "It was a Britisher that did them. But don't worry: we're holding up our end. I'm in charge here, and I'm an American." He smiled gracefully with self-assurance. He was obviously enjoying himself, making good, as he felt, at a greeter's job. "Where are you from?" she asked as a man would ask. "Buffalo. Where do you hail from?"—he had caught up her hearty note and was being somewhat more American. "I originally came from Vermont, but I've lived mostly in New York and Washington." "Well, we have plenty of Yankees here—New Hampshire and Massachusetts. Just about the whole English-speaking world is represented in the hotel now! We've even got a couple of New Zealanders." "Oh, it ought to be so *easy!*—if they'd just get used to each other's accents. It's principally the difference in pay that makes things difficult, isn't it? They don't like to go on parties together, because the G.I.'s have more dough." "That isn't an obstacle here," he assured her. "Everything's free except drinks, and we've made prices that are well within everybody's means." "What about women?" "There are plenty of girls." "But money's quite a factor there, isn't it?" "They come to dances that we give at the hotel here and that are joint affairs, of course— and then we have our snappy U.N.R.R.A. workers!" Mattie had noted, and now she reminded herself, that his gallantry was at least partly professional—that his raising of his left eyebrow and smiling on one side of his mouth had obviously been carefully acquired and that he exploited them for effect; yet she couldn't help feeling pleased. She hadn't ever had enough of this kind of thing to be scornful or blasé about it: men liked her and were always all right to her, except when, as sometimes happened, she frightened them by trying to run them; but her normal role was that of the pal who, if she did not always pay for her dinner, never slipped into a position of dependency; and it was nice to be treated flirtatiously, especially in this situation—doing U.N.R.R.A. work out in the mountains— where you would not have expected to be.

"Let me know if you want anything!" he said, with a fascinating special twinkle, as he later sent her up to her room, with a boy to carry her baggage. "I'm sorry it's such a climb, but we hope to have the lift working soon. I think you'll like the room—it's got a swell view." They ascended soft, ample and shallow steps that swept imperially around three curves; and she was shown into an attractive bedroom, very new, very light, very blond, in which the twin beds with blue blankets and the glass-topped tables and bureau were of

pale unpainted wood, and the tall blinds of the big French window
opened portals to a blue mountain landscape. It was a place so much
created for winter sports that she seemed to herself out of key, until
resisting the pressure of solitude, she began to assimilate herself to a
girl who should have come there for that. She had once been a pretty
good skier, before she had hurt her knee, and she imagined young
Fascist couples—those dark-haired vivacious young women with
their flashy but handsome young men—revelling insolently in
privileged holidays: their dashing ski-runs and deep relaxed evenings,
their intimate laughter, exciting love. In happier conditions, she
thought, she could have done with a little of that. Her most serious
love-affairs had never quite carried her off her feet and had always in
the end let her down. There had been, first, a Jewish settlement
worker; then a middle-aged business man who was unfortunately
permanently married; then, most recently, a liberal journalist, who
had become a New Deal official and afterwards a captain in the
Allied Commission, assigned for duty to Rome. Though their
amorous relations had petered out, she had looked forward to seeing
him there, and had not been able to help feeling hurt when she had
found him inhabiting an apartment with a pretty Italian girl of
nineteen—Mattie was thirty-four—who kept house for him as if
they were married. No: she had never had the kind of devotion or
been given the kind of good time that a girl had a right to expect.—
Unless of course those young Fascist blades had been all fund-
amentally phony.

But yes, Aquila did seem romantic as she stood gazing out the
window. She had never been in Europe before, and this was turning
out so much more like a pleasure trip than she had expected it or
thought it ought to be. She had only been in Italy a couple of weeks,
and she had found herself thrilled no end when, setting out in the
jeep from Rome, she had first become aware of the fine layers of
hills, one rising behind the other, in their delicate and varying tints
of gray, and then had seen, under low-hanging clouds of a silver
dullish and pure, the lovely silhouette of a mountain so dim and yet
outlined so firmly that it might have been drawn by an artist and
washed in with watered ink. Later they passed wide-skirted women
balancing baskets and jars on their heads, unexpected little statues of
the Virgin bricked-in over stable-doors, and a tonsured Franciscan
monk riding a bicycle with his robe fastened and it had made her a
little giddy to see the almost sheer olive-groves and vineyards
cultivated with such precision on what seemed such precarious slopes,
and by those hill-towns, all in one formless piece and riddled with

heir tiny square windows, that seemed so much of the same brownish-grayish substance as the barren rocks on which they were based that they might almost have been the mere caves of cliff-dwellers or even the nests of birds. To an American, they were hardly acceptable as habitations for human beings, and, though she she tried to think them picturesque, her first instinct was to find them repellent: one especially that had crumbled to rubble under bombing or artillery attack inspired her with utter disgust like a clay wasps'-nest incompletely swept down. Then there were landscapes that would have taken her unbelievably into a mediaeval story-book world—with their steep hills, crowned with little walled cities, spiked or specked with various plantings or circled with vegetation and ribboned with dry white roads that wound down from the town to the plain—if she had not corrected the fantasy by recognising that the quaint old pictures which she had seen in museums at home had been perfectly realistic: the country really looked like that. And now, as she stared out the French window at these impressive Abruzzi ridges that combined in so special a way hard temper with soft colour—as if there were steel underneath blue silver, yet a blue so etherealised that one peak, with its pencilled veins of snow, seemed to merge into the slate-blue heavens; as she looked, she felt lifted and freshened just the way she had sometimes been when she had gone back home to Vermont for a visit and had seen her own mountains again. And these mountains were so clean and upstanding!—how could the people who lived among them not be so? How could Italians, who were descended from the Romans and had that beautiful and hard-boned country, allow themselves to get roped in by such an obvious fraud as Fascism? And yet it must have given them something they liked. Had she not, in imagination, been sharing their fun in that skiers' hotel? They were *simple*, after all!—they had been misled. It both exasperated her and broke her heart! And her fancy now made her a leader who was warning them and forcing them to fight for their rights.

There was a knock. Mattie opened. A tall girl in a blue dress stood there "I'm Harriet Locker," she said. Miss Locker was the field head for U.N.R.R.A., to whom Mattie had been told to report. She came in and gave Mattie a handshake which consisted of a single pump, after which her hand dropped to her side. She had a small ruddy gray-eyed face and bare reddened roughened legs, and wore a dark-blue béret on one side. She seated herself on a bed. "Are you all right?" she asked. "Have you had some lunch?—There's nothing to be done till five." Quickly and quietly she went through

her briefing. Mattie was sure she was going to like her so much!
She had always admired the English: she herself was long-faced and
athletic, energetic and not easily daunted; and she had hoped to get
along with them well. It was true that her friend in Rome had made
bitter and indignant complaints about their policy with the Italians
and their treatment of their American colleagues; but at the
moment she was rather in reaction against his whole point of view—
he had done such a lot of talking, always making someone else to
blame, and had never really lived up to his principles!—and she was
quite willing to find the British friendly. How she loved the informal
authority, the casual-seeming firmness and sureness, with which
Miss Locker mapped the situation and indicated Mattie's duties!
An American would have been more assertive—either as a career
woman imposing herself on you or a "character" inviting you to
share with her her amusement, her impatience or her enthusiasm;
and how much more impressive it was not to exhibit your zeal or
your competence, but simply to do a good job without calling
attention to yourself or confusing the problem with personal feelings! And how this girl seemed to be hitting all the nails on the head!
The only thing that she had not made clear, Mattie realised when she
had questioned her about the scope of their work, was her own very
responsible position as the sole representative for U.N.R.R.A. in
four wild and inaccessible provinces.

"Of course they're supposed to do things themselves," said Miss
Locker, "and one is here merely to supervise." "But you have to
crack down on them sometimes, I understand." "Oh, things have
been going quite smoothly." She seemed to hesitate a second—
then went on drily to an official confidence: "There's one lot of
food that hasn't turned up, and it may have gone astray." "Sold to
the Black Market?" asked Mattie. "One can't be sure what's happened. I've been prodding them about it, but can't get a clear story. It
ought to have been distributed two weeks ago, and they keep on
making excuses. But they've promised to produce it tomorrow, so
we'll see. It's not always easy to know what's being done, because
the stuff doesn't go through our hands." "But still"—Mattie
affirmed with great confidence the democratic policy of U.N.R.R.A.
—"they've got to learn to take *hold* and handle their own affairs!"
"They're complaining," Miss Locker replied, "that we don't give
them enough direction. They say they got on better with the Germans
because they told them exactly what to do." "But then, they've been
taking orders from the Fascists *so long!*—and the whole regime was
so crooked that they take to the Black Market like mad!"

It was not until a minute or two after she had expressed herself so strongly that it occurred to her that it might not be quite proper, the very moment of her arrival to lay down such positive opinions. Miss Locker had changed the subject, and Mattie saw that she was rather shy and that it cost her a certain effort to put their relation on a natural basis of two young women working together. She tried to meet the nice girl halfway, and when her new chief addressed her as "Mathilda," she said, "Everybody calls me Mattie,"—adding, with a quick grin: "I'm not going to call you Hattie, though!" But the other did not smile in return: the look in her grey eyes was blank, as if she did not know how to take it. "I must watch my cracks, I guess," thought Mattie. "I'm going to have a bath," she said, "and then, if you don't need me till five, I think I'll go out and get a load of the town." Harriet looked at her without replying. Then, "You can go in the jeep," she said. "I'll show you about, if you like."

Mattie, as they drove through Aquila, was dazed with wonder and fun. The town looked as if it were constructed of hard planes of shade and light that made the most violent contrasts. Above white blinding side-walkless streets stood façades built of local stone that had a richness despite their austerity, with their juxtaposed orange and sepia, burnt sienna and cafe au lait, neutral liver and greenish grey, that made a double scale of colours, one darkened and cold, one glowing. The tall doorways were impressively hooded with heavy ornamental architraves, and the windows, well-proportioned and brown-shuttered, were capped with a variety of pediments that resembled, now triangular crests, now crowns with twin peaks, now coronets, and contributed to a standard of dignity that—surprisingly, she thought, in that mountain town—attained something akin to grandeur. It did seem queer and not quite comfortable to keep driving through a place of that size and never once to pass a corner drug-store or a Woolworth's or an A. & P.; but Aquila had a unity and a harmony which made it seem all to have been built in one piece like those wasps'-nests in the hills that had given her the creeps, but which here imposed themselves upon her and compelled her to respect and admire. This, she saw, was what architecture could do—not merely lay out a plan as at Washington, but dominate a whole city and actually provide the medium in which human beings lived.

"It doesn't seem to be much damaged," she said. "There was an Austrian in command," explained Harriet, "and he evidently

behaved very well: he didn't blow things up when he left. The
Germans shot him for it. The electrical plant was mined, but the
inhabitants dug it out." "They look as if they had guts," said Mattie.
Straight, hardened, lean and tall, they were quite different from the
Italians of Rome: why of course! they were mountaineers, like the
people of Vermont and New Hampshire. She wasn't sure they
weren't a tougher breed, because the New Englanders had been
certainly degenerating, and these people seemed to have remained the
same for hundreds and hundreds of years. "One can't always depend
on them," said Harriet, lowering her voice to a murmur, so as not
to be overheard by the driver, though he apparently understood no
English.—"That's where they wander up and down," she glanced at
a long domed colonnade, with attractive-looking cafés and shops
displaying unfamiliar objects that Mattie would have liked to
examine.

"Go to the right," Harriet ordered the driver. He half-turned, but
did not answer. "To the right," she repeated. Mattie helped her out
"*A destra!*" she said loudly and clearly. "*Più lontano*," he replied
" 'More something,'—I don't get it.—Oh, 'further'!"—as he flapped
with his right hand forward. "They always want to do things their
own way," said Harriet. "What does *più* mean? They're always
saying it," Mattie explained to her the driver's phrase. "Then there's
a *pòi*," her companion went on, as if to ease off her momentary
interest by slipping into a lightly derisory attitude toward a language
full of babyish monosyllables. "And something that sounds like
po." "*Pòi* means 'then,' " said Mattie,—"and there's a *può* that's
the third person singular of the verb that means *to be able*." "Is that
what it is?" said Harriet, her voice now quite devoid of interest
and she somehow made Mattie feel that she had been a little showing off and that the meaning of Italian words was not a subject in
which it was suitable to evince too keen an interest.

The Fascists, it became apparent, had done a good deal for
Aquila; an influential Fascist had come from there and had seen to
it that the town was well-equipped. Harriet pointed out a stadium and
a swimming-pool, with a faint smile which indicated amusement at
the idea of Italians' pretending to go in for real sports like Englishmen and to which Mattie found herself responding with a little
ironic twist of one corner of her wide and good-natured mouth
"Our men are using them now," said Harriet. Then they drove up
before the G.I.L., the Gioventù Italiana del Littorio: a long building
with a shrimp-pink façade and a triple row of slotlike windows
from the roof of which were flying, side by side, the British and the

American flags. It was pretty perhaps rather than imposing, but you had to admit, she thought, that the Fascists *had* given them *something*. She rather admired the ramplike stairways (on one of which, however, she noted, with reprobation for what it implied, a big decorative map of l'Africa Orientale Italiana); the verandah that stretched at the back, furnished comfortably with steamer chairs and commanding a marvellous view; the dining-rooms and school-rooms, into which they looked, full of unpainted "functional" furniture, in which children were still being taught and fed; and the club-room hung with photographs of old school groups. A number of these photographs had been destroyed, an American soldier told them, because they had had Fascist slogans underneath. "It seems kind of a shame," said Mattie, "that some of the kids should lose their class pictures." "They can't expect anything else," said Harriet quickly and firmly.

"Drive to the castle," she told the driver. This was a word he could understand. The castle was a flat grey stone fortress, surround-ed by a dried-up moat and guarded above the door with the epony-mous Aquila eagle. "Pretty grim!" commented Mattie. "I don't think we can use it as a country club!" Harriet made no response: "I've lost her again!" thought Mattie. They walked back to get into the car, and Mattie smiled at the driver. "*Ecco il Gran Sasso d'Italia,*" he gestured in the direction of the mountains,—"*dov' era imprigionato Mussolini.*" "*Lei è allegro,*" she asked, being careful to use the polite form, "*che Mussolini partito?*" "*Era un buffone, vigliacco,*" he answered, starting the car. "They drive like Jehus," said Harriet, in a way that Mattie couldn't help feeling was intended to detach her from the driver. "Where is San Bernardino?" she asked. "I'm afraid I don't know," said Harriet. "The Major says it's a beautiful church,"—Mattie took out a guidebook he had given her,—"that it's something you ought to see." The driver made a sudden sharp turn and stopped before a square stone façade—announcing, "*Ecco San Bernardino.*" Harriet was plainly annoyed, but she did not express her annoyance. "Do you want to see it?" she asked. "I'd like to go in for a minute, but if we have to get back, it's not—" "*I'll* have to go back, I'm afraid, but if you don't mind walking and will be on hand at five." "I've got an hour and twenty minutes,"—Mattie briefly flashed up her wrist-watch, "and—" "You won't get lost?"—her chief again cut her short—"It's just down that long street we were coming to before we turned off here. Since you speak Italian so well, you can ask if you go astray." She left Mattie feeling, for a moment, a little silly over her efforts at Italian and somehow a

little guilty for her desire to stop off at the church. She wondered
whether Harriet Locker—who had, after all, been to see the castle—
were not some kind of clergyman's daughter, so that she shunned the
monuments of Popery on principle. Yes: she might perfectly well
have come from some vicarage or rectory in the country such as you
read about in English novels. She was very provincial, of course,
and that was the reason, poor dear, that she hadn't learned a word of
Italian. And Mattie pushed open the dark old door and invaded San
Bernardino.

Inside, the deep cool shade was wonderful; and, though in
Catholic churches at home she had always thought of cheap perfume,
the sweetness of the incense here seemed disinfected by the ancient
stone, and the candles burning in silence conveyed sanctity as well as
peace. She made the rounds, at first a little self-consciously, of the
tombs with elaborate carvings which were confusing and too fancy
to please her; a crowned madonna that she thought really touching,
that idea of the Queen of Heaven so full of love for her child!
and a big terracotta panel of the Resurrection, in which seraphs and
saints and angels seemed to be foaming and coagulating like curd,
and which she was thrilled to discover from the guidebook was
supposed to be by Della Robbia, the man who had made the cherubs
a dear travelled aunt in Topsfield, Mass., had had them in her
dining-room. But what Mattie had not at first taken in, going from
one of these sideshows to the other, and what suddenly lifted her
spirit as she stood in the aisle and looked up, was the magnificent
gold-and-white nave that opened before and above her. An arcade of
high white arches, between each two of which, as if inlaid in the
woodwork, stood a white column with a gilded Corinthian top, gave
way to a white windowed clerestory and supported a gold coffered
ceiling which had a sword-raying sun in the middle and which
framed, on either side of this, a succession of sacred paintings of
which the colours seemed softer and more charming, the figures more
appealingly human, for the great wrought ornate brooches that
encased them. And this white panelling, this sober design, that
arrived at felicity through purity, was close enough in tone to the old
Congregational churches in which, on New England "greens," she
had sung hymns and listened to sermons, to make her feel now half
at home; and as she slowly moved down the aisle, she had almost
the reassuring sensation of having just stepped out of a marsh onto
indubitable solid ground. Here was something that had kept strong
and comely, that had sustained the dignity of man, till it did seem to
touch that Divine which, in the days before bombings, before

settlement work, before statistics on unemployment and wage-scales, the human race had not hesitated to postulate. What did it matter if religion was not really true? You were grateful enough for something like this—which had been spared, in these days by the merest chance, through the compassion or the good taste of one Austrian, who had perhaps admired the little mountain city and who had paid for its survival with his life!

She approached the foot of the nave and saw before her an open back-door, of which she had not been aware at a distance. Set thus in the dark wall of shade, a small rectangle, clear-cut and bright-lit, it gave a view, above a hillside that dropped sheer below, of the hillside that rose higher just opposite: a sudden vivid green-and-blue vista, that seemed itself a kind of church picture, painted devoutly in the age of faith and placed there where it could always be looked at, where it could always be seen at its best. She stood still, and tears came to her eyes. So in those days they had humanised, had focussed for art, even the sun and the trees and the grass, even the towering mountains, and, in humanising them, had offered them to God!

And now it was time to go back to the hotel.

II

They had a friendly breakfast together, comparing notes about settlement houses, and got off in good time in the jeep. Mattie remarked on the strange lack of odour of the Italian countryside, which caused her something like a feeling of frustration, as she missed the American humidity that always brought out so heavily the smells of vegetation and earth. Harriet agreed to this: you smelled things much more strongly in England, too. "There are no dogs either," she added. "They've eaten them, I suppose," said Mattie,—"or else had to let them starve." "It's been hard to feed them in England," said Harriet, "but the people would never eat them." It turned out that Harriet possessed two dogs, which she evidently adored. One was a Sealyham and one was a sheep-dog. Her mother was looking after them at home, but she was lame and couldn't take them for walks. Harriet was afraid that they weren't getting proper exercise. Mattie had had two Scotties, one of which—"oh, he was so cute and such a *scrapper!*"—had been killed by a car, it had broken her heart, and the other of which, given her later, she had had to leave with her sister when she had gone to do war-work in Washington.

Harriet paid no attention to the scenes among which they were

F

passing—she had of course had plenty of time to get used to them—
and the effect of this impassivity on Mattie was somewhat to check
her exclamatory tendencies. Yes, you had to take the ruin for
granted; this hideous and dismaying prospect was where your work
began. There was no nonsense about the British, even on an errand of
mercy, and that was the way to be. But all this country had been a
battlefield, and almost everything connected with peacetime had
been blown into smithereens. Frivolous villas in pink or blue that
had once been frilled with little iron balconies and red crenellated
roofs, had been crushed in like brittle molluscs, and the pretty
terra-cotta statues that had sometimes posed in niches outside had
had their heads and their hands snapped off. In one place, a grand
iron gateway, flanked by large marble urns, led to a fragment of
pretentious façade with a doorway of carved marble and the grill-
work of two upstairs windows, but nothing whatever behind it—
though a plain little mud-coloured church had somehow remained
intact. The bridges had all been blown up, so that the car would have
to bump down a bank, where a precarious path had been broken
through, and would find, among the pale dusty pebbles of the dried-
up river-bed, chunks of masonry, crumbled and dusty, that could
hardly be told from the dirt. Among the only things still in good
order were the supplies of unused shells and bombs piled up here
and there beside the road and, in one place, a whole field of German
tanks that, pointing their guns like proboscis and mottled with
dirty green, looked—as Mattie refrained from remarking—like a
herd of queer grisly cattle.

But the road had the appearance at certain points of having had
enormous mouthfuls bitten out of it, and she remembered that the
driver, on the way from Rome, had told her that there were still
some live mines and that it was better to avoid the shoulders.
Their present driver was definitely reckless, and, as Harriet did
nothing to restrain him, Mattie assumed that, since the day before,
her chief had given up hope of controlling him. "I'm going to tell
him to keep in the middle," she said in a low voice and began to
consult her pocket lexicon. Harriet made no reply and let Mattie
expostulate and gesticulate; but when she said afterwards, "I think
we're quite safe," she made Mattie wonder again whether she hadn't
made a fool of herself.

They spent the night in a town called Chieti, which was a good deal
less civilised than Aquila and seemed to Mattie quite mediæval.
The cramped and offal-strewn streets had no pavements, and they
were raucous with shouts and howls. It was the first thing that had

scared her a little. At the hotel, which was also small and dirty, the old room-clerk looked like a rat. When she and Harriet separated to go to bed, Harriet gave her some bug-powder. "You'd better keep your door locked," she warned her. "I missed a garment once after I stayed here." And Mattie, rather nervous for her, was kept awake most of the night by bands of young men who prowled the streets singing at the tops of their voices. At one point, she got up to look at them. They did not seem to be swaggering so much as she had thought they were, but slowly drifting arm in arm, so that she felt more sympathetic toward them. Was it some kind of politics, she wondered, or merely some youthful whoopee? But why were so many of them abroad on a weekday?—and why did they keep going all night? Was it something so romantic and gratuitous that a New Englander couldn't grasp it? In any case, it was evidently something not directed by the Allied Commission.

The next morning they went on to Orsogna, the place where the food supplies had disappeared. Though Mattie had now seen already a good many smashed or battered buildings, she was not quite prepared for Orsogna. Here, what had once been the public square was a barren expanse of dust, no longer surrounded by houses but vaguely bounded by piles of bricks and plaster and a few upright morsels of walls, with the shutters hanging askew by one corner and the wiring of fixtures and balconies shredded like spiders'-webs. Inside these wrecked human cells, the swifts had stuck their cell-like nests, and they were flitting in and out, busily intent on their households and delighted with the new quarters thrown open to them while the only sound to be heard was the incessant bleating of a goat, tied up near the place where the car had stopped. The goat seemed badly diseased: it was raw in great patches of a horrid pink, and Mattie tried to exclude it from her consciousness.

A handful of people who had been hanging around gathered quietly near the car, and others emerged from the ruins. They were barefoot, and such clothes as they had were ill-fitting and patched and discoloured, yet they made a fairly decent appearance. They were not voluble, Mattie noted, but seemed rather restrained and sober. An official called the *sindaco* came out, evidently a kind of mayor—wearing a well-curled white mustache and dressed in formal bourgeois black. Harriet talked to him through an interpreter, whom she had brought along from Chieti: a girl from Bridgeport, who had married an Italian and gone to live in Italy. Harriet tackled the food at once. It was known to have got there two weeks ago: why hadn't they given it out? They had been waiting, the *sindaco* explained, for

instructions to come from Rome. But they had had their instructions
from Rome. Yes, but only a few days ago. Then why had the
distribution not been announced at once? It had been: they had put
up posters. He handed her something written in longhand, very
archaic and clerical-looking. But where were the announcements?
—she looked around: there was nothing on any of the walls except
clumsily painted-up slogans of *Viva Lenin* and *Viva il Comunismo*.
That had been several days ago, he said, and they had taken them
down since. "They've never posted any announcement, you see,"
Harriett murmured to Mattie. Well, why weren't they distributing
the food?—They had said they would do it at half past ten, and she
had come expecting to find them doing it. The *sindaco* said he was
sorry—there had had to be a little delay: some of the people worked
in the fields and couldn't be there in the morning. The distribution
would take place this afternoon.—"He says that they'll positively
do it," the American interpreter explained. "Tell him," said Harriet
"that I'll come back at three." Mattie understood the *sindaco* when
he replied, "*Alle tre precise!*"

In the meantime, they went on to another town. Mattie felt sorry
for Harriet. If the food had really disappeared and they were unable
to produce it that afternoon, she would have to raise Cain with the
sindaco without knowing any Italian and would then have to take it
up with U.N.R.R.A. headquarters in Rome, who might think she
hadn't been on the job. Mattie was just going to try to say something
helpful when Harriet said something herself: "Tell him we're sure
to need petrol before we get back from Tollo. Tell him to get some
here." Mattie asked, after a moment's silence: "Are there many
towns in as bad shape as that?" It was the first time she had ventured
to comment. "About thirty in this province," answered Harriet.

Tollo, though it figured on the guidebook map as a name the same
size as Orsogna, made the latter seem a thriving metropolis. Whatever had been there once was now pulverised level with the road and
of exactly the same colour. The only thing standing was a kind of
shed, which had been recently knocked together, and to which a few
women and children who had been living under haystacks or in huts
in the fields had come to apply for the handout of lard, flour and
sugar, dried codfish, dried milk and dried beans, so meagre that it
had had to be limited to expectant or nursing mothers and to children
under the age of eight. When the U.N.R.R.A. workers appeared,
everybody smiled and applauded, and Mattie could not help feeling
pleased. She tried to talk to the women, and the interpreter helped her
out. One of the burstingly pregnant ones had already, it seemed, had

ten. The mother's face proudly beamed as if she expected congratulations. But Harriet only said: "One would think they wouldn't want so many." "Oh, lo-ok!" cried Mattie, delighted, over a tiny two-year-old girl, who was practicing to carry the big earthen jars, for which, it seemed, the word was *conche*, by balancing on her head a little aluminum bowl. Harriet was too much preoccupied with her position of responsibility to do more than give a fleeting smile. "Yes: she *is* rather sweet," she said.

On the way back, they stopped for a moment and ate some sandwiches that Harriet had brought along, and Mattie produced some American chocolate, to which Harriet seemed to react with more eagerness than Mattie had seen her show about anything but the thought of her dogs. "You're lucky," she said, "to have your PX's. We haven't had any proper sweets in England for ages." "I must give you some of my peanut brittle,"—Mattie tried to explain what this was, and Harriet replied by describing how their nana used to make them taffy—Harriet called it "toffy"—"It was awful fun," she said. She seemed to feel so much interest in this subject—"It's the Camp Fire Girl touch," though Mattie—that her lieutenant did not hesitate to pursue it. "And marshmallows!" Mattie exclaimed. "They have them now at the PX in Rome. I'll get you some and show you how to roast them. It's quite a trick, but when you get them just right, they're absolutely delicious. They have a sort of golden-brown toasted crust, and inside they're all melted and goozily!" But then she was pulled up short by the thought of the dried milk and codfish that they had just been giving out at Tollo. "Well," she declared, "it'll be interesting to see what we're going to find at Orsogna!" "It will indeed," said Harriet—"*jolly* interesting!"

But at Orsogna things seemed quite in order. The distribution did not begin at three; but barrels were being rolled out and upended in a low dark room that had a counter and looked like a general store. A large pair of old-fashioned scales was being set up on the counter; and lists of names were submitted to Harriet, written out in the same ornamental hand as the pretended distribution announcement. The *sindaco* went through some motions of checking up on the contents of the barrels to show that the right quantity of everything was there.

Harriet got somewhat confused between pounds and kilograms, and Mattie tried to straighten her out; but she felt that her attempts to be helpful were resisted, perhaps resented, by Harriet, and she finally gave it up, though she had the impression that Harriet was not getting her problems right. "*Alle quattro precise!*" the *sindaco* declared, holding up four fingers.

"When they say *precise*," said Mattie, "you're supposed to add an hour and a half." She glanced around and caught the eye—brown and friendly, not blackly foreign—of a small man in a khaki shirt "You're American?" he asked her in English. She was delighted he had spent sixteen years in the States, and what a relief his straight way of talking, his garage-mechanic's Jersey accent, were to Mattie's expansive nature after the diffidance of the rag-swathed and gaunt-faced natives! A great many people from Orsogna had gone to America, he said—about a thousand out of a population of six thousand. The town itself had been built up, in the years before its destruction, mainly by American money that the emigrants had sent back to their families. "He asks"—he interpreted the question of another man standing by—"why you don't make Italy the fiftieth state." "The forty-ninth," Mattie corrected. "I wish we could," she answered. Harriet had turned away, and Mattie, who had not known how to include her in the conversation, had for a moment a twinge of feeling that what she had said might have been in bad taste. "Do you want to take me around the town," she suggested to the nice little man, "and show me what's happened to it?" "Sure thing!" he eagerly answered. "Would you like to go around?" she asked Harriet. "This man's been in the States and speaks English." "I don't think so," said Harriet hastily, swallowing her words Mattie noted, like a character in a Noel Coward play. "I'll just stay here and keep an eye on things." "You don't mind if I go?" "Not a bit." Mattie felt a shade of disapproval, but did not allow this to stop her. "Great Scott!" she thought, "it's certainly important to see how these people are living." And she went off with the little man.

Orsogna, he told her as they walked, had been held for some time by the Germans, and besieged and bombarded by the British, who had driven the enemy out and then allowed the Italians to take it themselves. But by that time there had been little to take. The Germans had ordered the people to leave, but some two hundred had stayed behind, and the Germans had killed almost all of them He showed her one of the rare houses that were still intact. A man and his wife and daughter had lived there, and they had refused to go away, so the Germans had taken them out and shot them. But in other cases they had simply put bombs in the cellars and blown the families up with the houses. A hundred or so had been killed by shells, two or three hundred by mines. Some had gone to live in Padua, others were lodging about the countryside with friends. The people who were left in the town had established themselves in such basements as still had roofs or the very few habitable rooms, or, as at

Tollo, they slept in the fields. "They live like pigs," he said. "They raise a little corn and wheat, that's all. They haven't got no farm implements nor nothing," If they could raise a certain sum in lire for the purpose of rebuilding the town, the government would supply the rest; but even the smallest house cost about a hundred and fifty thousand lire, and that was a lot of money now. In the meantime, the town administration, he said, had been Communist and now was Socialist, and he seemed to have a typically American contempt for this un-American kind of politics: "All they do is bum around and drink. They fight with each other—that's all they do," he said. "And who gets the graft?" asked Mattie. "Who sells the U.N.R.R.A. supplies?" He shrugged and struck forward his underlip. "We don't know if it's somebody in Orsogna or somebody in Chieti. Nobody knows where the clothes have gone. They're sent and they never get here!" "I thought it was the food," said Mattie. "The food came, but they don't give it out till to-day. If you didn't come, may be they never give it out. The clothes don't come at all." "Is the *sindaco* a Socialist?" "He's a Socialist, yes." "Then I suppose he isn't a crook." Her friend gave another great shrug and protruded his underlip.

They were walking toward the end of the town, amid a brownish desolation of masonry that was melting into the pale mud. What had evidently once been a wide street presented but a few scraggy splinters of trees. A carpenter was working on the roof of a house that had not been too badly wrecked: the only attempt at repairs that Mattie had so far seen—perhaps the only place where repairs were possible. And, as they moved towards the edge of the town, she found that she had, more and more, to struggle with a peculiar reluctance, an impulse to rescue herself from an abyss of disgust and horror into which she seemed to be heading. Though she had dealt sometimes, in her settlement-work days, with the last degradations of poverty, these had at least been a recognisable element of the pushing and pulsing city, and, though she had often seen revolting diseases, she had been able to cheer up the patient, or, at least, to cherish the faith that science would discover a cure; but here, she was abashed to realise, it was only by an effort of will and a warning to herself to be lucid, that she could contemplate the carcase of an organism, this city where people had lived, so completely crushed down and ground out, that she could admit to her conception of the world in which she herself had lived the actuality of this wholesale negation practiced by man on man. Something in her did not want to be there, did not want to know about it, only wanted to get away! Among the shape-

less and monotonous clay-coloured mounds and the less frequent
still-upstanding fragments—about which she found herself reflecting
that, if they had been eaten away by the sea, the effect would have
been more symmetrical—you could look out on the blue Abruzzi
and the green hills that rose beneath them. "This is a nice view from
here," she remarked. "Yes: people used to say that Orsogna was the
most beautiful town in Chieti Province."

On the way back, he showed her the school. This was a creation
of the late regime and seemed to her, as a public building, a very
pronounced improvement on anything else of the kind of which she
had seen the remains. Well, the Fascists *had* been modernising Italy:
you couldn't blame people for being impressed by them. She looked
in at the roofless white walls of some large auditorium or common-
room and deciphered inspirational texts from Cicero, Saint Francis,
and Ovid: "*L'anima umana si sente ispirata verso la campagna perchè
è il simbolo della libertà*"; "*Fanciulli, voi siete l'aurora della vita, voi
siete la speranza della patria, voi siete sopra tutto l'esercito di
domani.*" There were only four or five rooms left now—none of
which had any glass in the windows—that could possibly be used for
schoolwork, and in the bigger ones two or three classes were being
held at the same time. The children were taught in shifts, and those
who were not in the classrooms waited their turns outside. Here,
among the barbed-wire brambles, this youngest generation of
Italians, who had been told that they were the dawn of life and that
the countryside was the symbol of liberty, amused themselves by
playing with unexploded bombs as if they had been nursery-blocks.
"Gosh!" Mattie exclaimed. "Is that safe?" "They take off the caps,"
—her guide smiled—"so they can't go off any more."

Would she like to see the house, he asked, where the Germans had
made their headquarters? It had survived because the German
soldier who had been left behind to blow it up with its stores of
ammunition had failed to obey orders and had tried to buy his own
security by surrendering himself to the Italians. They went in, and
Mattie's first impression chilled the back of her neck with horror,
but she compelled herself to be objective. The point was that the
German lookout had been in the top floor of this building, and, in
order to prevent the enemy from identifying it by the smoke from the
chimney, they had broken a hole in the flue, so that the smoke had
all poured through inside, and several rooms had been blackened—
with startling white patches where the plaster had chipped—so that
they looked like chambers of Hell. Every room had its dirty pallets:
a dozen or more people now lived there—glad enough to find place

or a bed in this hideously transmogrified dwelling, which the in-
ader had seized and made use of for the purpose of turning the
retty little town into a strategic point on a battlefield and a centre of
oppression and torment, and which still kept the flavour and, as it
vere, the shape of the aliens who had now departed. It was with
queer fascination and repulsion that Mattie stared, in the abandoned
ness-room, at a wall scrawled with jokes and cartoons, of which
he couldn't always quite make sense:"*Kamerad! Kennst du Knäcke-
rod?*," "*Schön war die Trat in Orsogna*," "*Was macht die Fussball
Braut am Sonntag Nachmittag?*" The drawings depicted the local
ife: a lazy native lounging crosswise in a basket on the back of a
onkey, and a woman with a *conca* on her head. All the figures had
potato-noses and looked, not in the least like Italians, but like the
ypes in German comic papers. This was what they had thought of
Orsogna, and this was how they had amused themselves. They were
uman, it was good to remember: first no doubt, bored and badly
ed; then surrounded by an embittered enemy, suffocated and smok-
d like herrings, and lodged above an ammunition dump, they could
ardly have enjoyed Orsogna. But then she thought how they had
one through the street, planting bombs under all the houses and
lowing them up one by one. She was glad to get out of the place
nd not sorry to see daubed on the front: "*Viva Stalin!*" "*Viva
Matteotti!*"

The British had not found this look-out, but, since the tower of
ne of the churches was the highest point in the town, had assumed
hat the Germans had been using it, and had shot it down, wrecking
he building. Mattie was asked it she wanted to see it—she had an
scort now of several men, all of whom had been in America; and she
vaded in among the debris and looked about at the white plaster and
aked bricks, and up at the three round domes that were cracked
hrough like the shells of boiled eggs. The broken places showed the
ure blue sky, and the swallows, incessantly chirping, were flying in
nd out. There were mutilated plaster cherubs, still perched over
mpty niches, from which the saints had in time been removed, and
he figure of a bishop, with mitre and staff and two fingers upraised
n blessing, which had miraculously remained unbroken. But the
onfession-boxes were shattered, the top of the pulpit was gone, and
nderfoot lay a scrambled grey mass of fallen beams, flaked or
rumbled plaster, bits of gilt, and wrenched-out wires. Mattie
hought about the church in Aquila and wondered what this one had
een like. What was left seemed so pretty and touching. An old
voman came in with a basket full of some kind of wild white flowers.

She had brought them, it seemed, for the bishop, who was the patron saint of the town. They explained to the woman that Mattie was an American who had come to help them. "*Portateci in America!*" she cried in a high voice. "*Portateci in America!*" "We want that the United States should take Italy," said one of the men who had been there. "If you don't take us, the Russians will take us!" "I wish we could," said Mattie. A brick fell a few feet off with a sharp rather wicked crack. They went away, and left the old woman praying. "Well," thought Mattie, "those paintings and things are certainly a darn sight pleasanter than what you have to study for social planning, but there doesn't seem to be any other way to get through to the Good Society!"

They were walking in the opposite direction from the end of the town which they had first explored. This had evidently been the smarter section, where the well-to-do people lived. There was a wide alley still lined with small lindens, which must have been a kind of park where people came to stroll in the evenings, but where they met now only a morose-looking man driving in a flock of sheep. He acknowledged her guide's salutation without the least sign of friendliness or interest. So this avenue which had once represented a certain degree of refinement and luxury had been sent back to the most primitive countryside. The remnants of the tinted façades, with their satyr-masks or little nude nymphs, were evidences, cheap though they seemed, of the cheerful ubiquity in Italy and of the survival through two thousand years of an ideal of pleasure and elegance, and it rather depressed her to realise that, with everything smashed up like this and herself come as an angel of mercy, she would never be able to taste it. Suddenly she felt as she had at the humbler end of the town: choking with dust and death. "It's time for me to go back," she said.

She found Harriet standing by while the last preparations were made—her businesslike and boyish béret drooping a little above one shoulder and one foot stretched out to the side, so as to rest on the edge of the sole and, by a posture as inconspicuous and as far from the feminine as possible, to take the weight off the other leg. She had, Mattie noted, her usual air of an authority so completely indifferent that it seemed sometimes hardly to make the connections that were necessary to influence things; and yet there was something about it that Mattie could not help admiring. She wrote down the name of her guide, and thanked him and said goodbye; then, incapable of Harriet's calm, she went in behind the counter and examined the gigantic scales. One of the sides was dropped with a load of the round brass weights, and when she lifted these off, she discovered that the balances did not hang even. "These scales are cockeyed!" she said. "Look," she called Harriet over—"they're about a quarter of a kilogram off!" she spoke directly to the American interpreter: "Tell him theses scales don't balance." The two men who seemed to be presiding came up and inspected the scales. They were extremely quiet and grave. Mattie watched them, making vigorous suggestions. When they were about to take the whole thing apart, she appealed to the interpreter to stop them: "Oh, why don't they just use a make-weight? We've been held up so long already! If they fool with it, it may never work." "I don't think that will do," said Harriet. "None of the weights makes the difference quite right. It ought be made to work properly.—Yes," she directed the interpreter, "tell them to go ahead." But their tinkering did not help, and eventually Mattie supplied a stone that exactly made up the difference.

The distribution now began. Mattie had occupied herself, while waiting for the scales to be fixed, in transposing pounds into kilograms for the quantity allotted of each of the commodities; and she now began checking the number of women who were to be served in the various categories. Harriet stood looking on, and presently, to Mattie's surprise—it had hardly been three-quarters of an hour—murmured almost inaudibly but decisively that there was no point in staying any longer. "You don't want to check?" asked Mattie. "I've done that," she briefly replied. They departed, Mattie feeling dissatisfied and Harriet, she thought, out of humour. "But then," she explained to herself, "she doesn't know where she is with the Italians, poor lamb! It's just as if she were in darkest Africa!"

III

That evening they were sitting after dinner in the interpreter's house in Chieti, where Harriet had her local headquarters and where she kept a room—drinking a bottle of whisky which had been given her by a brother. Though she answered Mattie's questions about him in the offhand British way—he had been all through the war, it seemed, and had lately been sent to Bari—it was plain, Mattie said to herself, that she absolutely worshipped this brother; and, warmed by the genial gesture and the idea of family affection into forgetting a slight previous tension, she soon let herself go with her chief. "I don't see" she suggested heartily, "why it wouldn't be a good idea to get some of those Americanised Italians that can really be depended on and put them in charge of things out there." "Florence's husband has been in America,"—Harriet dropped her voice—"but he wasn't very reliable about the food. He was the person who told me it was gone." "I guess he had something there"—"Do you think he was interested in some way?" "What? No: I mean that there was something in what he said." "But they did have the food, you see." "The man who took me around said it wasn't the food that had disappeared, but that a shipment of clothes that was supposed to have come had never been even seen." "The clothes have been distributed," said Harriet. "How do you know? Where you there?" "I had to go to another province—but they showed me the announcement and the lists." "I wouldn't say that that proved much of anything, judging by our experience to-day. If you hadn't gone out there just now and put them on the spot, I don't believe those nursing mothers would ever have had a smell of those things. I'll bet those scales were that way because they had them rigged. I don't see how we can even be sure, for that matter, that they gave out the whole amount—because we didn't stay to the end, and we don't know that those barrels weren't padded. I gathered from that man that I talked to that there was some skulduggery going on." "They always expect too much. They're quite childish about it," said Harriet. "In one town, a man found a dollar in a suit that had been sent from America, and the others were all complaining that they didn't get dollars, too—they thought they'd been stolen." Mattie laughed, but said inwardly, "She's sidestepping the issue." "One of us," she went on aloud, "ought absolutely to be on the job at every one of those distributions. We could each of us take two provinces. We ought to see that the signs are put up on time and we ought to be right there on the spot when the stuff is supposed to be given out—but I don't think it's any use to try to get anybody to do anything in the early afternoon—nobody works in the middle of the day." "I don't see why we should encourage their laziness." "But they've evidently *always* gone to sleep after lunch. They must have been doing it for thousands of years. I suppose you might just as well expect them to give up eating spaghetti." "They might have a sounder diet. They don't get enough meat and greens. The tuberculosis rate is frightfully high, you know." "Well, in any case, *we* can't expect to make them change their habits about things like that—just a couple of U.N.R.R.A. workers!" But Harriet would not be downed. "We've had to show them the error of their ways," she said, "as far as politics were concerned. I don't see why we should let them expect to idle away half the day when there's so much work to be done.

hat's not the policy of the A.C.—they make them be on duty all day."

Mattie did not reply at once. For the first time in her relations with Iarriet, she was brought up against something that gave her pause. he put out her cigarette in an ashtray and was glad, for some eason, to see that it had been bought in Atlantic City. She glanced owards her empty tumbler. She could have done with another drink; ut it was perfectly evident that Harriet drank slowly and only took ne. "If anything goes wrong in Orsogna,"—Harriet picked up the hread—"I think we know whom we have to thank." "That *sindaco*, ou mean?—I wouldn't trust him around the corner," "I'm afraid here's a hooligan element that's been getting rather out of hand." Who are they ? " Harriet lowered her voice, though it had already een a scurrying mutter: "They're Communists, I believe. You saw he things they'd written up on the walls. I suppose those signs that ay 'W Stalin' mean 'We want Stalin.' " "Those are two V's, not a V," Mattie explained. "They stand for *Viva*, *Long live*, it seems.— ut it comes to just the same thing," she added, not wanting to ppear pedantic. "The fact that they're Communists, though, oesn't mean that they're going to steal things. In fact, I should say at Communists were more likely to be conscientious about handl-g supplies like that than the ordinary politicians." Her lover, the Jew Deal official, had been also a Fellow Traveller, and had ersuaded her on one occasion to vote for some Communist andidates; and, though she was now out of harmony with him, othing had ever upset her assumption that the Soviet Union and s leader had the interests of the masses at heart. "The *sindaco* told e," said Harriet, "that the Communists about here are ruffians," He would," Mattie took her up knowingly. "He's a Socialist, and e represents the bourgeoisie. You can tell by the way he dresses. I'll et he used to be a Fascist!" "I don't see," demurred Harriet, "that 's any use their trying to be Communistic now." "No: they won't ave much of a chance with the Allied Commission here. But who nows what they may do when we go? Unless you want to stay on definitely, as I know some of the English do." "One can't let the ussians dominate—because that's what it would come down to," id Harriet. "Well, all I can say," declared Mattie, "is that if I ere one of those young guys in Orsogna"—she couldn't help ntrasting her ideal of them with her disillusioned view of her New ealer—"and I'd seen Mussolini flop and then had had my whole wn wiped out by a couple of foreign armies fighting back and rth across it, I'd be saying '*Viva Stalin*!', too. I certainly wouldn't to the priest to have him tell me to submit to God's will. These

churches are perfectly lovely, but if I lived in a place like Orsogn
I'd certainly come to the conclusion that my patron saint wasn
much help, and that, if I wanted to keep a roof over my head, I
better do something about it myself." "Their saints *are* rather absur
aren't they?—But Communism would mean a dictatorship, wouldr
it?—and that's just what we want to get rid of." "Well, I suppose,
I were an Italian," Mattie answered, "I'd think the A.C. was
dictatorship and that I'd rather be told what to do by a Communi
Central Committee that was at least made up of Italians. Our tin
little U.N.R.R.A. handouts aren't going to put them on their fee
they're only a drop in the bucket. It's just like settlement work, ar
there are moments when it gives me the same futile feeling!" "
helps to keep them from anarchy," said Harriet. "Listen, honey
Mattie warmly exhorted,—"it's not going to be enough just to ke
them from having riots. We've got to back the progressive elemen
and help them get a democratic set-up or they'll decide to do som
thing themselves."

"They'll have to be taught first," said Harriet, "to recogni
what's for their own good.—I'm afraid I must turn in now." Sl
picked up the bottle to put it away. "We ought to get off at nir
tomorrow—we have to drive all the way to Pescara. Florence
husband will take you over." "God knows," declared Mattie,
she got to her feet—"I'm not for dictatorships any more than yc
have to have them.—As a matter of fact, the people I talked to ov
there seemed to be much more full of the idea of having Italy annex
to the United States." "I should think," suggested Harriet mildl
"that that would hardly be practical from your point of view
"It does sound rather silly," said Mattie, "but they actually told r
in Rome that there was an Italian organisation with a fairly lar
membership that is trying to arrange to have Italy made a part of t
United States—and, after all, I suppose that Hawaii will be admitt
to the Union soon, and that's almost as far off as Italy."

"Did you sleep all right last night?" inquired Harriet, as Mat
was leaving. "Don't you want to take some bug-powder?" "Well
she answered, "there was a certain amount of racket on the part
some roistering blades that paraded the streets all night—but
didn't particularly mind it.—Communists, maybe," she added witl
grin. "When I spent the night there," said Harriet, "there we
incredibly rowdy Americans, who had struck up an acquaintan
with some women and were trooping about the halls all night
Mattie returned to the repellent hotel, feeling rather annoyed wi
her chief, but not sure that she really deserved it.

The next day, however, an incident occurred which definitely and, he thought, on good grounds, discouraged her sympathy with Harriet.

At Pescara, on the Adriatic, they supervised the giving-out of J.N.R.R.A. food by the nuns of a local convent to the children of the shermen and sailors. As usual, they were met with the applause which warmed Mattie but now made her embarrassed, because she elt they were doing so little and living so well themselves. The nuns an a regular soup-kitchen and they seemed to be doing a pretty good ob. The kids were lined up outside with little tin cups in their hands, inging a piping little song about supper that had been taught them y the nuns. They certainly needed food. Mattie had read in books bout children that looked like little old men, but she had never ctually encountered this phenomenon, and some of these children vere horrifying in their resemblance to senile goblins. Never, robably, having known for a day the well-being and freedom of hildhood, they were shrunken and bony and stooped, and their ices, staring-eyed and creased, seemed never to have expressed nything but anxiety. She studied them, but she could not help irning away to a pale but somewhat healthier little girl, who, fraid to go in with the crowd, was clinging to the black skirts of her other. Mattie talked to her and tried to encourage her, but either er Italian was too bad or her manner too brusque, for she only ade the child shyer.

And, as usual, she soon became interested in something that did ot interest Harriet. She and the American interpreter got into a onversation with two nondescript-looking young men who turned ut to be engaged in removing mines. They could not have been aved for a week and were bristling with dark wiry beards; and they ere dressed in the queerest assortment of odds and ends of clothes— ne was barefoot and had nothing on but an undershirt and a pair f shorts, while the other wore sneakers, a béret and a dirty white nitted sweater that suggested old fashioned football. But they were ght-knit and strongly built and burnt to an African bronze, and Mattie found them attractive. The one in the undershirt had a athery unyielding face and talked entirely inside his mouth, as if e had set up a rampart against the mines and tried to keep himself hind it; but the other, with his juvenile garments, gave the impres- on of a bearded school-boy, and he had evidently grown up during e years of the war, for his eyes had that same curious glaring ok, at once desperate and lacking in purpose, that she had seen in arving children. With him she had a long lively talk, and, assisted

by energetic gestures, she seemed to be making great progress i
understanding and being understood. This young fellow was th
kind of male who peculiarly appealed to Mattie: a little guy with a
the guts in the world—it was so that she always saw them—ye
vulnerable and needing help, a good kid not quite equipped to tak
care of himself in the world.

It was "*un lavoro; molto pericoloso*," he confessed when she said
"What a job!" They had an American mine-detector, which was
thing like the handle and hoop of a nettingless butterfly net. The
would walk with it, holding it out, and when the hoop came above
mine, it would set up an electric buzzing in a telephone clampe
over the ears. Then they would try to dig down on one side and ge
at the mine from below. But the detector only registered for metal
it was no good for the wooden or bakelite mines; and they had onl
this one detector. Otherwise, they just had to look out for the place
where the earth was depressed and probe the ground with a rod. If th
rod struck on something solid, they would make a big circle aroun
it and take out a whole chunk of earth. Everybody, both German
and Allies, had exercised the utmost ingenuity, and this made it ver
hard for the diggers. The Germans had even mined their ow
cemeteries, rightly thinking that this would be the one spot in whic
the enemy would assume that there were none. The worst kind wer
the ones that jumped: a first explosion sent the thing up in the air s
that the charge had a clear field and the second scattered the mine
When they had got them out of the ground, they first had to mak
them safe by sticking a piece of wire into a hole just below the pir
They showed the ladies—Harriet had now come up—a bomb tha
they said was still live, the size and shape of a dingy brick, an
Mattie's friend, while she inwardly gasped, pulled the cap off wit
his teeth, then took out the wire and exploded the cap with a ban
that made her jump and left her heart beating. Harriet walked awa
without comment, taking the interpreter with her; but Matti
allowed the men to conduct her to the place where they lived. It was
little shack next door to the convent, and so wretched that it mad
her sad. All they had were knocked-together board beds, with n
mattresses and dirty old blankets, and a few pin-ups from Italia
papers plastered on the cracking wall. They told her that they g
for their mine-digging only twenty lire a day, the equivalent of te
cents, and Mattie wanted to give them money but felt that this woul
not do. If she could only supply them, she thought, with some mo
glamorous American pin-ups, say some of the big coloured spread
from *Esquire!*

It was so hot that they were able to work only up to ten o'clock in the morning and after six in the afternoon, and now it was time for them to get back on the job. And Harriet was approaching the jeep. Mattie said goodbye and grinned and wished them all kinds of luck.

"Those boys have got nerve!" said Mattie, when at last, after some delay, due to the driver's having disappeared, they jolted off on their homeward journey. "After all," Harriet firmly demurred, "they've got an American mine detector, haven't they? When our men were fighting through here, they had to take their chance." "But the war's all over now—and they get only *twenty lire* a day!"— A dull detonation stopped her, and it was followed, in another second, by a louder and uglier one, which thudded point-blank on the eardrums. "I hope that isn't those boys!" said Mattie. "There'd be nothing we could do," said Harriet. But Mattie was deeply disturbed: "I think we ought to stop and make sure, though!" "The nuns would be able to look after them. They must be prepared for accidents. They have a hospital in the convent." "If you don't mind, I'd like to go back and see. There might be *something* we could do, and we wouldn't want to—" Harriet cut her off: "I don't think we've got time, you know—we have to make another stop."

And Mattie for the first time was made to feel, freezingly and indefeasibly, the force of Harriet's superior authority. She stiffened; and, after a moment, her companion added priggishly, crisply: "I don't think they can be frightfully careful—the way they were showing off." Mattie made no reply. Rigid and tense with anger, she was silent all the rest of the way.

At Aquila, two evenings later, just as they were finishing dinner, Harriet announced as if casually: "I have to make a trip tomorrow, and I'm going to leave you here to look out for some trucks that are coming. Rather than have us both making these jaunts, I think it will be much better for one of us to stay here all the time. You can go over things with Mr. Morelli and keep tabs on the hospital and the convents. You know, I'm not sure that that Mother Superior who gesticulates and rolls her eyes is giving the boys all they're supposed to be getting. That place isn't so clean as the others, and I don't have much confidence in her. You're so good at getting to the bottom of things—I think it would be worth looking into."

On the way out, they ran into the Major, who invited them to have a brandy. Harriet declined and went up to her room, but Mattie let him take her to the bar. It would be a relief, she thought, to talk to another American, especially since she knew that he and she were

companions in frustration now. During her absence, a British
colonel had been assigned to the staff of the rest home, and the
Major, now outranked, found himself superseded. "Well," said
Mattie, after glancing at the soldiers standing up at the bar, "I
suppose that all our boys will be playing cricket now!" "Not so bad
as that," he maintained. "Well," she declared, "if they don't mix, it
certainly isn't *our* fault." "They do, up to a point," he answered.
" 'Up to a point' is good," she interjected. "We're getting satisfactory
results," he mechanically, officially, insisted, and it touched her to see
how his enthusiasm had dropped since she had left the hotel. She had
learned from a conversation with one of the G.I. guests—but
restrained herself from bringing it up—that there was hardly a case
on record of a soldier, either British or American, who had chosen
Aquila for his furlough; they had had to be ordered there. "You and
me, too," she bitterly said. "I'm just going to be an office-boy, it
seems. She wants me to stay here and take telephone calls while
she travels around and does all the real field-work!" She told the
story of the food and clothes. "This is strictly between ourselves,"
she said, "but I'll bet that if I went over to Orsogna and jabbered
pigeon Italian to them and made them see that I really meant business,
I could get things straightened out in no time!—And it's mostly
our money, too!" "She's a little bit dim," said the Major. "If you
must use those British expressions,"—Mattie, by a sudden revulsion,
found that to be an American meant being anti-English. "Wishy-
washy is what I'd call her—and downright stupid, too! I must
have frightened the liver out of her when I was talking to her about
Communism the other night." "That's the worst thing you can
possibly do—give the impression that you're what they call a
Bolshie." "I tried later to make it clear that I was just an old-fashioned American who wanted equal opportunity for everybody and
trusted in F.D.R." "The trouble is that a lot of them think that
being American itself is some kind of Bolshevism. You have to make
them realise that Americans can be just as good-mannered and
quiet and just as conservative in many ways as any English person."
"That's not my type, I'm afraid," said Mattie. She finished her cocktail and flared up again: "And when we do that, they just take
advantage of it. I think that we ought to go to the mat with them and
have something to say about things in Italy." "Don't ask me to agree
with you," the Major warned, with his smile on one side of his mouth,
which had formerly contributed to his charm but which now had a
crestfallen wryness. "I'm here to promote cordial relations. —
You're wrong about her, anyhow: she admires you—she told me so

when you first arrived. You're what they'd like to be but don't get a chance to be." "So in the meantime," she persisted pugnaciously, "they want to keep us down!"

The ranking British colonel saw them and came over and was introduced to Mattie. He sat down with them and had a manhatten. "I really don't know," he said, "how we'll get on with our stuffy old whisky-and-sodas after our diet of American cocktails—though, like so many other excellent things that come from your part of the world, I do think they sometimes let one down after starting one off with a rush." He beamed in the complacent way that the British invariably have when they feel that they have scored off a foreigner who will be helpless to defend himself. But he had reckoned without Mattie. "Just a red-faced old lush," she was thinking, "who was no use to them anywhere else!" "What do you mean: we let you down?" she demanded. "Not in any serious way, my dear lady." "I'd like an example of what you mean!" "Well, well," interrupted the Major, automatically conciliatory, "nobody had let anybody down." "We're both letting the Italians down, if you ask me,"—she switched the subject,—"after all our talk about the Four Freedoms. We don't let them form a government of their own—we don't even let them make speeches!" "As for the Eye-tyes," the Colonel pronounced, "I think they deuced well get more than they deserve when we send them such charming young ladies to minister to their needs!"

"I wanted to say, 'Nuts'!" growled Mattie, when the Colonel had excused himself and left them. "It wouldn't have helped," said the Major; and, confronted by his Anglicised trimness, she was seized by that fierce impatience which had always at last overtaken her with the men she had begun by loving, and which supplanted the instinct to protect and prop: the indignant conviction that they were not the men that she would have in their place, that they did not really have what it took. There must be American men with passion and with backbone, she thought but, not only did her own bad luck always involve her with the other kind but she had so often had to sympathise with her girl-friends for being married to that kind, too! The drinks had gone a little to her head. "Oh, come on!" she taunted the Major. "Are we men or are we mice? Did we beat the hell out of these limies at Lexington and Bunker Hill just to let them push us around after we've saved them from being chewed up by the Germans ? "

But the Colonel and two other British officers needed a fourth at bridge, and the Major was obliged to join them.

6

ROMAN DIARY : RUSSIAN EXILES

A RUSSIAN friend in the States had suggested my looking up, in Rome, a cousin of hers who had been living there since the Russian Revolution; and, having located her with a certain amount of difficulty, I went one day to see her. Her house was somewhere out on the Janiculum, almost at the edge of the city, and I had recourse to a P.R.O. jeep, driven by a reckless Italian, who, till I made him restrain himself, hurled the car through the streets like a missile, ferociously cursing the pedestrains and forcing the bicyclists out of the road by pretending to run them down. His attitude was evidently based on the fact that he was working for the winning side and felt he had nothing to fear, and it gave me an idea of the insolence which the people must have had to put up with from the underlings of Mussolini.

On my first visit, I made the mistake of letting him drop me at the foot of the hill and walking up the long succession of flights of steep and backbreaking stairs. Approached in that way, the address proved peculiarly difficult to get to, and when I did find the little villa, it seemed to me that I had penetrated to something very remote from my correspondents' hotel and the offices of the Allied Commission. When I was face to face with the household, I saw that I had had no idea of the condition, during the years of the war, of the ordinary civilian in Rome.

But these Russians represented, also, privations not of recent date. Mme. de L., whom I had come to see, had left Russia in 1919, with her husband and her adopted son, and in company with a friend, the Countess R., whose husband had been killed in the Revolution and who had had with her her four children. The family of Mme. de L., I learn from a Russian history, had been at one time the richest in Russia, They had benefited, in the eighteenth century, by the extra-ordinary favour of the Tsar, who had made them immense grants of "inhabited estates," and by the middle of the nineteenth century they had owned three hundred thousand serfs. The country place of Count M., one of the splendours of eighteenth-century baroque, had had as a rival in Russia only the Arkhangelskoe of Prince Yusupov and had been comparable, "if not with Versailles, at least with Potsdam or Caserta." Mme. de L. and her husband had lived a great deal in Rome before the Revolution, and they returned there in 1919, to make a household in common with the R's. Mme. de L. took in "paying guests," and they lived mainly on the proceeds from this. They had to practice the severest economy, and the younger generation suffered. Three of the Countess' children, who had had years of inadequate feeding, died of tuberculosis. Mme. de L.'s son had married and gone to America. Her husband had died during the second war. In the war years, there had been no more boarders, and they had moved to a smaller villa.

I did not, however, know all this at the time, and I was not quite prepared for the state in which I found Mme. de L. and the R.'s. It was true that Mme. de L, as she told me, had been afflicted for years with ailments which partly accounted for her emaciation; but the thinness of the Countess R. and a sister of hers who now lived with them, the paleness of an R. daughter and grandchild, showed how desperate their fasting had been. Mme. de L. used the phrase "dire hunger" but said that things were much better now: she had weighed only forty-five kilos and recently she had put on five. But Mme. de L. stood six feet tall, and her figure was now almost a skeleton. Her skin was yellow as if she had jaundice, and it had wrinkled in a peculiar way which seemed due, not to old age merely, but to a collapse from the shrinkage of flesh. Her great grey eyes were blocked out in her face by the straight eyebrows that ruled above them a dark rather majestic line and by the discoloured patches below them; but they reminded me—in that atmosphere of Russia that so persistently though fadedly endured there—of Pushkin's description, in *Eugene Onegin*, of the eyes of the young Lensky when he is dying after the duel and they become like the windows of an empty house, blinded-up and covered with chalk, when the owner has gone away—save that one of Mme. de L.'s eyes was also swimming in blood as if a vessel had burst. When I saw her from the side or behind, she had the look of an old black crow, with her long back and her humped bony shoulders, her thin straight black-stockinged ankles and her slippers which she had worn so long that they were heelless and gave the impression of her feet's not being shod but merely, like the feet of a bird, composed of some hornier substance. On the furniture were shabby prints; a screen shut off her narrow bed; on the wall hung a Genovese tapestry. I did not see anywhere the "ikon corner" that such old-regime Russians usually have; but in the corner where she had her chair she had put up a picture of the Tsar, photographs of members of her family, and a view of some mountain landscape. On the table beside the chair were a volume of Dickens in English, a carafe of very harsh red wine and a box of loose tobacco and papers, out of which she made her own cigarettes. This was one of the few parts of Rome that had been fairly badly bombed, and the windows of the house had been shattered. In Mme. de L.'s room, some of the gaps were patched with a glass that was completely opaque and others had been boarded up. Through a pane that was still intact, one could see the house across the street, which had had one whole side sliced off, and, beyond this, one could look away over a newly built-up part of Rome, in which the principal objects of interest were a big Benedictine monastery, a yellow arc of monotonous apartment houses and the cypresses of the Protestant Cemetery, where Keats and Ronald Firbank lay: those two Englishmen of brilliant plumage, escaped from the coop of England and dead pathetically, still young, in Rome.

Yet, against this desolate background, her tone was quite cheerful and stout. She showed humour and a sharp good sense, and her voice had an agreeable timbre which combined the gentle Russian humanity with the full-throated deep Russian register. After two months of the Italians and the British, I found it rather a relief to talk to her, for an American, in certain ways, seems much closer to-day to the Russians than to any of the Europeans. Up to the beginning of the first World War, Americans and Russians both, however much they loved their country or however strong their faith in it might be, tended to occupy a provincial position, or acquiesce in a provincial attitude, toward the civilisation of Europe. But, to an American in Europe at the present time, it seems just the other way. The little European nations, among which England now must be counted, have fallen into the provincial role in relation to the larger societies of the Soviet Union and the United States. This had already begun to be evident before the recent war, and it is even more striking to-day, when England and Germany are no longer formidable. Each of these countries, during the years of the war, had been locked into its own boundaries, compelled to feed on itself and kept concentrating all its attention on the defense of it national existence. Even the Germans, who overran the other nations, could bring them nothing but the plundering and bullying inspired by spite. If they had possessed any creative ideas, they might have been able to impose their "New Order," since Europe needed so badly to be unified; and their failure marked the definitive bankruptcy of old-fashioned nationalistic conquest. We are left with a lot of small nations that seem barbaric and ridiculous nuisances, with their traditional family feudings: the quarrel of France with Germany, the

competition of Germany with England, the dispute between the
Italians and the Yugoslavs, etc., etc., etc. America and Russia to-
day, with all the defects of their civilisations, do constitute more
advanced systems to the extent that they have succeeded in organising, in more or less synthesizing, a great variety of kinds of people—
so that men find themselves here in a position to think at least about
what kind of *societies* they want instead of about how they are to
manage to maintain themselves as autonomous nations. But the
Russians have always had it in common with the inhabitants of the
United States that they were half outsiders in Europe, visitors and
curious observers; and I had particularly felt during the last ten
years with all kinds of intelligent Russians how far our two peoples
were emerging out of the ancient compartments of prejudice into
bigger associations that were capable of wider and more lucid
views. Even White Russians in exile have felt this—since their
starving self-confidence has been stimulated by the Russian defeat of
the Germans and by the recent imperialistic tendencies exhibited by
the Soviet Union. With Mme. de L., at any rate, I found that I
could talk more freely about Europe and the Europeans than with
anybody except an American.

She understood what one meant about Italy. Yes, the tourists had
spoiled the Italians: they had encouraged them to be idle, to live on
their past. There was far too much of the past in Italy. You couldn't
pull down an old building in Florence that was rrrotten, rrrotten,
rrrotten! without letters from English spinsters protesting at the
destruction of the picturesque. The Fascists *had* wanted to do something about cleaning up and modernising Italy, and they had been
better, she believed, than the Nazis because they had wanted to
encourage the individual. She had approved of the Germans,
though, too, up to the time when they had invaded Russia and she
had realised how brutal they were.

She would like, she said, to go to America: the only thing she had
now to look forward to was seeing her family again. Her son wrote
her every day but the letters took a month or more, the packages of
food even longer, She asked me, her face lighting up, as it did not do
often, with an eager smile, whether my family were good correspondents. I suggested that, since she knew our ambassador, he
might possibly be able to help her if she wanted to go to the States;
and she startled me a little by replying, "There'd have to be some
dirty work at the crossroads first!"—though I was later to find out
that her talk was sprinkled with Americanisms, which she had picked
up from her "paying guests," students at the American Academy.

They contrasted rather queerly with a mannerism which I had noted before in the Russians from the upper ranks of the old regime. Russians, when they are speaking their own language, are likely to say *yes* five times—as the French tend to say *oui* three times and the Germans *ja* twice—if they are hurriedly affirming something that somebody else is saying; and Mme. de L., if one told her anything, would do this with a note of impatience, as if it were not possible or not proper to inform a person of her position of anything she did not know. This was not, in Mme. de L'.s case, in the least impolite or unamiable; it was a trait like her towering stature that she had not been able to help carrying with her.

Distressed by her starved appearance and remembering how much more comfortable were her Russian friends in America, I tried to encourage her to make the trip. But she said it might be better not. She knew she couldn't live in America on five hundred dollars a year, which was what she could just do in Rome; and she could go about here in rags, which she shouldn't be able to do in New York. Somewhat curbed by her *yes yes yes yes yes*, I left most of the talking to her. The room was getting darker with twilight, and her voice gradually dropped to a murmur. She had to spend most of the day in bed, and I suppose that it had cost her an effort to get up and receive a visitor, for she now seemed to relapse from the admirable poise, the quick perception, with which she had greeted me. It was a little as if she were talking to herself, but pursuing a train of thought that had been started by the consciousness of herself suggested by the coming of a stranger. She was saying, as I sat in silence, I rather tardily realised, that it might be that "the ones who had been killed" had been "more fortunate than the ones who survived." But then— she picked herself up again—with a Russian, after all, it was different than with people of other kinds: when one happened to find one-self badly off on the physical and material plane, one could go on to another plane.

I did not want to tax her too much and soon left.

But she insisted on my coming to dinner, and I called on them several times. "The Italians and the French are conventional," Mme. de L. explained. "They won't ask you to dinner to eat what they eat. But we don't mind asking people to eat what we have ourselves." I think that they must, nevertheless, have made some special preparations for me; but their menus indicated the limits of persons who live as they do: on one occasion, borshch, stuffed tomatoes, plums, a little loaf of grey butterless bread; on another, a bowl of spaghetti with pale pinkish sauce, a salad of chopped-up

ettuce, and little preserved cherries, with the usual bread and wine.
I enjoyed it after the mess of the Hôtel de Ville, which was betraying
every day more outrageously the depredations of someone or other
to the advantage of the Black Market and coming to consist exclusively of leaden and greasy raviolis and unidentifiable cuts of
cartilage.

Before dinner, we would sit and have sherry in the living-room
which was also the dining-room, between walls that, in the Russian
fashion—like the Hermitage gallery in Petersburg—were completely
plastered over with pictures: the inevitable Russian water-colours,
painted, no doubt, by some member of the family, and the usual long
Russian engravings of the endless perspectives of the Neva and the
barracks-like palace at Oranienbaum. After dinner, we would sit out
of doors in a garden behind the house. Here they had planted some
carrot and beet seeds which had been sent them, by an old boarder,
from America, in a poor soil in which things did not always grow.

I now encountered the other two old ladies, whom on my first
visit I had barely met. They had the appearance of good fairy god-
mothers—though one of them, of whom I learned afterwards that
she had been in her time a great beauty, gave restive little signs,
almost childlike now, of what must once have been a wilfulness of
coquetry. We listened after dinner one evening, just before the British
elections, to a radio speech by Clement Attlee, which came through
to us rather dimly, interrupted by strains of dance music and spasms
of voluble Italian; and they commented, as if to reassure themselves,
on Attlee's unexpectedly well-educated voice. The British Labour
Party, said one, wasn't really Socialist, was it? In any case, said
another, the Socialists were much milder than the Communists.
She had always, she asserted, believed that the public utilities ought
to be nationalised—and, after all, if all that money that the governments had just spent on explosives had been put into hospitals and
schools and parks! . . . They were puzzled by the failure of Fascism:
the people had been satisfied with it, and the government was not
really intolerant: they had sent out to the malarial region a sanitary
engineer who was known to be anti-Fascist (there had been, I
learned later from U.N.R.R.A., but one sanitary engineer in Italy),
only exacting from him a promise that he would not make any
criticism of Fascism. I suggested, thought I knew it was futile—they
had grown up in the world of the Tsar—that freedom of criticism
was a cardinal issue. It seemed cruel to tell them that socialism was
what Europe certainly needed. Their lives had been so difficult and
frightening. Having escaped from the Bolshevik terror, they felt

the enemy again threatening them here. They had established themselves in Rome on a meagre but stable basis; they had made, with
their children and grandchildren, a solid little Russian group that had
weathered the rigours of exile. And now, in their old age, they found
themselves pressed by want even beyond the narrow restrictions to
which they had accustomed themselves; and anarchy seemed creep-
ing in around them. They told me—what I had already heard elsewhere—that there had lately been gangs in the streets who had been
catching well-dressed people and stripping them. A man was supposed to bring twenty thousand lire, a woman fifteen thousand. This
had happened, not far away, to a professor of their acquaintance.

The phrase "displaced persons," in one of our conversations,
caught Mme. de L.'s attention. She considered, she said with a laugh,
that *they* were displaced persons. I wondered, as I saw them there,
whether they wouldn't have been better off in America. Certainly
I though , the young people would. A daughter of Countess R. was
giving Italian lessons; a boy wrote plays in Italian. Neither seemed
Italianised; they were simply uprooted Russians—for a Russian
cannot become an Italian. But in America he can become an
American on the same footing with everybody else. (Since this was
written, the grandson has married an American girl and come to live
in the States). The conception of the American system as a solution
to the social problems which had disrupted and tormented their lives
loomed even to the two old ladies who were closer than Mme. de L.
to the order they had left behind. There had been people, one of
them said, even in the old days at home, who had had the idea that
Russia ought to be governed like the United States.

*   *   *

I had dinner with Bill Barrett from our Embassy, and he told me
that he had lately been called upon to interview some hysterical
Russians who had come in from the Displaced Persons Camp just
outside Rome. They were engineers and school-teachers and such
people who had been living in Poland before the war and who had
fled and come down into Italy. They now had the status of displaced
persons, and the Soviet authorities had claimed them and were going
to have them sent back to Russia. Barrett had looked into the matter,
and his inquiry had led him to the desk of a British officer of the
Allied Commission whose function it was to deal with these problems.
There he learned, to his astonishment, that the Americans and the
British had, at Yalta, made with the Russians an agreement record-

ing to which we were bound to hand over to the Soviets any Russian who had left Russia since 1927. Such people, for reasons not clear, had been assigned to the status of prisoners of war. This agreement had never been published (and might never have been made known to the world if the Vatican had not gotten wind of it and "broken the story" to an American correspondent in March, 1946). Intended ostensibly for the rounding-up of Russians who had fought with the Germans, it could be used, also, to secure the deportation of mere disaffected persons of the kind who had been appealing to the Embassy and of the members of unorthodox political factions and people who had fled from the purges.

I reflected that a man like my friend the ex-Soviet official Alexander Barmine, if he had landed among the displaced persons, might have been, at the insistence of the Soviets—since he had left Russia after 1927—surrendered by us for certain execution. Fortunately he had come to America and was now a United States citizen. I had just seen him before I left New York, and he had warned me, not entirely in jest, that, since I was known to have criticised Stalin, I should, if I went into territory where the Russians were in occupation, be careful about exposing myself to the hazards of standing on the platforms of moving trains. On the voyage over, I had read proofs of the new English version of Barmine's autobiography: *One Who Survived: The Life Story of a Russian Under the Soviets;* and had admired the concreteness, the compression and the feeling for human realities which had enabled him to cover in a minimum space so extensive a field of experience and at the same time to give so definite an impression of everything on which he touched. In this and in its moral sincerity it had seemed to me in the great tradition of Russian revolutionary memoirs, the tradition of Herzen and Kropotkin. A child of the Revolution but now confronted with a new Russian despotism, he had written an exile's book which might well become a classic; and his career and the conclusions one drew from it were vividly present to my mind.

Barmine, born in 1899, was the son of a schoolmaster and a gamekeeper's daughter. His parents had divorced and remarried, and he had grown up without a real home and soon found himself embroiled in the happenings of a period of Russian history chaotic to the last degree. He fought in the civil war on the side of the Bolsheviks, and at nineteen was made a commissar on the basis of his success in getting the villagers to give them food by persuasion and honourable dealing at a time when Red Army soldiers rarely came back from such errands alive. He attended the Red Army

Academy in the years when old tsarist officers, recruited to the
Revolution were attempting with a certain scepticism to transform,
"a lot of young peasants and workmen into infantry officers in six
months," while their training was at any moment likely to be interrupted by the necessity of going away to take part in some actual
fighting. He was later, at one time or another, as assigned by the
Communist authorities, a soldier who held several commands,
consul general in Persia, official Soviet agent in Belgium, Soviet
director general of imports in Italy and France, and president of the
trust that controlled the exportation of the products of the motor and
aviation industries. He thus saw a good deal of the business and the
officialdom of the Soviet Union; but, though a member of the
Communist Party, he played no political role. At the time of the
Stalin-Trotsky split, he was content to leave everything to the higher-
ups, on the principle that it was always correct to back the findings of
the Central Committee. Rather unusually non-political for a
Russian, his assumptions were still based on the methods of the first
years of the Revolution, when, for example—in 1919, "the most
critical year of the Civil War"—it had been possible, fifty miles from
the battle for a public debate to take place, without "passing the
bounds of courtesy," between Bolsheviks and Mensheviks; and it
was not till very much later that he could see what a "decisive part
in causing the final downfall of all Lenin's real companions-in-arms"
had been played by the blocking of every attempt to organise an
opposition with the argument "that any weakening of Party unity
might provoke a crisis of which the forces of counter-revolution
would take advantage." In the meantime, as he discovered with
amazement on returning to Russia from service abroad, the big
officials of the Stalin government had acquired splendid country
houses, with tennis courts, Rolls-Royces and servants, while the
ordinary Soviet workers in whose name the Revolution had been
made were still compelled to spend ninety per cent of their wages on
food which, from the point of view of the countries in which
Barmine had been living, was miserable in the extreme.

In the summer of 1937, Barmine was chargé d'affaires in the
Russian Legation in Athens. The political purge was in progress, but
in Athens they knew little about it. All they knew was that dozens of
ambassadors and heads of government departments were being
arrested and shot. Their own chief had been summoned to Moscow,
and it was now a very long time since they had had any instructions
from him. One day they received a communiqué which informed
them that Tukhachevsky and seven other Red Army generals had

been executed for treason, and Barmine learned a few days later from
a friend who had arrived from Moscow that some twenty of the
younger generals, former class-mates of his at the Academy, old
comrades of the civil war, had also been summarily shot. The staff in
the Greek Legation had been listening to the radio in silence, and
they pretended to accept the charges that had been brought against all
these men; but it had suddenly become apparent to Barmine that
Stalin, in his passion for power, had set out to destroy systematically
all the Soviet officials and officers who represented the Leninist
generation and who could possibly oppose his policies or contest his
leadership. He expressed to one of his assistants his astonishment and
his horror, and the outburst relieved his tension. But soon after this
conversation the assistant was recalled to Moscow, and Barmine
became aware that his friends in the Foreign Office were no longer
communicating with him. An order to seal the minister's papers and
have them sent to Russia was put through over Barmine's head, and
one day he surprised his code secretary rummaging among his
papers. He wrote to the Foreign Office asking to be relieved of his
duties, but received no reply from Litvinov. Instead, he was invited
one day to dine on a Soviet ship which was lying in the harbour at
Piraeus. He declined and went fishing, but the captain of the ship
with several other men waited for him on the dock, and when he
returned, he had to sidestep a second attempt to get him on board the
ship. A man from the Legation, however, whose real function was
beginning to dawn on Barmine, insisted on spending the evening with
him and talked to him suggestively of the ease with which it had been
possible in China to frustrate or murder officials who had attempted
to run away from the Embassy.

Yet for some reason the mesmerism of Moscow did not succeed
with Barmine as it had with so many other officials—though it was a
spell that had behind it a tradition as old as Ivan the Terrible with
his bellowings of "I am your God!" "My sense of personal dignity,"
he writes, "was revolted by the alternatives: to submit to kidnapping
or to walk out. After the stories I had just heard, I knew what was in
store for me. I had to decide where I would be of more help to the
Russian people—perishing in one of Stalin's prisons or living as a
free man somewhere in the world, knowing the truth and speaking it
out." He eluded the manoeuvers of the G.P.U., wrote a letter of
resignation to Moscow, walked into the French Legation and got a
visa as if for a holiday, and boarded the train for Paris.

In Paris he wrote to the Central Committee of the French League
of the Rights of Man, reporting the step he had taken and explain-

ing the reasons for it. "For nineteen years," he said, "I have been in Soviet government service. . . . I have fought for the Soviet regime and dedicated all my energies to the cause of the Workers' State It is quite obvious to me that a reactionary dictatorship is now in control of my country." And he wrote and published in France—in 1939—the book which is now, for the first time, appearing in the United States.

These memoirs—what is altogether exceptional in the writings of Russian Communists—contain no political apologies, no casuistry of the Party conscience. It is all the more comprehensible and all the more convincing to the English-speaking reader for its freedom from that rather creepy atmosphere of Marxist polemic and theory in which we do not find ourselves at home. So practical and so direct all his acts and reactions have been, so sensible the conclusions he has drawn from them, that one feels, as one does not do always in the case of Russian careers, that, in the circumstances, one would not have behaved differently or arrived at different views; and it seems almost inevitable that Barmine should (at the end of 1939) have gone on to the United States.

I had seen something of Barmine in New York and had been struck by a certain convergence of the Soviet with the American type. It was not only that the new Russia of the Soviets, in spite of it socialist beginnings and of its supposed disapproval on principle of our capitalist business and our bourgeois democracy, actually envied and aimed to emulate our industrial organisation, our brisk methods and our material prosperity; it was also that a man like Barmine, tall, straight and well set-up, sanguine in the physical sense, bred out of what seems quite another race than that of the ordinary Moscow pygmy, had behind him, as have so many Americans, a tough and vigorous rural stock. For both of these reasons, perhaps, he approximates—though rather more accomplished than most American executives are—to an ideal at the opposite pole from the old-fashioned type of Russian official, a type of which many examples are still to be seen in the Soviet Union. Barmine is not nervous, not volatile, not theatrical, not evasive, he is not even, for a Russian, very flexible or very sensitive to psychological atmospheres—as was shown by his not grasping sooner the full implications of the purges and the danger of talking about them. He is in some ways much like an American, and he perhaps finds himself more at home here than the modernised Communist official can sometimes be in the Soviet Union among conditions often nearly as primitive as that life of the sixteenth-century which, to the Eliza bethan travellers of Hakluyt's *Voyages*, seemed barbaric in comparison with England.

Yet the product of Marxist schooling and the Soviet commissar have marked characteristics of their own that are unlike anything in America and perhaps quite new in the world. Barmine has been cast in a mould and can hardly now be remelted. The proud self-confidence of the Communist official, taught to believe that the future belongs to him and set off from the common herd almost as much as a member of the old upper classes—an assurance which has come more and more to present a hard mask of arrogance—appears in Barmine as a challenging dignity, a brusquely ironic tone, an air of knowing all the answers; and the tradition of Communism betrays itself in the bad habit which he sometimes reverts to of trying to talk his opponent down by sheer emphasis or loudness of voice, when his own point of view becomes hard to defend, instead of conducting a sober discussion; and in his resorting to what is technically known as the "bedfellow" line of argument, which relies on producing the illusion of having put you irremediably in the wrong by associating you with some odious person who holds either a similar opinion to yours or an opinion which may be confused with yours. The indoctrination of Leninist Marxism which such Russians as Barmine received went deeper perhaps than the teaching of any of the Protestant churches usually does at the present time and almost as deep as the Catholic dogmas. To us who have first seen the world through the windows of the bourgeois economy, the Marxist view must always come as a heresy and require a certain effort to be valued and understood; but to Barmine it was the social cosmogony, the story of history and the basic morality, which it required an effort to correct. He has told me of the shock that it was to him to discover, in the collective nurseries, where the toys which had been brought by the parents had been pooled and made common property, the instincts of acquisitiveness appeared in these children who had never had contact with the bad appetites of capitalist society; and of the disquieting doubts suggested by his realising at last in the factories that disunion and sabotage were not invariably and inevitably due to motives of political obstruction, but could also, all too obviously, be prompted by jealousies and personal ambitions. Of late years I have sometimes heard him talk as if he were disillusioned, not merely with the government of Stalin, but with the ideals of socialism themselves; yet it is a little like the pupil of the Jesuits who, emancipated though he may think himself, can never lose either the conviction of sin or the intellectual discipline

they have given him. So Barmine, by a conditioned reflex, will
respond to certain kinds of stimulus by plugging the old Communist line of insisting on the permanent scandal of the contrast
between rich and poor in a capitalistic society—only to pull himself up with the admission that the poverty of Stalin's Moscow is in
just about the same proportion to the standard of the privileged
groups as the poverty of Tammany's New York; or—the other way
around—he will start talking of international affairs with the incisive
and cynical realism of Lenin during the first World War—only
influenced by our own propaganda, by the pressure of the American
newspapers, to fall flat into some ready-made attitude, to my mind
quite unrealistic, dictated by the supposed desirability of our
following the line of the British.

He is, I think, less out of place in the United States than he would
be in any other country. He can say "we" as an American citizen in a
way that would hardly be possible for a Russian in England or
France—in a way that is not wholly different from the way in which
the Soviet official talks about the Soviet as "we": in the sense that—
as in the case of both countries—the "we" are not an old-fashioned
nation but a great geographical unit which is engaged, to use the
Communist language, in a project of "social engineering." "We" are
trying certain forms of government, going ahead on certain assumptions, rather than straining to save something that is simply there, like
the hierarchy of an English county or a set of French peasant holdings.
But he, too, is a man uprooted like any exile of the old regime, like
any emigrated "displaced person"; and that position is an extremely
uncomfortable, an extremely frustrating one. A former officer of the
Red Army, a former worker for Soviet prestige abroad, he was not,
in the recent war, any more able to defend his country than if he had
been an old tsarist general; he could no more serve the State with his
brains than if he had been an excommunicated Menshevik. Nor has
he, still a foreigner in the United States, still suspect from his Soviet
origin, had the chance there to work at a job that gave anything like
full scope to his abilities. He cannot, to be sure—as he could be, if
he were a displaced person in Europe—be deported to the Soviet
Union; but the injury he has suffered through exile must remain
beyond a certain point irreparable. And his commissar irony, his
Marxist reactions, persist, like Mme. de L.'s imperious *yes* and her
authoritarian instincts, as the insignia of former power, to remind us
of the fate of those who, having been trained for positions of leadership, have not been allowed to fill them.

*   *   *

Coming back from Mme. de L.'s one day, I saw chalked up on a wall the following confident legend: "*Viva l'anniversario del 7 novembre quando la libertà è stata data al popolo russo.*" Well, I reflected, if the Bolshevik terror had brought the freedom of the Russian people, one could not, after all, complain. But the truth was that, thirty years later, the Russian people were a good deal less free than the man who had scrawled up that slogan and who at least did not run the danger, even under the rule of the Allied Commission, of being executed or imprisoned for life, as he certainly would have been in Russia if he had been caught making public an opinion equally subversive for the Stalin regime. The Russians are to-day not free either to talk, to print or to vote: they have to do, and they are supposed to think, whatever the government tells them, and they have no means of changing the government. They cannot even have recourse to strikes. There is so little freedom in Russia that even persons of heroic character and irreplaceable talent are no more safe there if they differ from the dictator than they were in the days of the Tsar. First there was Alexander I, who exiled Pushkin for an ode to liberty; then there was Nicholas I, who exiled Lermontov for praising Pushkin, who mounted the throne over the corpses of the Decembrists with their petition for constitutional government, who imprisoned and expelled Herzen, and who sent Dostoevsky to Siberia; then Alexander II, who shut up Kropotkin in the Peter-Paul Fortress and transformed a geologist into an anarchist, and who would have imprisoned Tolstoy if he had not been lucky enough to have an aunt at court; Alexander III, who turned the student of zoölogy Ulyanov into a conspirator and would-be assassin and hanged him when his plot was discovered, and who prevented his brother Vladimir from graduating at the university; and Nicholas II, who sent to Siberia Lenin and Trotsky and a whole generation of the ablest and most brilliant young Russians. Then there was the first Bolshevik government who executed or drove into exile, for technically different reasons but in the same autocratic fashion, hosts of Mensheviks and Social Revolutionaries, aristocrats, landlords, officials, and representatives of the various departments of the professional bourgeoisie (many of them, in all these categories, just as capable and just as public-spirited as the intransigent Marxists that turned them out) and who bedevilled the men of genius that had believed in the Revolution and tried to help do its work till the life of a Mayakovsky had become as unhappy and hopeless as that of Lermontov or Pushkin had been; and finally the satrapship of Stalin, who deported and murdered Trotsky, executed Tukhachevsky and conducted a wholesale massacre and imprisonment of everyone who still held to the Leninist faith and so was likely to question his tyranny. For more than a hundred years the world of the West has been strewn with Russians who have represented the brains and the conscience of Russia—men and women who could rarely be so useful abroad as they would have been at home. And in spite of my liking, for the Russians, my sympathy with the hopes and principles with which the Soviets started out, my admiration for their exploits in the recent war, I remembered with impatience how ridiculous it was for them to think themselves civilised, or for others to think them so, so long as a change of government is allowed to involve in their country the slaughter or extirpation of everyone who happens to oppose it, so long as it is still made a crime to differ from the head of the State. So long as this is true, we and they, Americans and Soviet Russians, for all the things that we have in common and however intelligent and emancipated the individual Russian may be, will never be able to co-operate as peoples. You cannot have a society of equals where one man, by informing on another, can always silence him or ruin his career; and you can have no international understanding between a state run by political police and a state run by independent citizens.

7

ROMAN DIARY : BRITISH OFFICIALS

I WANTED to find out something more definite about our pledging ourselves at Yalta to give up to the Soviet Union all Russians who had left there since 1929, and I called on the British major with whom my friend at the Embassy had talked. Like all the British, he was leery of journalists and very firm about refusing information. He admitted that it was true that Russians of whatever age or sex could be claimed by the Kremlin as prisoners of war, but about the precise terms of the agreement he said he was not authorised to speak. He was, however, extremely loquacious. He could, he declared, "write volumes" about what had been going on, if it were not for his official position; and he proceeded to parade for my benefit a personality which he obviously conceived as both formidable and fascinating.

He was an Irishman, superficially Anglicised but furiously exhibitionistic. His accent was completely English, but his eloquence unmistakably Irish. He had the build and the crouch of a bruiser and a British beefsteak complexion, and he fixed me, as if to hold me petrified, with a pale blue but glaring eye—stopping after every statement to watch for my astonishment or approval. His talk was full of dark intimations. "I thought we were fighting for freedom, didn't *you?*" he demanded. "But I've never seen so many dirty tricks in my life!" He evidently referred to the Russians. He had been twice in the Soviet Union as a Metro-Vickers engineer, but he hadn't he said, when I asked him, been involved in the 1933 trials: he always kept his politics in his pocket! But these trials had hardly been political, and many of his comments left me blank. He talked as if, on matters of politics, he entertained the strongest sentiments, but I was totally unable to find out what these uncompromising opinions were. He said challengingly that he hadn't voted once in the last fourteen years, because there had never in all that time been a candidate who was the kind of man he'd like to see run things. This dated his abstention from the moment of the apostasy of Ramsay MacDonald; but when I tried him on the subject of Churchill, usually a touch-stone for pro-Labour men, he promptly and emphatically answered that "everything would immediately collapse" if Churchill were to die or be defeated. I came to the conclusion at last that he had no real opinions at all, but merely an overwhelming impulse toward self-assertion. When I later asked L.M. about him—they messed in the same hotel—he answered that the Major was "a child of nature."

I soon abandoned any effort to interview him and simply listened while he let himself go. He had been in all the countries, he gave me to understand, and had mastered all the languages—he could learn any language in three months. In the East, he said, they called him "the wild Irishman"—unquestionably I knew, he propounded, how fast a reputation travelled? But they all knew that he was completely honest and that when he said he'd do a thing, he did it. He had once held five thousand blacks at bay absolutely single-handed. If an Arab came into his office and didn't wear a hat, he wouldn't say anything to him but would simply get up and kick him, because his not wearing a hat was a sign of disrespect—and the Arab wouldn't do it again. In the Sudan, he assured me proudly, he'd been fined twice for beating natives—£25 and £50. He didn't like to beat people up, but sometimes it had to be done. It was no use trying to punish them by holding out on supplies, because they'd always manage to get some food and to "enjoy their vices" anyhow, and it would only mean that somebody else would have to go without food. He'd asked the judge, on one of these occasions, how much it would have been if he'd killed the man, and the judge had said £5. (I learned later from a reliable source that it was true that the penalty was less for killing than for beating a native: if the man was still alive, he had to be taken care of and gave rise to more trouble and expense.)

I finally tore myself away from his eruption of talk and his magnetic gaze, which were at the same time pugnacious and coquettish. He was a perfect example of the Irishman who, escaped from the old problems of Ireland, no longer oppressed and a rebel, finds himself in a position to bully. He reminded me of New York police captains and of that Irish General Dyer who gave orders for the Amritsar massacre and later boasted that he had meant it to be worse.

*   *   *

At a dinner of the Ritrovo, a "cultural" club for bringing Allies and Italians together, I sat across the table from an important South African general. He was young-appearing, tall and blond; talkative, waggish, a good fellow. He told me at once that he was an Africander and would keep saying from time to time, in the course of our conversation: "I'm not an Englishman, you know." There was something a little pathetic about it, because his accent was completely English and that rather lower middle-class English which seems to condemn British colonials to an irremediable inferiority (the Australians are better off in speaking cockney). And he was certainly pro-British enough. I was told afterwards by another South African that he was supposed to be "socially ambitious" and wanted the post of South African ambassador to England.

He surprised me by a line of attack that I had not had to withstand before. He assured me that the United States was really a British dominion and that all the British dominions would now have to stand together for the principles of "fair play" and to "see to it that people like the Germans didn't go about bullying people." I denied our dominion status and replied that, in any case, wars were not really fought for the purpose of defending moral principles. He readily admitted that this might be true, but immediately returned to his propaganda. South Africa and the United States had, he insisted, one great thing in common. We had both rebelled against England, and the English had never forgotten it. The Boers had fought the English just as we had, but then they had made peace with England, and England had stuck by the terms of the peace, and the South Africans knew they could trust her. The implication was that the English had learned their lesson and dropped their old methods, and that we need not be afraid of them now. Yes, he went on, the United States had a lot in common with the dominions—everything but a king (giving me a broad wink)—and it would be a good thing for us to have one! We gave our president more power than a king. The king, in the case of South Africa, was powerless to appoint a prime minister except on the advice of the South Africans.

I talked after dinner to an intelligent marchesa who had long been an earnest republican and was supposed to have played a role in getting rid of the Fascist regime. She had heard my conversation with the General and expressed her amazement that an American should have taken so calmly the suggestion that the United States have a king. But I had been getting used to British impudence. She, I suppose, as a patriotic Italian, had been suffering from it acutely.

*　　　*　　　*

Bob Leigh rather relieved me by declaring that Sir Osmond Gower was a "story-book Englishman," and that if you gave him a comic hat, he could make money in a music-hall any day. Leigh himself is part English, part Irish. He went straight into the army

from Oxford, where he had specialised in Classics and studied some
kind of academic history about which he was now indignant because
it had nothing whatever to do with the history he had found himself involved in when he came to serve in the war. He has had a
heavy dose of the war; has been all through it from France to Italy.
At one time he tried to write something about it but lost his manuscript with his baggage somewhere—which very much discouraged
and depressed him. He is intelligent and well-informed and his
Irish element constantly stirs in him a satrical point of view on many
things that the English take for granted. He is particularly amusing
about Sir Osmond, whose accommodations he had to provide for on
the occasion of the veteran proconsul's arriving for a brief stay in
Rome. He had heard of Sir Osmond's brilliance—he has been
praised by Lawrence of Arabia—his dexterity, his tact, his languages,
his knowledge of the Near East, his appreciation of literature and
music; and the young major rather looked forward to meeting him.
But, though Sir Osmond's accomplishments were undoubtedly great,
his personality turned out rather wearing. He had stopped, on his
way from the East, with the intention of delivering a lecture on his
memories of T. E. Lawrence. It happened, however, to be V-E
Day, and it was intimated that this was an occasion when the troops
might not care to come to lectures; but nothing could deter Sir
Osmond. He was deeply offended and indignant when only fourteen
people turned up—he had brought with him a Roman princess—
and said at first that he would not speak at all, but allowed himself
to be persuaded by the Princess and the Major to give them an informal talk. The next day he peremptorily demanded that an
audience be produced. The Major did his best to point out that the
men were recovering from their festivities and might be almost as
little interested as the day before; but Sir Osmond, with bland
insistence, asked whether the officer in charge of entertainment were
not in a position to command attendance, and, as he seemed to be in
a position to command the entertainment officer, several hundred
rather sulky men were detailed to listen to the lecture.

I met Sir Osmond one evening at dinner, when Bob Leigh was also
present; and was astounded by his preposterous vanity. He was now
anxious to realise a further ambition of delivering a third lecture—
this time on "The Four Great Books of the World"—and inquired
of an Italian professor, who had also been invited to meet him,
whether the school with which the professor was connected would not
care to arrange for this. When Sir Osmond learned that the school
was designed for a different purpose: to provide instruction on

Italian subjects for American and English soldiers, he did not—though elaborately affable—take it in very good part. Well, since they wanted only to *insegnare* not to *imparare*—since the school was only *senso unico!* (he introduced the Italian words as if he were dropping into some local patois, toward which one's attitude was bound to be humorous)—he saw there was no chance. But, after all, the *Divina Commedia* was one of the great books!—and he told us that he had just been reading it in the plane in which he had flown to Rome. He read it, he said, once a year, and his manner seemed to suggest that it was a work with which nobody present could have any very great familiarity—and, especially, gave us the impression that there was some sort of peculiar merit in relishing Dante in a plane. I brought up the only passage I could think of that could possibly connect Dante with aviation: his account of his flight into Malebolge on the back of the monster Geryon, in which he anticipates the sensations of circling down in a plane by noting that it was only by the wind on his face that it was possible for him to tell how they were moving; and the effect of this upon Sir Osmond was to impel him to recite at length the description of the appearance of Geryon, which was not the passage in point. He then went on to remark that he supposed that Dante's admiration for Virgil was one of the most curious instances in literature of a great man overrating a much lesser man—an opinion which seemed to me to weaken the legend of Sir Osmond's taste, since it is difficult to see how anyone who really appreciated Dante could fail to see the greatness of Virgil or to understand the debt—in the accent and texture of the writing, in the staging of the dramatic effects—of the later to the earlier master. And he told us of the classical honours which he had won in his youth at Cambridge, and declared that there had been a time when he could recite any ode of Horace if you fed him the first line—he believed he could do so still. (Bob Leigh had to restrain an impulse to take Sir Osmond up on this and try to stump him with the opening of an epode). He had been to see the Holy Father, and the latter had expressed surprise that an Englishman should know the classics so well. He had explained that Horace went with port wine and was highly esteemed in England.

Our hostess being an American married to an Italian prince, Sir Osmond now proceeded to a waspish little poem by Dunsany on the absurdity of the American Mrs. Simpson as the inamorata of Edward VIII, and announced that he considered it equal to the Greek epigrams of Leonidas of Tarentum. This was followed by a humorous anecdote about "the then head of my family, Lord Bramwell."

Lord Bramwell had been sitting after dinner and had been disturbe
by a servant, who said to him: "There's a fire in the library, sir.
Lord Bramwell had answered: "I'm quite warm here"; but the poin
was that the house was on fire. He must have thought, from ou
reception of this, that we had failed to understand the point, for h
repeated: " 'There's a fire in the library, sir.' 'I'm quite warm here
The house was burning down!"

The whole thing was a sort of performance, and I saw what Leig
meant about the music-hall. While Sir Osmond sat back, bein
brilliant and wagging his white moustaches, the audience wer
supposed to applaud and laugh: that was the only use he had for h
companions. On foreign affairs, in general, he was everything tha
was most correct from the point of view of British interests and c
giving the right impression, but with a guile which could hardl
have imposed on babies—though that was what he seemed to tak
us for. He assured us that the insurgents of E.A.M. in Greece, wh
had been ruthlessly put down by the British, were disreputab
ruffians and brigands; and in denouncing Marshal Tito, whom th
British were trying to dislodge in Jugo-Slavia, he brought out as
triumphant clincher: "Why, Tito's not even his name! His re
name is Josip Broz!"

I found later a little paper-bound book containing chapters fro
Sir Osmond's memoirs, reprinted for army reading—chapters whic
told of his years in Palestine and discussed the Zionist movement. I
preparing this popular edition, intended for the use of the army, S
Osmond had not taken the trouble to eliminate the Hebrew an
Arabic—to say nothing of the Greek and Latin—with which, to u
Bob Leigh's phrase, he could not resist throwing his weight aroun
and the twisted allusive style made rather hard reading in any cas
But I got out of his snarled-up narrative a clear perception of some
thing which Sir Osmond, thought he tried to obscure it, could n
help allowing to come to light. I closed the book with the realisatic
that the British had brought the Jews into Palestine solely for th
purpose of providing themselves with an ally against the Arabs, wh
were menacing their access to the oil wells. And I saw that S
Osmond himself was simply a British imperialist agent, playing th
British game and disguising it with his Greek and Latin, his cultiv
tion of poetry and music. Was not he himself, I asked myself nov
sometimes embarrassed by this? was that the reason for the confuse
presentation of the Palestine question in his memoirs? Did he ta
refuge from a sordid episode, of which he knew the underside to
well, in the memory of his trips at Cambridge? Was he prouder

having known Lawrence of Arabia than of the whole of his work in
the East? Yet were Englishmen of this sort, I wondered, ever really
embarrassed? An outsider could never know. They have been making
it for so long a habit to establish themselves in foreign countries,
keep the natives at arm's-length and gather up, along with solider
loot, the cultural possessions of the region, which they take carefully
back to England and deposit in museums and libraries—as Lord
Elgin did the frieze of the Parthenon—somehow creating the impression that the English have a much better right to these languages and
literatures, these works of art and facts of archeology, than the people
who originally produced them, while these nations themselves are
dealt with strictly according to the dictates of British commercial
policy.

Later I learned that when Sir Osmond had been governor of a
Greek island that had been made into a Crown Colony, the inhabitants, recalcitrant to British rule, had rebelled and burned
Government House, destroying Sir Osmond's library. But in those
days it was still very hard to make any impression on the English.
When the news of Sir Osmond's loss reached England, another
distinguished scholar-diplomat, retired, shipped his travelling
library out, with an apposite quotation from Virgil, so that Sir
Osmond's equipment was again complete and he did not lack for
classics.

*   *   *

Young Leigh, as I say, seemed to react to Sir Osmond in much the
same way in which I did. Yet, in talking to him, I would feel in him,
from time to time, in spite of his sensitivity and humour, what
seemed to me the well-defined sproutings of the very same mental
traits which in Sir Osmond had flowered so flamboyantly as to become rather unusually conspicuous, but which were evidently the
inevitable armament for the business of imperial domination. I was
perfectly aware, for example, of the weakness and corruption of the
Romans and Leigh, who was the officer in charge of the public,
utilities of the city, came into much closer contact with them than I
did and was in a position to be more annoyed by them; but I thought
that he was inhibited by his official position from exploring and
enjoying Italian life in the way that would seem to be normal for a
young man still in his twenties. He read up modern Italian literature,
but found it uniformly unsatisfactory; he went about a good deal socially, but complained that it was impossible to have any fun—to go
anywhere or talk satisfactorily—with well-bred Italian girls, because

they were guarded so grimly by their parents (it never seemed to occur to the British that the parents of young girls in countries which had just before been occupied by the Germans might regard them, too, as invaders to be resented and never trusted). Italy, he said, was like the frog in the fable which, in an effort to compete with the ox, had blown itself up and burst—and now they talked about their rights and ambitions! And in certain connections, it seemed to me, he instinctively resorted to the method, which I have noted in an earlier chapter, of diverting attention from some matter in which the British were open to criticism by denouncing the injured party on grounds that had nothing to do with the case. Thus the appointment of Count Sforza as Foreign Minister in the Bonomi government had been vetoed by Churchill the winter before, apparently for the reason that Sforza was not prepared to submit to the terms demanded by the British; but when this young major talked about Sforza, he took the line that he was simply an impossible person: egotistic, high-handed, wrong-headed—a description which did not tally with other accounts of Sforza I had heard.

One evening when we met at the Silones', just before I went back to England, I decided to try to smoke Leigh out, to get him down to the basic assumptions which underlay the cleverness and tolerance that these Englishmen from Oxford and Cambridge so agreeably display on the surface and which I usually found so genial that I did not want to prod below them. This proved to be a difficult task, and it took the combined efforts of Signora Silone, Bill Barrett and myself to make him admit his position. When I questioned the British policy of clamping a military government on such countries as Italy and Greece and frustrating their natural political development, he answered that the English troops were sure to be withdrawn soon from Italy, because the soldiers wanted to go home and forces would be needed for Germany; but, in the meantime, it was a good thing, in any case, for them to keep on holding down the North, where the Partisans had become so unruly—since, if political meetings were allowed there, there would surely be horrible riots and a lot of people getting killed. Barrett pointed out that there were a lot of people getting killed, anyway: the Partisans went gunning for Fascists at night. To this Leigh replied that, if they assembled at meetings, people would be massacred wholesale. It was his echo, I thought, of the traditional attitude, all too familiar to me, that everything done by the English abroad was done at great inconvenience to themselves and for the benefit of the natives. But did not the English I asked, have an interest in what they were doing in the,

Mediterranean countries? Well, the English, he explained, were busybodies who couldn't see strife or confusion without wanting to restore order. There had been the other day, for example, a brawl in the Piazza Barberini. The Americans had gathered about and egged the combatants on, whereas the English had been worried, felt responsible, thought that something ought to be done to stop it. I reminded him that the British—as in Syria—had never hesitated to instigate violence if they could obtain any advantage from doing so. Yes, he said, but they'd begin to be uncomfortable if they found there were more Syrians than Arabs—he seemed to imply that this feeling would be due purely to an instinct for fair play.—In any case, it was easy, he said—becoming more realistic—for Americans to be impartial about what was going on in Europe because, Germany now being beaten, they had nothing important at stake. Americans were just as hardboiled as anybody else when it came down to things in which they did have an interest and they were capable of talking, on occasion, their own kind of hypocritical cant, which was just as repulsive as the British brand.

With reservations, we assented to this; but asked why it seemed so difficult for enlightened young people like him to contemplate the position of England as a member of a European federation. Signora Silone urged in her soft and gentle voice that England, with a Labour government, could play such a wonderful role of leadership in organising a socialist Europe! He replied that conversations like this were conducted on two levels: an idealistic level and a level of political realities—I interrupted, insisting that the international socialist movement was one of the fundamental political realities, and that, if it did not seem so to him, it was because he had not come into contact with it. He admitted that this was true, but said he was going to vote for Labour—in spite of the fact that he didn't believe that they had any chance of winning and thought that, if they did get in, they wouldn't be able to accomplish much.

Silone had come in during the conversation, fatigued and rather *battu*. As a member of the Central Committee of the Italian Socialist Party, he had been struggling with the crisis, now protracted for days, over forming a new interim government. The aim was to swing the balance away from the monarchist bloc to the side of the republicans; and what with the five political parties of the Committee of Liberation that were always combining in new alliances and what with the vanity and rivalry of the leaders, the problem was a complicated one. The delay, said Signora Silone, was making Italy look ridiculous, but no one even got to meetings on time. Rome in summer, said Silone, reminded him of Smyrna. Like most serious and energetic Italians, he seemed thoroughly disgusted with the city, where the Vatican was lodged like a polyp and where all business got bogged down and obstructed. He had sunk to a couch and had begged us to go on talking English, which he did not understand; it would enable him to rest a little. From time to time he smiled politely, and at one point he made connections and intervened in the conversation. I had brought out a malicious idea which I had worked up to tease the English: the suggestion that England might comfortably survive as a small agricultural country, with little industry and a reduced population, very sound and clean and trim like Denmark, strong in democratic schools and wholesome rural co-operatives; and he quietly broke in to curb what he took to be naive illusions about the economic innocence of small "independent" countries. The good Swiss, he pointed out, sent their capital abroad for investment in Swiss-Italian and Swiss-South American companies and thus were living, without working themselves, on the sweat of other people's labour just as much as the more obvious beneficiaries of colonial exploitation. Lenin had pointed this out in his book on imperialism.

At any rate, we made Leigh confess that he could not face with equanimity what he called the decline of England—which implied, by inexorable logic, the breaking-up of the British Empire, since the immediate consequence of that would be a decline in the standard of living. But he added that we Americans were criticising Britain today "from a very comfortable position." And how were the British to know that America wasn't going to swoop down and possess herself of profitable fields which the British had been induced to relinquish? Hadn't we let down the men of good will like him by coming to Europe in the guise of liberators without having any line of our own that could be opposed to the old policies we complained of?

The British under Churchill, I knew very well, would have fought any liberal aims that we might have tried to bring to Europe, and done their best to prevent us from carrying them out. But that wasn't young Bob Leigh's fault, and he was right about the weakness of our foreign policy. I told him, as we were leaving the Silones' and walking down the many marble flights from the floor on which they lived, of an evening I had recently spent with a well-known American woman journalist, who, agreeable though I had otherwise found her, had disturbed me by crying up the Christian Democrats, the most ambiguous of the Italian parties, evidently knowing very little about them and attracted, so far as I could see, merely by the benign connotations of the two component parts of their name. She had also, toward the end of the evening, announced challengingly that the foundation was long overdue of the United States of Europe, and that we ought to go straight home from the restaurant and design an appropriate flag. This was the kind of thing, I admitted, that we were sending to Europe just now, at the same time that our occupying army wanted to get home as quickly as possible and take as little responsibility as possible and sometimes offset this lady's benevolence by raping and racketeering. I was dissatisfied, I said, with all this. "We've had it!" Bob Leigh grinned ruefully, as if to wash his hands of the whole thing. This—like "The natives are hostile"—is one of the British catchphrases of the war which illuminate their state of mind. It has, however, come to be used by both armies for such everyday announcements as the PX supplies have been exhausted or the mail has been all sorted out, and I had never heard it applied before to the downfall of Western civilisation. Once, he went on, he would have talked like us. It had seemed to him that the other countries had ideas and ideals and movements that would come to the rescue of Europe where England was deficient or failed; but he had now seen quite a lot of the world—French, Italians, Americans and Russians—and they were just as much out for themselves, just as limited and crass in their objectives, as the British could be accused of being. I told him that this showed an advance, because it meant that he was beginning to learn not to take national differences seriously and that he was ripe for international socialism. Otherwise, I declared, he might be well on his way to becoming a Sir Osmond Leigh. He retorted that I ought not to be sure that I was not myself going to end by becoming a Sir Edmund Gosse—a gibe which was probably deserved if it was aimed at a certain complacency which I fear I had been displaying.

*   *   *

I found one morning a remarkable item in the British army paper, the *Union Jack*. It was an article called *An Idea* by a man named Peter Wilson, which began by explaining that, having defeated Germany, the question now presented itself as to what was to be done with her next. "Many revolutionary theories," the writer said, had been suggested and discarded. But I have not seen a return to a theory which worked . . . in the eighteenth-century—the Mercantile System. . . . America then as now was a big producer of cotton. Great Britain insisted that she did not manufacture her raw cotton into finished goods, but exported it by means of British ships back to the

Mother Country. (The non sequitur of tenses here matches the logic of the historical argument.) In Britain the raw cotton was spun and woven into goods of all kinds, manufactured and designed by British craftsmen. These were then transported back to America, their country of origin, and were sold to the settlers there." He believes that this system was a huge success, and that it ought to be adopted with Germany.

8

LONDON IN MIDSUMMER

FLEW back to London in the middle of July and, being
tached to the Army now, was given an army billet. This was a
eadful little hotel in Half Moon Street, which accommodated both
mericans and British. The elevator was so tiny that you could
rdly get into it with another person and so flimsy that you could
el the boards of the floor giving under your weight. I took to walk-
g up and downstairs, though in the confusion of dark stairways
d corridors that were shut off from one another, I would sometimes
d myself in a *cul de sac* and have to go all the way back down and
art up another flight. My room, which looked out on low chimney-
ts, was a cubbyhole of yellow walls that contained a little prison-
e daybed, with the greasy marks of heads above it and a horrible
own cover impregnated with pounds of dust; a wooden washstand
at had no towel: you were supposed to supply your own; a brown
rpet with a rhomboidal pattern, also much stained and full of dust;
d, in one corner, a small dung-coloured coal-grate which contained
all and dismal gas-logs. In the other corners large piles of dirt had
en swept up and left in plain sight. Down below in the dining-
om, the clothless tables seemed never to have been wiped, for they
re soiled with innumerable spillings of soup, gravy, eggs, jam and
; and you were waited on by slovenly skivvies so pallidly un-
petising that they made the meagre food seem more tasteless.
soon discover that this odd little nexus of streets just off the Green
rk is one of the headquarters of the London whores. Most of the
ee- or four-story hotels are evidently *hôtels borgnes*, and the
vious conclusion is that my billet is a converted brothel. In the
ddle of all this, at the foot of the street, you find a little Christian
ence church, which manages to look almost as old and gray as
other church in London.

*   *   *

is nearly as hot here as in Rome; and the worst of it is that,
ereas in Rome you can at least go around without a jacket—
e in summer a shirt with insignia is regulation in the Mediter-
ean—here in London, as is characteristic of onerous British

convention, you have to do all your walking and travelling in
buttoned-up and belted uniform, with you shirt always soaked
sweat.

At night there is still almost as little light as there was before t
end of the war, and a section that has been badly blasted, like t
Tottenham Court Road, looks gruesome in the late-gathering dar
ness: its bare and wry trees with tufts of leaves at the tips of t
branches like the legs and necks of plucked fowl; its masklike fro
of bombed-out houses, with their dark eye-sockets and gaping jaw
There is a peculiar desolation and horror about finding these carca
of streets unburied in the midst of an inhabited city.

Piccadilly is crawling with life, but equally repellent in its differe
way. The summer murk, stagnant and tepid, is eddying with t
aimless movement of the British and American soldiers and t
deteriorated London tarts that circulate slowly or clot in grou
The purposes of the fighting accomplished, the tensions of warti
relaxed, these uniformed and dog-tagged men now find themsel
immersed like amoebas in the swampy backwater of England. Wh
has the war worked up to?—nothing, vacuity—to these young ma
afloat in the foreign streets, with no training in directing themsel
and with no strong impulse toward self-direction, merely respondi
to a rudimentary instinct to adhere to these floating females who
faces they can hardly make out.

*   *   *

How empty, how sickish, how senseless, everything suddenly see
the moment the war is over! We are left flat with the improverisl
and humiliating life that the drive against the enemy kept our mi
off. Where our efforts have all gone toward destruction, we ha
been able to build nothing at home to fall back on amidst our o
ruin. Where the enemy are roofless and starving, where we ha
reduced their cities to rubble, we get now not even useful plun
or readily exploitable empire, but merely an extension, a m
wearisome load, of harassing demands and duties.

The novelist Graham Greene said to me the other day that th
sometimes thought to themselves, now that the war was over:
one could only hear the hum of a robot bomb!" Life had b
dramatic because dangerous. Everything one did was pointed
was lived with a special awareness, because it might be the last th
one did, and now they missed this: life was safe but blank.
doubt Greene's rather saturnine nature, his addiction to the pecu

excitements of pursuit and persecution, count for something in his nostalgia for the buzz of the V-1's; but then, Greene himself and his themes are partly products of the conditions of the period, of which a fundamental insecurity has been so much a permanent feature that, once having adjusted themselves to it, they do not know how to live without it.

G. struck the same sort of note when she complained that the headlines were dull. One was used to reading of cities in flames, infernal concentration camps laid open, German officials killing themselves and their families; the murderous and crushing revenge, like the progress of a gigantic tank, for the assault on one's own cities. And now the crescendo had ceased: the nerves no longer felt the stimulus that had been shocking them every day like the insulin and electric current which, applied to schizophrenic cases, was supposed to give them lucid spells. She had written me of the disappointing flatness of the V-Day celebration in England and of her own depression and apathy at the parties where people had tried to be gay; and now she told me ghastly stories of men she knew who, after years in German jails, had just got back to England. One of these had turned Communist in prison, and was now so appalled and unsettled by what he found at home that his first reaction had been to long to go back to prison, where he had at least known which side he was on and had been able to remain true to his principles. Another had come back to his wife and had stayed with her only two weeks. During his absence, she had had a lover, to whom she had become accustomed, and had taken rather badly to drink. He, on his side, had always been a gambler, and imprisonment had encouraged this taste. In prison he had done nothing but gamble and had even used to bet with his friends on which and how many prisoners were going to be converted by the Roman Catholic priest. He found he could not get on with his wife, left the country and came to London, where he completely gave himself up to gambling. A third man had been playing the women's roles in the shows that they had put on in jail, and his companions, who had not seen a woman for years, began behaving toward him in daily life as if he were an attractive girl to be treated with consideration, relieved of unpleasant tasks and courted—with the result that he had gradually developed, in response to the pressure of this attitude—he was apparently not a case of congenital homosexuality—a feminine personality of which he found that he was unable to rid himself. He hardly knew to which sex he belonged.

(I later met, in the United States a young man who had spent, five years in prison-camps and had talked with a woman but once, and then only the Mother Superior of a convent, of whom, through a little grating, he had been able to see only the hands. On rare occasions when they heard women's voices, these had sounded extremely queer. After so long a confinement, he said, during which one had been always under orders, with every moment of one's time assigned, it was incredibly painful and frightening to find oneself at large in London and to have to do things for oneself. It required a great effort of thought and will even to bring oneself to the point of walking down the steps to the Tube, buying a ticket and boarding the train).

*   *   *

G. herself, who is always wound-up and looks physically rather frail, seems to have felt the nervous pressure increase instead of lessening since the end of the war. She has a job in the department of "economic propaganda" and has worked in London all through the bombing, when, as she says, you sometimes thought you "couldn't stick it." A house a few doors from her flat was blown up when she was at home one night. But, now that the war is over, she suffers more than ever from claustrophobia—feels oppressed by day in her office and is dismal with people at night. In between her regular work and dinner, she takes lessons in Italian and Turkish, in the hope of getting herself sent out to Italy or the East.

She is an extremely bright and able girl, with the same sort of all-around competence that the young Englishmen from the universities have. The English women I have met in London have been in general a pleasant surprise. The clever ones are more sympathetic than the same kind of people at home, because they usually have quiet manners and do not try to compete with the men. When they are beautiful, they are beautiful in a feminine way that is a relief after the dashing and aggressive "style" which is directed, on the part of our women almost more, perhaps, at women than at men. At the same time, I note that G. has one habit which American girls have and which I have come to regard as significant of a change in the status of women. When she is standing and wants to rest, she puts forward one foot with the toe up, resting it on her heel, where the more maidenly older pose involved bending in one knee and leaning one thigh against the other. But these English girls talk the men's language: the crisp laconic schoolboy code that makes everything matter-of-fact or droll, and that has its own kind of charm after the challenging wise-cracks of our women. G. combines this with something else which seems to me extremely old English, a more formal turn of phrase in a style probably characteristic of her clergyman father, now dead, which is matched by her beautiful handwriting, with its distinctly detached letters, its deftly twisted ampersands and its incised serifs and shadings. "I think I talk like a don, you know," she says; and she tells me that she can never decide whether to regard herself as "the gamine type" or "the serious type."

She has also—what does seem to me unusual here—along with her matter-of-factness, a volatility of mood and expression of a kind that always enchants me in women; the beauty that seems to derive from a spirit that inhabits the body rather than from the body itself. This spirit, in G., sleeps or wakes, fades or flushes, is *mèchant* or merry, flits about through a repertory of several roles, and has its moments of strength and of weakness. Sometimes she looks frightened or a little out of focus, with the two sides of her face not in harmony: one pert, the other chagrined; sometimes on guard and alert, like a keen-eyed quiet baby fox that makes quick silent darting movements; sometimes lovely with delicate colouring or electric with the kind of intensity in which feeling and intellect mix. Sometimes, dressed to go out, her hair caught up from her forehead and ears and done in a knot at the back of her head, she looks grown-up and very handsome, with the hard English chic.

One evening, just before dinner, I made her keep still and wrote down a little sketch of her as she sat in her living-room: "Pale slight figure in grey suit and white collar, with slim legs that show pink through grey stockings and too-large old white high-heeled shoes that are the best that can be had in wartime. Against yellow lamp-light, her profiled face shows greyish-pink, too. Very fine though rather irregular features. Sharp and longish nose, with a hump and dip in the bridge, that is assertive and shows curiosity. Sharp shoulders, perhaps mainly due to tailoring; soft, delicate and palely-veined neck under pointed little forward-thrust chin, with slight rounded flesh underneath. But the lower part of her face, with its very small mouth, is less strongly developed than the upper. Soft yellowish hair that grows low on her forehead and—worn thus with a feminine tossed effect—has a suggestion of lion's mane; it is balanced in colour by the gold of the bracelets on one of her wrists, as she sits with her capable non-tapering fingers clasped about her knee. But the features that give her face its chief accent are her little diamond-bright blue eyes that might almost be used to cut glass or as points for

Johanssen gauges. Under her finely drawn-in eyebrows, they look
sometimes cold and sharp-pricking, sometimes twinkling and cute.

Her figure has disproportions of largeness and longness with
smallness and shortness, which, instead of being disconcerting, are
altogether a part of her attractiveness—because they seem to
correspond with her complexity. I found, for example, on this visit
when I had bought her some silk stockings from Italy, that her feet,
which I had remembered as tiny, were several sizes bigger than
had thought. And this discovery at once disappointed me in that it
seemed to destroy the image of an exquisite little figure that I had
carried from my previous visit, and pleased me because it added to
her piquancy and revealed a firm base in substance for solid qualities
of intellect and character with which I was coming to credit her.

Her way of receiving these stockings and some other things I had
brought her from Italy seemed to me very English and, especially,
very post-war English. There were an antique veil for the hair and an
antique black lace fan, two pairs of ear-rings, the stockings, the new
book by Silone, whom G. greatly admired, and an Italian magazine
that had in it a short story by Moravia called *Il Uffizio Inglese*,
which, perhaps with a certain malice, I wanted people in England to
read, a carton of cigarettes from the American PX, and two bottles
of some sparkling Italian wine—which were received with a coolness
and a minimum of comment that might have made me feel that I had
overdone playing Santa Claus if they had not at once been whisked
away as if sucked up by a vacuum-cleaner. It would be beside the
point, with the English, to complain of ungraciousness of manners
since what they aim at is a dryness and curtness that has nothing to do
with grace; but it was interesting to note the difference between G.'s
way of receiving presents and the transports or emphatic approval
of the ordinary American girl. The attitude of Leonor Fini, the
painter, whom I had got to know in Rome and who had asked me to
bring her some paints and brushes from London, was also quite
different from G.'s. In the magnificent Italian way, she offered me
my choice of her drawings, any one of which was valued at more than
the materials I had bought her; and, when I hesitated between two,
insisted on my taking them both. When I afterwards showed an
interest in a handsome new album of Pollaiuolo, she made me take
this, too, declaring that she had two copies, and, as I was leaving,
remarked that she would send me some new books in which she
thought I might be interested. I do not in the least, by these contrasts,
intend to be invidious at G.'s expense. The incident was one of many
which made me see how the privations of the war had intensified to a

ravenous voracity the appetite for property of the English, for whom permanent family possessions, tangible personal belongings, a steady supply of food and goods, have always been important in a different way than they are to Italians or Americans. It was not, I am sure, that G. had not appreciated my gifts—she later, in the, same inexpressive way and with no suggestion from me, did me a great service, which I shall tell about further on; but, even aside from her "British phlegm," she was too dead serious about things like silk stockings to put on a polite little act.

*   *   *

When I had just come to London in April and was taken one evening by English friends to dine in a first-class restaurant, I ordered "roast duck" as a dish that sounded attractive and normal. I noticed, however, that the Londoners approached the menu with a certain quiet wariness, and that none of them selected duck. The duck, indeed, when it came, turned out to be disappointing: it consisted of little dry and tough slivers from a bird that seemed incredibly thin for even a poorly-fed barnyard fowl. The other day, when I was walking with G. through one of the narrow streets near Holborn, we found ourselves inhaling a foul stale smell, and, looking round, saw a little market, on the shelves of whose open windows were laid out rows and rows of dead crows. That was apparently all they sold in that shop.

*   *   *

I took G. somewhere in a taxi in the rain and, as I was dropping her, saw a well-dressed woman who was waiting to get a cab. I was going in her direction and took her to Oxford Street. Seeing my war correspondent's insignia, she asked me where I had been, and, when I said that I had just come from Italy, she inquired how things were there. In very bad shape, I told her. "But they're very light-hearted about it, aren't they?" I replied that this was not my impression. She said at once that she had understood that the Italians were "very unwilling to do anything for themselves." I don't remember whether I answered that the Allied Commission in Italy were making it extremely difficult for the Italians to do anything for themselves; but it seemed to me that this lady's remarks were typical of the attitude of the English toward the damage that has been done by our side. It is true no doubt, as was said to me by an Englishman on my

earlier visit to London, when the Allies were advancing on Berlin,
that the English so hate destruction that they have been made to feel
uneasy and guilty by the ruin they have created in Europe; but it is
equally characteristic of the English that they should always try to
present the picture in such a way as to make it appear that their
opponents don't really mind having their buildings and people
blown up or that it is somehow the fault of the negligence of those
foreign and inferior races that one should find them in such a mess.

*   *   *

I was a little taken aback one evening for which I had had vague
other plans to find that I was going with G. to a new opera by
Benjamin Britten which was being done at Sadler's Wells. She had
bought the tickets herself and said nothing about it in advance. The
only thing I had heard by Britten had been a *Requiem* that had not
much impressed me, and I did not feel particularly eager to sit
through an English opera called *Peter Grimes*, based on an episode
from Crabbe. G. did try, with her usual lack of emphasis, to get me
to read the libretto, of which she had procured a copy, but she did
not explain that this work had been creating great interest in London,
where the critics, who, like me, had at first not expected anything
sensational, had been roused from their neat routine to the point of
hearing it several times and writing two or three articles about it.
But she knew that I ought to hear it, and it is one of my debts to G.
that she made me go to *Peter Grimes*, which I should otherwise
unquestionably have missed.

For, almost from the moment when the curtain went up on the
bare room in the provincial Moot Hall—which no overture had
introduced—where the fisherman Peter Grimes was being examined
at a coroner's inquest in connection with the death of his apprentice,
I felt the power of a musical gift and a dramatic imagination that
woke my interest and commanded my attention. One of the rarest
things in the world is the first-rate musical genius who expresses
himself naturally in terms of the theatre. There have been Mozart,
Musorgsky and Wagner, but has there really been anyone else?
To be confronted, without preparation, with an unmistakable new
talent of this kind is an astonishing, even an electrifying, experience.
The difficulty of describing *Peter Grimes* to someone who has not
heard it is the difficulty of convincing people whose expectations are
likely to be limited by having listened to too much modern music
that was synthetic, arid, effortful and inadequate, that a new master

has really arrived; of conveying to them the special qualities of a full-grown original artist. In my own case, I am particularly handicapped by lack of technical knowledge and training, so that I can only give an account of the opera's spell without being able to analyse it intelligently. The best I can do, then, is to report my impression—subject to expert correction—that Britten's score shows no signs of any of the dominant influences—Wagner, Debussy, Stravinsky, Schönberg or Prokofiev—but has been phrased in an idiom that is personal and built with a definiteness and solidity that are as English as Gilbert and Sullivan (one can find, for an English opera, no other comparison in the immediate past). And the result of this is very different from anything we have been used to. The ordinary composer of opera finds his conventions there with the stage; but, when you are watching *Peter Grimes*, you are almost completely unaware of anything that is artificial, anything "operatic." The composer here seems quite free from the self-consciousness of contemporary musicians. You do not feel you are watching an experiment; you are living a work of art. The opera seizes upon you, possesses you, keeps you riveted to your seat during the action and keyed up during the intermissions, and drops you, purged and exhausted, at the end.

The orchestra, in *Peter Grimes*, plays a mainly subordinate role, and the first effect on the hearer, during the opening scene in the Moot Hall, is of a drastic simplification of opera to something essential and naked, which immediately wakes one up. There is no Wagnerian web of motifs that tells you about the characters: the characters express themselves directly, either conversing or soliloquising in song, while the orchestra, for the most part, but comments. The music is a close continuity, though articulated rather than fluid, of vivid utterances on the part of the personages and—except in the more elaborate interludes—sharp and terse descriptive strokes, in which from time to time take shape arias, duets, trios and choruses. These—almost never regular in pattern and never losing the effect of naturalness—have their full or fragmentary developments, and give way to the next urgent pulse of the blood-stream that runs through the whole opera. In the same way, the words of the libretto, by the poet Montague Slater, which are admirably suited to the music and which the music exactly fits, shift sometimes into the imagery of poetry but never depart far from the colloquial and are sometimes —with no loss of dignity—left perfectly bald and flat. But we soon come to recognise in the music the extraordinary flexibility, the subtlety and the variety, which are combined with a stout British craftsmanship that has a sure hand with mortise and tenon and that knows how to plant and mass a chorus, and with a compelling theatrical sense, an instinct for tempo and point. And —what is most uncommon with opera—we find ourselves touched and stirred at listening to an eloquence of voices that does not merely charm or impress us as the performance of well-trained singers but that seems sometimes to reach us directly with the emotions of actual people. Nor do these voices find their expression exclusively through the singers' roles: one of the most effective devices of *Peter Grimes* is the use of the orchestral interludes that take place between the scenes while the curtain is down. Thus at the end of the first scene in the Moot Hall, where you have just been seeing Peter Grimes consoled by Ellen Orford, the school-teacher, the only being in the town who cares for him, the orchestra develops a theme which seems to well up out of Ellen's heart, and then rises and falls with a plangency that, sustained through the long passage with marvellous art, conveys, as if her spirit were speaking, her sympathy and pain for Peter. And at the end of the scene that follows, when a storm has been heard coming up as Balstrode, the retired captain, has been trying to remonstrate with Peter over his plan to take another apprentice and prove to the town that he is not a monster, the winds and the waves break loose the moment the curtain falls, fiendishly yelping and slapping in a way that represents with realism—Britten was born on the Suffolk coast—the worrying raving crescendo of an equinoctial gale but that howls at the same time with the fierceness of Peter's rebellious pride and of the latent sadistic impulse of which he is half unconscious but to which the new situation will eventually give free rein. The sea's restive and pressing movement has been all through the scene that preceded, and in the next, in the local tavern to which the people have resorted for warmth and cheer, the hurricane wildly intrudes whenever anyone opens the door, and at last, with the entrance of Grimes, rushes into the room to stay. This long act, which is brought to its climax by the silence that greets Peters' appearance and that concentrates the hostility of the town, and by the arrival of the orphan whom, the carrier refusing, Ellen has herself gone to fetch and for whose welfare she hopes to make herself responsible—this act has an intensity and an impetus that carries one through, without a moment's let-down, from the opening to the end.

Nor is what follows much less effective. The whole drama is a stretching of tension between the inquest and the inevitable crisis when Grimes will, if not deliberately kill, at least cause the death of, he second apprentice; and I do not remember ever to have seen, at any performance of opera, an audience so steadily intent, so petrified and held in suspense, as the audience at *Peter Grimes*. This is due partly to the dramatic skill of Britten, but is is due also to his having succeeded in harmonising, through *Peter Grimes*, the marsh helpless emotions of wartime. This opera could have been written in no other age, and it is one of the very few works of art that have seemed to me, so far, to have spoken for the blind anguish, the hateful rancours and the will to destruction of these horrible years. Its grip on its London audiences is clearly of the same special kind as the grip of the recent productions of *Richard III* and *The Duchess of Malfi*. Like them, it is the chronicle of an impulse to persecute and to kill which has become an obsessive compulsion, which drags the malefactor on—under a fatality which he does not understand, from which he can never get free, and which never leaves him even the lucidity for repentance or reparation—through a series of uncontrollable cruelties which will lead, in the long run, to his being annihilated himself. At first you think that Peter Grimes is Germany. He is always under the impression poor fellow, that what he really wants for himself is to marry Ellen Orford and to live in a nice little cottage with children and fruit in the garden "and whitened doorstep and a woman's care." Above all, he wants to prove to his neighbours that he is not the scoundrel they think him, that he really means no harm to his apprentices, and that he will make a good family man. But he cannot help flying into a fury when the boy does not respond to his will, and when he gets angry, he beats him; and his townsmen become more and more indignant. At last, shouting, "Peter Grimes!," they go on the march against him, determined to capture him and make him pay, just at the moment when he has paused and relented, and when their approach will precipitate, in his dash to escape, his pushing the boy so that he falls over the cliff, which is finally to settle his fate. (A comparison of the text of the opera with the story as told by Crabbe in *The Borough* shows that Britten and Montague Slater—though they have used here and there a few lines from Crabbe—have put Peter in a different situation and invented for him a new significance. The outlaw fisherman in Crabbe is married, though his wife does not figure in the story, and he has no connection with Ellen Orford, who is the heroine of a separate episode. The mainspring of the original version is Peter's rebellion against his father: he is in Crabbe completely anti-social and has no hankering for middle-class decency.) But, by the time you are done with the opera—or by the time it is done with you—you have

decided that Peter Grimes is the whole of bombing, machine-
gunning, mining, torpedoing, ambushing humanity, which talks
about a guaranteed standard of living yet does nothing but wreck its
own works, degrade or pervert its own moral life and reduce itself to
starvation. You feel, during the final scenes, that the indignant
shouting trampling mob which comes to punish Peter Grimes is just
as sadistic as he. And when Balstrode gets to him first and sends him
out to sink himself in his boat, you feel that you are in the same boat
as Grimes.

*   *   *

Every night when I walked back to Half Moon Street, I ran the
gauntlet of the innumerable prostitutes that lined Piccadilly and the
Green Park. They would brush you with "Come heah, Sweetie!" or a
simple "Hullo!" in their low quiet London voices that, with their pale
dimly-looming forms, made them seem a part of the night like moths.
There was one of them who gave me the impression of being more or
less a lady, for she talked the schoolboy language like G. and would
say to me, "Can't I tempt you?" as if she were offering me a cake or a
drink. One night when I had lost my way in the queer little tangle of
streets behind the Christian Science church, a tough, short and
stocky blond wench, almost like some hussy of Rowlandson's, of
whom I had asked the way and who was going in my direction,
steered me good-naturedly to my sordid hotel. She tried to take
advantage of the occasion to do a bit of business, but I replied, in a
attempt to discourage her, that I had just been to see a friend. "In
other words, you've had it," she said. "Charming!"
One night, wandering back at loose ends, I picked up a really
good-looking girl who accosted me in French. She was the only such
woman that I had yet seen in London who was not frankly down-at-
heels and disreputable. A vigorous well-filled-out brunette with a
bright smile of strong white teeth, she was wearing a brown suit, a
bèret and relatively little make-up. She came from Montmartre, she
told me, and had been in London since 1939. Her aim was to go back
to Paris and open a lingerie shop. During the day, she worked
wrapping up parcels at the French Red Cross; and for the purpose of
her traffic at night she did not use the harlots' hotels, but had a well-
kept room in a house that was inhabited entirely by French girls. It
was impressive, as a feat of French character, to see how these girls
stuck together and how astutely they had organised their affairs.
Everything here was on a higher level of decency than among the
native prostitutes of London. I was talking about this, when I got

back to Rome, with Alberto Moravia, the novelist, who had lived for a time in England, and he said truly that the point was that in France prostitution was a recognised profession which did not involve the loss of self-respect, whereas, in England, a woman who took to the streets was consigned to the dregs of society and could no longer keep up any standards. She was now simply a *tart* or a *whore*, which is quite different from being *une petite femme*—what Odette, my French friend, always called herself. The English girls, as a rule, looked blowzy and behaved vulgarly, and they mostly gave the impression of being diseased. But Odette was in good shape and handsome, and conducted her commerce with men with the same sort of efficiency and dignity with which she would have run her shop. She was scrupulously hygienic, and had availed herself of every resource to eliminate both squalor and risk.

It was all like a little chunk of Paris embedded in darkest densest London. Though Odette had been in England six years, she had learned only a few words of English and talked French in a polite and conventional way that would have done perfect credit to the proprietress of a *pension de famille*. She had on tap all the correct formulations, and when she used, as she did not do often, a word of argot that she saw I did not understand—as when she tactfully remarked, in connection with the outburst of de Gaulle against Britain over its attitude toward French interests in Syria, that she "didn't know what de Gaulle had taken into his *ciboule*"—she would immediately explain what this meant. She described to me with clarity but discretion the characteristics of the various nationalities as she had encountered them in the course of her business. The English were very cold: unbuttoned, buttoned up, and then goodbye! the Canadians were "*ordinaires*." Some of the Poles were nice. But "*il n'y a que les Français, les Belges et les Américains pour faire l'amour*." The Americans were rather "*bruyants*," but then they were "*loin de chez eux*" and no doubt behaved better at home; and in any case, they were gay to go out with and really liked to have a good time. She would have nothing to do with blacks, and one night when she had been spoken to by an officer who turned out to be a Negro, she had said she had another engagement.

I saw her several times and used to pay her to stay on and talk, but merely talking made her nervous and restless, and she would begin knitting energetically on a sweater that she told me she was making for the director of the French Red Cross. If she had had to buy it, she said, it would have cost her several pounds, but this way it cost only a few shillings. She discussed her expenses and savings

with exactitude and in detail, and declared that, what with the over
head of her high-grade room, she wasn't able to save very much; bu
I am perfectly sure she saved something.

*   *   *

I had lunch in an old London club, full of dark staircases and
antique engravings, very pleasant in its privacy and comfort, and
quite different from the elevator-served and more hotel-like clubs o
New York. The lunch was much the best and the most abundant that
I had had anywhere in London. They had managed to keep themselves supplied with excellent vegetables and cheeses and various
kinds of meat, as not even the best restaurants were, and seemed
secure in their privileged position.

When I left with the friend who had brought me, we stood on the
curb for some minutes trying to catch a taxi; but at last, just as we
thought we had one, a man snapped it up under our noses, and we
decided to give it up and walk on. My companion must have known
the man, for he remarked: "It's a kind of Hell—eternally waiting in
the street while one watches all the people one most loathes getting
into taxis and driving off." He was not naturally an unamiable man,
and it seemed to me that his comment was typical of the general
state of mind to which England was now reduced: a combination of
competitive spitefulness with exasperated patience.

*   *   *

I looked up Harold Laski and went around with him to some
Labour meetings in the industrial towns outside London. From the
houses of grey "roughcast" or yellow brick, with their small bay-
windows and dull red-tiled roofs, the pale men and women and boys
and girls emerged in gray or blue or khaki to sit quietly and listen to
the speakers with concentrated and anxious attention. These
occasions seemed a great deal more serious than anything else of the
kind that I remembered to have seen in America, including even
labour-union meetings and the rallies of the Left-Wing parties. The
routine of a presidential campaign looked, beside them, like per-
functory clowning.

Laski put on a very good performance, and he received a resound-
ing ovation. People crowded around our car to get a glimpse of the
professor from Oxford who was working for their side and who was
just then being denounced by the Beaverbrook press. The situation

was that Churchill had invited Clement Attlee to be present at the Berlin Conference, and that Laski, the chairman of the Labour Party had announced that, if Attlee attended, it would be as an observer only, and that the decisions made by the Conference would not affect the future foreign policy of Labour. This statement had been seized upon by Beaverbrook as a pretext for raising an alarm against the sinister hidden hand of Socialism, which, in the event of a victory for Labour, would be manipulating puppet officials. But he had apparently made no impression on the supporters of the Labour candidates, for whom Laski had now come to speak. These people were much too badly off and had much too grim a prospect before them to be excited by the antics of journalists. The only thing that mattered to them was that the Labour Party was promising quick action on housing, education and jobs. Churchill, as Laski reminded them, had said that he was "in favour of the traditional Britain, with a few measures of practical construction"; and now Laski was declaring that "mass unemployment was incompatible with democratic institutions," and that they "must never again allow such a degradation of conditions as had occurred between the two wars." As for foreign affairs: he was loudly applauded when he told them that the people of Europe and Asia, "bound in chains," were "reaching out for the Four Freedoms," and that the Labour Party, if elected to office, could not undertake to follow the policies of the party that had allowed China and Spain, Czecho-Slovakia and Abyssinia, to fall victims one by one to the Japanese and the Fascists, and that was still, in Italy and Greece, backing the reactionary elements and trying to reinstate the very kings who had delivered their countries over to the Fascists and who had no longer any popular support.

He reminded them that, in the "traditional Britain" which Mr. Churchill wanted to perpetuate, one per cent of the population owned fifty per cent. of the wealth; that, in the Army, only one per cent. of the officers came from working-class parents; and that in 1939, at the time war had broken out, sixty-seven per cent. of the diplomatic corps had gone to school at Eton. Well, they all knew that the Battle of Peterloo had been won on the playing-fields of Eton and that the Battle of Sidney Street had been won on the playing-fields of Harrow! (References to the Manchester Massacre of 1819, when soldiers charged with sabres a meeting held to petition for parliamentary reform, and to an incident in the twenties when Churchill, as Home Secretary, went personally, pistol in hand, after some foreigner, a political refugee, who was supposed to be a dangerous character). Yet I noticed that the speaker did not hesitate to call attention to his own upper-class education. I heard him explain more than once, in connection with social inequalities, that he himself, in being born, had "had the good sense to choose rich parents," who had sent him to a public school; and he made a conventional joke about his coming from "the best university—by which I of course mean Oxford." (I remembered that he had been telling me on the train coming down, about a book by some liberal peer, who showed brilliantly how impossible it was "to get a real education at Oxford.") Well, this kind of thing, I reflected, would never have gone down in America from such a speaker before such an audience; but I imagined that Harold Laski knew perfectly what he was doing, and that he was not merely aiming to create prestige by appealing to the deep-rooted snobbery which is supposed to prevail in England, but also, or perhaps solely, to disarm any possible resentment of his Oxford manner and accent. The alternative would have been, I suppose, to pretend to be apologetic about them—which would have been found a good deal more objectionable. In America, the differences in the way people talk, though considerable, are less noticeable than in England; and where the factory worker's son may very well go to some college, there is no clear issue of education. But in England the consciousness of class seems omnipresent and everlasting, and even in a campaign where the speaker is advocating "government ownership, under socialist control, of land and raw materials," this factor has to be exploited or circumvented.

But I felt about Harold Laski, as, in Europe, I had already felt in connection with certain other figures, literary, artistic, or political, whom I had met since the end of the war, that the processes of disintegration had now gone so far over here that people, if they were capable of seriousness, had now to be serious in a way that our well-fed and well-defended intellectuals had never lately been forced to be in America. If one was capable of good sense and courage, those qualities were aroused, were demanded, by this hour of moral slump; and they emerged with a moral dignity that differed from the heroism of wartime. There has always been in Harold Laski an element of intellectual vanity, of self-indulgence in his own virtuosity, of a confidence in his own resourcefulness which plays sometime into a boyish sense of mischief, sometimes into the irresponsibility of taking himself, or letting others take the appropriate and ready legend for the outlying uncivilised fact (as in his willingness to ignore or not to recognise the totalitarian tyranny of Stalin or in his habit of casting himself for a role in all his anecdotes of illustrious contemporaries). At these meetings, his cleverness and his competence, his quick wits in dealing with the problems of the moment, combined with his long-range capacity for absorbing and retaining data as well as for sticking to principle, were displayed in a striking way. He was adroit at disposing of hecklers—of the hired and coached kind, set up by the Conservatives and the Communists; marvellous at answering questions—he had the answer on the tip of his tongue the second that the questioner had finished; admirable in the homes of the Labour people, with whom and with whose wives and children he had no stiffness and knew just what to say. But I felt now as I had not done before, merely in talking to him or reading his writings, that he was more than an intellectual radical who formulated plausible positions. I felt that there was something in him of the real fighter for human rights, and that this had survived, through two wars, an era of chaos and panic, in rather an impressive way. At one moment—I was sitting on the platform and in a position to study the audience—I caught sight of an elderly woman (she may not have been so elderly as she looked), who sat with chin and nose thrust forward, eyes intent yet staring, and with a peculiar kind of hungriness and gauntness that caused one to recoil from the suggestion of something that was just on the edge of not being quite familiarly human—as if she belonged to a quite distinct breed from even the poor people of peacetime communities, to a breed with ravenous eyes like an animal's that no longer took in the same things that the true human being saw but saw only with appetites that were simple and stringent. Such faces I had noticed in Milan just after the expulsion of the Germans; and I was coming, as they recurred, to recognise them as the type of wartime Europe. On the platform, erect before this woman and all her silent companions, stood Laski, slight, bespectacled, high-browed, making them promises which could not always perhaps be realised, amusing them with wise-cracks and stories which were not always absolutely first-rate, talking to some degree the mere cant of politics, yet certainly kept up and held to his post by some tension that magnetised and turned him toward that craning grey-faced chicken-eyed woman.

9

ROME IN MIDSUMMER

Rome, on my return from England, seemed more fetid and corrupt then ever. The whole stretch from the gates of the Borghese Gardens down through the Via Veneto, the Via del Tritone and the Corso Umberto to the Piazza Venezia has been, as Moravia says, converted into one great brothel; and in the evenings of the dog star summer, we all seem stewing like lumps of flesh and fat in a cheap but turbid soup that washes through this winding channel like the bilge of a Venetian canal. Prostitution, with the Americans here, has become, from the Roman point of view, so unprecedentedly incredibly profitable that many girls have been brought into the streets who might otherwise have stayed at home or worked at decent jobs. The standard price that they try to keep up seems to be thirty thousand lire—that is, thirty dollars; but in other respects the thing has certainly reached a very low level. Bill Barrett is under the impression that the soldiers go further here than has ever been done anywhere in peacetime in dispensing with even the most sketchy preliminaries: the G.I. simply overtakes the girl, cranes around to get a glimpse of her face so as to be sure she is not absolutely repulsive, then grabs her; she allows herself to be grabbed, but, backing against the wall, makes him stop for a discussion of terms. All the way along the Via del Tritone, these walls are lined with soldiers, who have been watching the parade every evening so that they have got to know the regular girls, and are fishing for the better ones, with whom they will attempt to drive bargains. If a respectable woman goes through here and hurries on without replying to greetings, she is likely to be followed by such jeers as, "She must be a hundred-thousand-lire broad!"

The hotels in the Via Veneto that have been commandeered by the A.C. are picketed by tarts and pimps. The air corps are great spenders on furlough and they are allowed to have women in their rooms, so that the aviators' hotel in this section is the centre of activity and gaiety. Women stream through the lobby, perch in the bar and flutter about the entrance like starlings. I saw one little girl coming out, wild-looking, red-haired and slim, who gave me the impression that she was having an intoxicatingly good time as well as making a great deal of money. In another of these hotels, one night some soldiers threw a girl out the window and broke her back so that she died. Such incidents have antagonised the Italians, and the "better class" of people are disgusted by the spectacle of the Roman women—and many who have come into Rome for the purpose—making such a display of themselves, and by seeing what was once one of the handsomest and most fashionable quarters of modern Rome turned into a squalid market, where the behaviour of Catullus' Lesbia "*in quadriviis et angiportis*"—which I have never seen in public before—is a matter of nightly occurrence. There is a sign on an American army club which says, "Reserved for G.I.'s and Their Lady Guests," and the Romans have picked up the latter phrase as a synonym for tarts. They say that the word *signorina*, from its constant use by the soldiers, has passed into disrepute.

*　　　*　　　*

In these days it is always reassuring to find people who have been working at the arts undistracted by war-work and unshaken in morale. One of the things I have enjoyed most in Rome has been calling, from time to time, on Leonor Fini, the painter. I had seen in New York a few of her pictures, which were half-Surrealist, half-Romantic; and to climb up to her apartment in an enormous old palace in the squalid Piazza del Gesù is to realise that Rome itself is not only intensely Romantic but even also rather Surrealist, so that such work loses the power to shock that was its aim and its pride in Paris. At night, with electricity economised, the place is entirely dark, and at first, among the many entrances that open on all sides of the courtyard, I would always become confused and have to summon the *portiere*. You need matches to achieve the ascent of the shallow and wide and deep interminable marble stairs, made for unimaginable grandeur, that the proportionately lofty arched windows illuminate only faintly; and by the glimmer, beneath the stone vaults and among the great funeral vases and the flower-carved entablatures, one has glimpses of Roman relics that appear, on their heroic scale, in a completely Surrealist key: the conventionally statuesque pose of a white naked hero with a sword would be followed by a similar figure in an unexpected half-squatting posture; a single finger from an ancient colossus, standing upright on a pedestal, loomed as tall as an ordinary statue; and a bearded man, seated on something and leaning forward intent on a book, had the appearance of reading in the toilet. As the staircase goes on so long that you finally lose count of the landings, you are likely to try wrong apartments and get the rooms of some lurking nobleman whose old butler peers out through the crack of a door apprehensively secured by a chain.

At last, taking a smaller stairway, you arrive, just under the roof, at what must once have been servant's quarters but is now a duplex apartment. One comfortable large room serves as both studio and living-room and looks out, in a commanding view, as I discovered on later visits, over the infinite lines and planes of the roofs and top stories of Rome, all grey-blues and dry pale buffs, which are matched, during the late summer sunsets, by the pale blues and pinks of the sky, in which the eternal swifts restlessly twitter and flock. The mood induced by the stairway and by my previous experience of Surrealists was so strong that when I went there first I mistook for a "Surrealist object" a large cat with a bandage on its head that was lying on the table like an ornament but that turned out to be alive when I tried to pick it up. And, as a matter of fact, the studio is remarkably and refreshingly free from what Signorina Fini, in speaking of another painter, once called the "*voulu*" aspect of Surrealism. Such "objects" as one did find about were mostly things she had used as models, such as a small glass case of moths; and the place, with its disorderly elegance, was quite free from the neo-Gothicism that one associates with, for example, Max Ernst. The pictures by Leonor Fini and her colleagues on the walls and tables and shelves had an element of fairy-tale enchantment and *commedia dell'arte* humour that prevented their being "modern" in the sense that Ernst and Dali are; and, in Rome, it seemed perfectly natural to pass to Signorina Fini's paintings from the late Rennaissance patterns, the decorated ceilings and strips of wall, that make a background in the Vatican Museum: hippogriffs that hang in a filigree of scrollery, vine-leaves and tendrils, winged sphinxes with the curling rears of seahorses, spindle-legged and needle-billed birds, hawk-beaked and double-headed eagles, feathery-tongued serpents with twining tails, cupids holding red spidery lobsters, allegorical figures or Graces that seem balancing like tight-rope walkers; and the satyrs' masks, the lions' faces, the unidentifiable female beings all compact of imperturbable complacencies. It was as if into this mythical world, conventionalised and quietly lively, Leonor Fini had brought an emotion more personal and more poetic, and motifs from a later time. Here the sphinxes are leonine, and immobilised in their first sombre broodings or the maiden surprises of girlhood—a girlhood cut off from the world and queerly turned in on itself; here great ladies with dishevelled long hair and long enveloping skirts sit silent and self-absorbed in the grand but bare rooms of palaces, from the walls or arches of which big fragments have sometimes fallen; and a tousle-headed dubious-eyed girl with a pretty throat and round full breasts has flowered from a twisted root that sends out fibres and bulbous sprouts, in defiance of a death's-head moth, two white paper animal skulls and a dead lizard with its pale belly up. These contrasts of brokenness and deadness with a warm and rich physical life that is unable to extricate itself are characteristic of Signorina Fini's painting; they seem to express a tragic paradox. This is a soul that is sullenly and fiercely and yet wistfully narcissistic, self-admiring and self-consuming, at once blooming and checked in growth. She is entirely a *female* artist, occupied much less with the work, which the man will approach as a craft but which in her case is unequal in skill and taste, than with her dreams, her awareness of herself, her personality and role as a woman. And for this reason her pictures of men are the weakest part of her work. With women she sometimes succeeds through assimilating them to herself; but her portraits of men that I have seen are invariably sentimental: mere images that rise in the mind of the smouldering sequestered girl who waits too long in the other pictures.

In one corner, beside her own work, hangs that of the Marchese Lepri, a young man in the Foreign Office, whom Signorina Fini first met in the early years of the war, when he was consul at Monte Carlo and who, more or less under her tutelage, has recently learned to paint. These examples of his painting show that he has been making a rapid development: some of the latest ones seem to me extremely good. Satirical and fantastic, they do not exploit any of the anomalies which are the tricks of the Surrealist School, but attach themselves to a tradition that is Italian, almost mediaeval. I told him this as I was looking at a picture—done recently and one of the best—in which a party of sodden people in contemporary evening dress are seen gorging at a dinner table that stretches back in a long perspective, while the walls and the floor and the table itself are cracking up below and about them—all painted with the precision and clearness of a loggia in some early religious scene; and he replied that he had hoped he had got into it "a certain actuality, too." On a table stood some drawings by Clerici: a young architect and classical draughtsman who has emerged from months of hiding in Florence to apply his firm and hollow line to violins spilling human intestines and bald indignant wigmaker's dummies.

I did not find at first in Signorina Fini any outward traits that corresponded to the elements of moroseness and frustration that often appeared in her work, nor in Lepri any disgust with the society breaking up around him. Leonor Fini is a handsome and voluptuous, an extraordinarily attractive woman—with large dark round eyes and abundant dark hair, which she arranges in a style that is copied from the ladies in Venetian paintings: gathered up and tied with a ribbon behind, but with a mass of it pushed forward on her forehead; and though she lived in Paris for years before the war drove her back to Italy, she seems always, not Parisian in dress, but magnificently and generously Italian. She was wearing, the first time I saw her, an emerald-green taffeta housecoat with a kind of white-lace filigree bodice, and a pair of very high-heeled sandals. She is quite natural and talks very well—with perfect freedom and ease—about people and pictures and books, too sure of her personal taste, too intent on her own painting, ever to have been involved in that sectarian esprit de corps, that ardour for group promotion, that has possessed some of the other Surrealists. Lepri, in his white summer clothes, is quiet and cool and modest with, apparently, the indifference to current events and the sceptical lack of zeal that are supposed to be typical of Romans of the cultivated upper class. I liked to see them, and they were always most amiable, and I would sit turning over the pages of Max Ernst's demonological *collages* of old steel-engraving illustrations from nineteenth-century novels or of bestiaries of curious woodcuts showing animals with human heads. It seemed to me that here was a centre of real creative life in Rome, a live spirit that had not been extinguished.

It was, then, with rather a shock that I discovered one day that their dearest hope was to get to the United States before the summer was over. "You don't like Rome, do you?" Signorina Fini had suddenly said to me. I confessed, feeling impolite, that I did not like it much. But "*I* don't like it," she told me. "I hate it!" She wanted to go to America and live in the country there. She had made a brief visit to the States, and she felt she could find there the freedom she needed—she described herself, I think, as "*sauvage*"—which she implied was impossible in Europe. Her position, as I knew, is, like Silone's, not that of a great figure in Italy. She suffers, like him, from the handicap of having made a reputation abroad while many Italian writers and artists were taking the wage of the Fascists or submitting to the Fascist directives. Such exiles, returning, are met with a mixture of envious malice and of the uncomprehending hostility of a conventional and antiquated culture, condemned also to provinciality by the restrictions of Mussolini. As for Lepri, however good a civil servant, he cannot look forward to much of a career in a government that seems likely to remain under the thumb of a foreign power or, if it escapes this, to go to the Left at a rate that he could scarcely follow. They are not at home, not serene—probably almost as uncomfortable as I am. The sullen women in the empty palaces, the swinish crew in the banquet hall, are the realities with which they live.

This is a period that is hard to accept, we are in it but we do not really believe in it. One day Signorina Fini showed me a copy of *Vogue* which she had just received from America and expressed an amused astonishment at an article on Buchenwald, with pictures of human incinerators, piles of tangled emaciated corpses and bodies hung up on hooks, followed immediately by new flowered hats and smart bathing brassières, with an article that ran over into the back among the cosmetics ads. This was embarrassing to me as an American, but her instinctive reaction to it was not itself, I thought, without a certain incongruity, for she had just been engaged in executing, with a good deal of finesse and elegance, a series of pen-and-ink drawings for the *Juliette* of the Marquis de Sade: slim figures of men and women hacking one another to pieces and performing other questionable acts. The Surrealists had cultivated deliberately a sadism of the parlour and the gallery; but now the times had overtaken and passed them in a manner so overwhelming that it was impossible for Leonor Fini not to be shocked by the impropriety of juxtaposing these wretched victims with the refinements of Saks-Fifth Avenue. The Surrealist exponent of such horrors who makes out of them objects of art that the lover of art will enjoy, with a shudder of pleasure or pain, cannot help being startled at finding them served up as if they were detective thrillers or merely a whet to the appetite in the enjoyment of articles of luxury.

*   *   *

My hotel, the Hôtel de la Ville, is at the top of the Via Sistina, and almost directly opposite, at the convergence of two streets, stands a curious flatiron-shaped house, in which D'Annunzio lived and to which, in the luscious eighties, the *femmes du monde* of *Il Piacere* are supposed, with faltering or eager steps, to have come to their rendezvous. A little further down the Via Sistina is the house where Gogol wrote *Dead Souls*, designated now by a plaque with inscriptions in Italian and Russian, that has been put up by the Russian colony; in the next street, the Via Gregoriana, is a house in which Stendhal lived when he was making his *Promenades dans Rome* and

which a couple of centuries earlier had been occupied by Salvator
Rosa; and in a building just below, at the foot of the Spanish steps,
is the room in which Keats died and which has been kept as a Keats
museum. Not far away are the houses where Scott and Bernini and
Goethe lived.

Now, at first I found myself rather stimulated by the thought of
these illustrious neighbours—especially since it seemed an environ-
ment, this region around the Piazza di Spagna, where men had really
lived and worked, not merely a Bohemian quarter where talent went
soft or ran thin. But the longer I have stayed in Rome, the more the
cultural accretions of its past have come to weigh on me and affect
me as cloying. The climax of this feeling was a visit I paid to the
celebrated Caffè Greco, which I had been told I ought to explore.
Though it went back to 1760 and had been frequented by no end of
great people, I could not like the Caffè Greco. Making a plunge
through those sordid rope curtains that I always find distasteful in
Rome I threaded my way through three dingy compartments,
which were narrow, inadequately lighted and lined with little black
horsehair seats forbiddingly and uncomfortably squeezed in behind
little grey-veined marble tables. On the walls hung bad portraits and
landscapes and not very impressive medallions of famous men who
had come to the place. One of the ridiculous little hallway-like rooms
that should all have been thrown into a single one was lit only by a
dismal filtration from the dirty gray panes of the skylight. The
waiter prides himself on his languages and has a humorous-familiar
tinge, as if he were playing a role in some comedy of the eighteen-
forties. He will show you the yellow old albums in which the great
men have signed their names, if your interest is sufficiently keen and
you back it with the hint of a tip. And you can pick up à little
leaflet with a description of the place in four languages, each of
which contains a list of names of celebrities of that nationality who
have been habitués of the restaurant. I learned from this that the
Caffè Greco had been visited by the following persons: Goldoni,
Canova, Leopardi, Carducci, D'Annunzio, Stendhal, Berlioz,
Corot, Gounod, Bizet, Baudelaire, Paul Bourget, Anatole France,
Byron, Shelley, Keats, Thackeray, Goethe, Schopenhauer, Mendels-
sohn, Liszt, Wagner, King Ludwig of Bavaria, Gogol, Thorwaldsen
and Mark Twain—as well as by many others only less famous.

But all these names and associations were too much for me to take
in at once, and my effort to react to them appropriately had upon me
the effect of an emetic and compelled me to disgorge, as it were, the
whole mass of lore that I had swallowed before in connection with

he genius-haunted past of Rome. For the moment my only thought
was that the Greco was chill, cramped and fusty, that it had no
more relation to those artists than the leather of their old boots, and
hat a more modern and more cheerful café should be installed in that
place instead.

*   *   *

I started, before I left Rome, Hawthorne's *The Marble Faun*,
which I had never read before, and I was amazed to find how close
his reflections—mostly transferred, I believe, from his note-books—
had run to the kind of thing that I was putting down in my own.
When I finally left the city, I was feeling, very much as he was,
decidedly "tired of the sight of those immense seven-storied, yellow-
washed hovels, or call them palaces, where all that is dreary in
domestic life seems magnified and multiplied, and weary of climbing
those staircases, which ascend from a ground floor of cook-shops,
cobblers' stalls, stables and regiments of cavalry, to a middle region
of princes, cardinals and ambassadors, and an upper tier of artists,
just beneath the unattainable sky (a description which still more or
less fitted such places as the Palazzo Altieri where Leonor Fini
lived) . . . disgusted with the pretence of holiness and the reality of
nastiness, each equally omnipresent . . . half lifeless from the languid
atmosphere, the vital principle of which has been used up long ago or
corrupted by myriads of slaughters . . . crushed down in spirit with
the desolation of her (Rome's) ruin and the hopelessness of her
future . . . in short, hating her with all our might and adding our
individual curse to the infinite anathema which her old crimes have
unmistakably brought down." It is true that I was also to feel—
although not until a year or so later, when I was back in the United
States—the nostalgia of which he speaks when he writes that, after
leaving Rome "in such mood as this, we are astonished by the discovery, by and by, that our heart-strings have mysteriously attached
themselves to the Eternal City, and are drawing us thitherward
again." But in the meantime, I was in a position to recognise the
perfect accuracy of Hawthorne's description of the effect of modern
Rome on a Protestant Anglo-Saxon.
Later on, when I was back at home, I read Norman Douglas'
South Wind, also for the first time. It seemed to me that this famous
novel had been very much over-rated—for though it is clever and
fairly well-written, it is really, it seems to me, hardly more than a
superior piece of journalism about the life of the foreign colony
of Capri. Douglas *is* up to a point successful in dealing with a subject

very similar to that of Hawthorne in *The Marble Faun:* the influence
on an Anglican bishop of the demoralising atmosphere of Italy. But
if one reads the two books side by side, one is made very clearly
aware of the relative superficiality of the later writer's treatment of
the theme. The contrast is inescapable because—what I have never
seen noted—Norman Douglas has reproduced the central incident
of Hawthorne's book and used it in just the same way to create a
moral problem. The parallel is so complete that one assumes it to
have been the result of some trick of unconscious memory, reviving
the impression of a story which had been read and forgotten in
youth. Thus in Hawthorne we have a woman, American but
perhaps with some non-English blood, constantly pursued and
plagued by a rascally discarded husband, who is in a position to
threaten her with "blasting" her reputation. The moral crux of the
book is the scene on the Capitoline Hill, in which she consentingly
stands by while an Italian who wants to protect her pushes him over a
cliff and kills him. In *South Wind*, an English woman is similarly
pursued and blackmailed by an undesirable husband, and the moral
situation is managed by having her push him over a cliff in Capri,
where she has lived for so long that she has presumably caught what
the author has already shown to be the local point of view on revenge
and the taking of human life. In either case, the problem presented is
how shall the crime be treated, not only by the persons responsible,
but also by those, New England or English, who happen to know
about it; and the conclusion in either case is that the languor and
animality of Italy are capable of dulling the conscience to a degree
where such an act of violence does not seem so clearly wrong as it
would in another country.

But the difference—a curious one—is that Douglas, the man of the
world, who has now been accepted for thirty years (since the appearance of *South Wind*) as the touchstone of sophistication, should have
made the whole thing too simple: a matter of black and white, with
the two colours simply interchanged. The Scotch moralist in Douglas
has always interfered with the epicurean Austrian (to assign, perhaps
rashly, his mixed tendencies to the elements of his mixed blood), so
that he cannot enjoy the pleasures which he makes it his business to
celebrate without betraying, at the same time, a need to justify his
self-indulgence by bringing charges of inhuman or anti-social
behaviour against people with sterner principles. But a hedonist
should not be peevish; and Douglas' doctrine of sybaritic Nietzs-
cheanism, at once too soft and too cruel to catch the real exaltation
of Nietzsche, suffers also from the handicap, in a Nietzschean fatal

of being nagged by a bad conscience. In *South Wind*, the point he would like to make is that the sun of Southern Italy puts the morality of the North to sleep and may lead us to regard as quite natural, perhaps even to approve as beneficent, actions that we should else-where condemn. But what it turns out that he cannot help doing is so to construct his fable that the killing by the woman of her husband becomes a positive moral act, which her brother the Bishop and the reader must endorse as not merely understandable but demonstrably, undeniably *right*—so that, instead of remaining a comedy or suggest-ing a psychological inquiry, the book ends as a melodrama, with the lady as surely a heroine as if she had killed to defend her honour. In real life, a woman who had done such a thing would certainly have had some qualms, and her brother would have at least been un-comfortable and his relations with his sister affected: the story would be only half told; and Hawthorne shows his insight and intelligence, his superior toughness of logic, by giving Miriam a complex character which makes her behaviour plausible as well as a great deal more interesting (Douglas' lady is all of a piece), and even partly redeeming the husband, who is less a Victorian demon than an unhappy and desperate *détraqué* (where Douglas' husband is simply a rotter); by having his Italian murderer driven finally to a Catholic repentance for his pagan Italian crime; and by presenting the painful embarrassment caused by both parties involved in the crime to their well-meaning American friends. It is here the provincial puritan, the grumpy American traveller, who complained about the emptiness of Italian museums and the shallowness of Italian painting and who wanted the nude statues clothed, who is the genuine man of the world where the cities of the soul are in question, and who knows that Anglo-Saxon and Italian share, after all, the same mixed nature.

Yet *South Wind* may be read with *The Marble Faun* as one of the best accounts ever attempted of the peculiar—and, to the Anglo-Saxon, dismaying—alteration in one's point of view that may result from a long sojourn in Italy.

*   *   *

Philip Hamburger, also here for the *New Yorker*, has just come back from a trip to Trieste. The British did their best to dissuade him from interviewing any Jugo-Slavs or visiting the back-country. If he hadn't had an American major with him, he believes that he wouldn't have got anywhere at all. The British called the Jugo-Slavs "Jugs" and Jugo-Slavia "Jugland." They talked about the natives in such a was as to suggest that they were hairy savages crawling around on all fours—as if they had once been good police dogs but had now turned into dangerous wolves, and that Hamburger and his companion were likely to be torn to pieces. The President of the Trieste Council had been locked up in jail by the British for reasons of "military expediency," and he was speechless with indignation. They always referred to him contemptuously as the "fisherman," because that had been his occupation—which had finally moved him to to protest: "Well, after all, Christ was a carpenter!" When the Americans finally, after waiting for days, had been allowed to see a little of the hinterland, a British general had attempted to brief them. The Jugo-Slavs, he explained, always carried their politics with them. Hamburger had asked whether the British didn't do that, too. The American major had become much incensed and described to Hamburger as follows one of the obstructions he had met: "A bicycle drove up, and out swarmed three top-ranking warmongers, all complete with pips and squeaks." From Trieste they went on to Klagenfurt, where they were treated, says Hamburger, at the British mess, as if they were captured enemy officers. After dinner, an altercation had occurred. The British had announced to the Americans that England would now have to fight the Russians, "and you people will have to help us." Hamburger and the major emphatically denied that they would have to do anything of the kind. One of the British—there is always one Englishman who is uncompromisingly opposed to what the rest of the English are doing, but who is helpless to influence the proceedings—suddenly blew up and denounced his fellow officers, telling them that they were two hundred years behind the times. This made things more acrimonious, and the Americans left the next day.

*   *   *

A few days before I left Rome, I was taken by American friends to dine in a Black Market restaurant. We ate at outside tables in a little enclosure on the street. The clientele all looked more or less as if they were Black Market profiteers themselves. We were sitting right next to the rail that fenced us in from the street, and I had my back to this, so that, absorbed in conversation, I did not notice at first that a crowd had gathered behind us and were reaching in to grab things from our plates. But the management soon sent out a bouncer, who knocked down an old woman with a blow on the head, and drove back the mob, mostly women and children, some of whom disappeared, while others, keeping their distance, stood and stared at the diners.

10

NOTES ON LIBERATED MILAN

WHEN I first saw Milan, at the beginning of May, it looked like a slice of Hell. Some of the shabby green trams were running and some of the inhabitants were going about their routines, but the whole place seemed stunned and stopped, and the bloodless undernourished people, dressed in any old cloth that could protect their skins, seemed to have been fixed, by the long months of the German oppression, the Allied bombings and the fierce civil war, in a condition of permanent strain. The children, especially, were appalling: they had acquired, as they were growing up, expressions of indignation and apprehension which were now as much a part of their faces as malnutrition was of their bones. The halfgrown boys in their teens, exhilarated at getting a chance to let themselves go against somebody, were cruising around in cars with machine-guns, looking for Fascist collaborators to shoot. A hotel in which the Germans had tried desperately to fortify themselves was still surrounded by barricades and barbed wire; and Americans who invaded the S.S. headquarters found their police dogs and pornographic pictures. Over the whole city hung the stink of the killing of Mussolini and his followers, the exhibition of their bodies in public and the defilement of them by the crowd. Italians would stop you in the bars and show you photographs they had taken of it.

The Albergo Diana of those days, taken over for the American Army, had the grisliness of all the reminders of the old holiday tourist Europe as one finds them still clinging to the carcase left by the recent convulsions and blastings. The cool white-tiled corridors of bedrooms, the views of the Villa d'Este, the coy little plaques in the wall that indicated by a series of pictures (thus avoiding complications of language) which button you were to press for the waiter, which for the valet and which for the chambermaid—all these comforts and amenities of the traveller seemed sickeningly stale and mendacious, like the few old shopworn volumes of Tauchnitz novels that some of the bookstores had brought out for the Allies. And the desk-clerks, lift-boys and waiters, though they were going through all their old motions and speaking an adequate English, as they had just been speaking an adequate German, were somewhat upset by the new arrivals (they would probably, as Hamburger

147

suggested, not have been at all surprised to receive the Japanese next)
and had little to accommodate them with. The maitre d'hotel in full
dress was presiding over homely dinners of bully beef and army
greens, reinforced by large hard wafers that rather resembled dog-
biscuits and were the sole local contribution.

To-day, however, two months and a half later, the Diana is
completely transfigured. A rest hotel for American soldiers, it must
be one of the pleasantest places in Italy. The hotel people have got
back into their smooth routine, and it seems quite natural to be well
taken care of. The food and wine are by far the best I have had since
I have been in Europe, and you eat, to the accompaniment of music
at wicker tables with blue-and-white-checked cloths, in a charming
outdoor dining room, full of the leafage of plants and vines and
shaded by chestnuts and oaks, in the branches of which is suspended
a sort of decorative roofing of Japanese mats. There is an admirably
equipped bar and a great atmosphere of parties and dates. The
Americans are capturing and bringing to dinner some remarkably
good-looking girls.

*   *   *

The women here, in general, are marvellous. They don't have the
natural chic which is almost universal in Rome, but, in general, the
quality is better. They give—like almost everything about Milan, in
contrast to almost everything about Rome—an impression of
independence and strength. They have broad backs, and there is a
splendid blond type—often but not always dyed—who wears a
shoulder-length *chevelure*. I was struck by one girl on a bicycle who,
riding without hands, raised her arms to smooth back her done-up
pale-blond hair; and I passed, at a table on the sidewalk, where she
was having a drink with a man, what seemed to me one of the
prettiest girls I had ever seen anywhere: another blonde, with lively
brown eyes and provocative arched eyebrows, who was wearing on
her bare feet, instead of the usual wooden clogs, a pair of red-
leather high-heeled shoes that she had somehow succeeded in getting.
She made me imagine what would be possible for them if they really
had clothes and cosmetics.

*   *   *

When I was here before in the spring just after the Allies had
arrived, the walls were covered with bills that said in English,
"Hurrah for the Anglo-Saxon Liberators." But there were also
inscriptions of a different kind, painted, it is said, by the Fascists, and

ese, I see, have been left up, though the others have disappeared:
Museo distrutto" or "Casa incendiata dai liberatori anglosassoni.
ilanesi, riflettete!" And they have invented a play on words:
Anglosassoni assassini." These reproaches meet you all over the
ty, wherever there have been buildings bombed. And it is true that
e Allies attacked Milan as cruelly and as indiscriminately as the
ermans ever did London. Most of this hideous damage was in-
cted in August, 1943, when we were trying to force Badoglio's hand
√ a series of pure terror bombings aimed at densely populated
stricts and could hardly have hit more cultural monuments if the
olicy had been to destroy them. The museum and the Scala have
een gutted, the finest churches are half reduced to rubble, some of
e best sculpture on the cathedral has been shattered, and of the
fectory containing de Vinci's *Last Supper* there is nothing left but a
ell.

*   *   *

Though the Scala is boarded and silent, the Scala orchestra and
era company are still performing in other places. I went to a
ala concert in the courtyard of the old Sforzesco castle, with its
eraldry of gold-crested blue dragons devouring anguished victims
d its immense and once formidable moat, now comfortably
anted with cabbage and squash. The orchestra played Bloch,
avel and Debussy, and Hindemith's *Mathis der Mahler*; and the
licate pieces were traced with an exquisite faithfulness that made
uch music in New York seem vulgar. The concert was jammed, and
e *canto funèbre* of the Bloch Concerto Grosso was incongruously
sturbed by the roarings of people who were besieging the doors. I
t into conversation with an exceptionally well-dressed man sitting
xt to me. He didn't care much for modern music, and Hindemith
is way beyond him. He had been very much alarmed, he said, by a
port that the Allies were to leave. They mustn't go away, he
sisted; he was, he explained, *un borghese*, and he knew that if the
lies deserted them, there would be terrible civil war and the
ommunists would bring in the Russians.

When I got back to the Diana, I went to the bar, which stands at
e side of the lobby, and found a very drunk American soldier
olding forth in a loud voice in a vein which was reminiscent of
nversations at home on a supposedly higher level. They said, he
oclaimed, that he was a mental case and that he needed psychiatric
tention—well, if anything was plain in that unit, it was that the
ajor was absolutely screwy and needed to be psychoanalysed

himself—and the Colonel, wasn't he nuts!—he needed to be analyse
too. He went on and on and on, standing at the bar alone, an
though he was using the dirtiest possible language, nothing was do
about him, because the policy in these rest hotels is to leave peop
as free as possible. The two or three other soldiers present occasio
ally threw a word or a laugh at him. There was a woman across th
room, but she must have been an Italian and unable to understar
what he was saying, for she sat placidly through it all.

*   *   *

I saw another of those horrifying children: a very tall and ill-fe
boy in absurd short pants—probably because he had no others
with drawn face, frowning brows, glazed blue eyes. They look as
they had been frozen by the Gorgon.

*   *   *

I noticed a book in a bookshop called *Arrigo Beyle, Milanes*
Stendhal adored Milan and wanted this inscribed on his tombston
He must have loved the boxes of the Scala, the close, long ar
solidly built-up streets, the pale pinnacles of lace on the Duomo, th
peculiar dry blue of the sky—"*sempre un poco stanco*," as a poem in
Roman paper said the other day—and the mountains beyond th
town, as I saw them the first time that I came here: a purified dimm
slate-blue, sharply outlined like an old engraving, but presented in
softened perspective, with the silvery snow on their ridges, or, as
have seen them on this second trip, scarcely by a shade darker tha
the blue of the sky behind them, so that the mottlings of snow see
a pattern on a background of taut silk. I forget about Stendha
adventures in Milan. He came here first with Napoleon's army, ar
he would have fallen in love with some countess. He would ha
done his incessant, inexhaustible, illegible, cipher-screened writir
that made his secret and personal life, and he would have bee
sustained from without by the energy, the sound relations, the u
right spine of the city. It does not seem out of keeping here to find
statue of Leonardo or a street named after Dante, whereas in Ron
the monument to Giordano Bruno seems to have fallen to the utmc
ignominy in the squalid and swarming market of the square
which he was burned.

*   *   *

Under the patched glass of the big Galleria, where the Milanese g
in the afternoon for ices, vermouth and cakes, I sat down, at one

e outside cafés, with a young American officer: a tall fellow in a
rest-green uniform, who had been hammered into hardness and
riousness by his experiences of the war. He seemed to have been
incipally engaged in laying mines against the Germans for our
le and in detecting and digging up the enemy's mines. I had
ready some sort of idea of what this exceedingly dangerous work
is like, as I had been down along the coast in Littoria, which is
ll planted with thousands of mines, ours and the Germans' both,
that large areas of that important region are impossible for
ltivation. The little pins that explode the caps are so sensitive that
e wind bending the grass is sometimes enough to set them off, and
e malaria-control workers and the mine-diggers as well as the
hermen and the country people are constantly getting blown up.

This lieutenant explained to me at length the mechanism and
chnique of mines, drawing me little diagrams and showing a very
en interest in the subject. There was the German kind that had two
arges, the first of which blew it out of the ground and the second
which caused it to burst in the air and scatter big pieces of shot
e ball-bearings. Later, they had improved on this with thick
gged cuttings of wire that gave a "terrible slash." The Americans
d taken over this idea and turned out a model that was even worse.
unting mines was a very delicate business. There was one kind that
d a hole in the pin that you could pass a wire through to prevent it
m going off, but if they didn't have that, you just had to take a
ance. You dragged them out of the ground with long ropes and
ploded them at a distance with T.N.T. If there were fragments of
ell around, the mine detectors weren't much good, because they
sponded to the presence of any kind of metal. For the "bakelite
s" that the Germans used later, the detector was no good at all.
en there were quantities of dummy mines that the Germans had
t in to fool us and that had to be removed with just as much care as
hey had been real ones. In the case of the leaping mines, you had a
ance to see what was coming and throw yourself on your face, and
e man who had done this had survived and received the Purple
art. Another had thrown himself against the mine to protect the
n who were with him, and they had named one of the new bridges
er him. The lieutenant said that he had once been blown yards
ay from where he was standing, and that another time, after one
these incidents, when he had gone over and started to talk to his
n, he had suddenly fainted away. With booby-traps, you had no
ide: you just had to suspect everything. Once a Britisher and an
nerican had gone into a suspected house to search it room by

room. The American had sat down on a bed and the whole hou
had blown up and left him among the ruins holding a piece of t
bed; the Englishman, who had been downstairs, had suffocate
under the heap before they could get him out.

But in spite of the shortcomings of the Germans, you did have
hand it to them: all these mines and things were wonderful wor
The lieutenant told me with pride that he had acquired a clockwo
time-bomb of the kind that had destroyed the Naples post office
week after the Germans had left. He talked about it as if it were a ra
book or print—said that there were only seven or eight extant. It w
made beautifully—all of aluminum. He had set it without t
explosive, and it had gone off within two minutes of the time.
realised in talking to him, how the younger generations of Americar
were being affected by the war. During the last war, in which we we
less deeply involved, there was, as I have said above, an humanitaria
reaction against the practice of war itself; but in this one the Germa
methods have ended by making everybody more callous and by inte
esting the practical Americans in the technical side of the business,
as if mechanised large-scale homicide were a normal occupation.

The lieutenant did not think much of the Italians, who, he sai
had laid down on the war just when the critical moment had com
He told me that, a few nights before, he had walked out of a bar wi
an Italian girl and run into a gang of young men who wanted to gr
her and shave her head—a penalty which has been sometim
inflicted for going out with Allied soldiers; but he had called sor
other Americans out of the bar, and they had completely cleaned
on the Italians. He said that it had been the best fight he had h
since he had been in Italy. He told me that American jeeps we
constantly being stolen, and blamed it all on the Negro soldiers, w
sold them, he said, to the Italians.

*   *   *

The following day, in the Galleria, an Italian at the next tab
spoke to me in very good English. He was neat, precise, gray a
well-dressed—evidently some sort of businessman. He felt ve
strongly that the Allies ought to stay and keep order in Italy. T
working class were threatening trouble—not because they we
naturally bad, but because they were misled by their leaders.

*   *   *

A translation of Karl Marx's *Das Kapital* has appeared in almo
all the bookstores. It is queer to see it displayed in the windov

etween a translation of Catullus and a new edition of Rimbaud—
nd along with Gide's *L'Immoraliste* and Barbey d'Aurevilly on
andyism. The Italians under Fascism seem to have been completely
at off from the main cultural currents of the time, and their reading
still out of date. It was curious to see, in Rome, how a novelette,
e *Agostino* of Alberto Moravia, which deals in the lightest and
ildest way with a Freudian mother-and-son relationship, could
eate a sensation in a city where new editions of Verlaine's porno-
aphic poems and the short stories of the Marquis de Sade were on
le in every bookstore. And here it is as if they had discovered
arx at the same moment as Gide and Rimbaud, and just as, in
erature, they regard the *fin de siècle* as very advanced and daring,
  in politics they are still in the period when Communism was
riously Marxist: they don't know that in the Soviet Union Marx
id Lenin have gone by the board, and that the Russians are un-
cely to encourage a genuine working-class movement aiming at
ina-fide socialism.
The class line-up that you find in conversation with the people
ppears even among these bookstores. One of the shops in the
alleria says, "*Libri socialistici non si vendono qui.*"

*   *   *

I went to see one of the American officials in the Allied Military
overnment. He was a Jew, a big, agreeable, well-meaning man, not
ite so well-posted and alert, perhaps, as one expects a Jew to be.
rrived at a moment of crisis. "Here's the story," he said. "There
is a jailbreak in the prison last Tuesday, and thirty-six men
caped—all Partisans, but none of them policial prisoners: they
re all in for regular crimes that ranged from robbery to rape. The
ards were Partisans, too, and so I'll have to change them for
rabinieri, which I've been wanting to do all along. But now,
cording to the reports we get, there's going to be a demonstration—
 supposed to start at four o'clock right outside in the square, and
en march to the prison and protest." Who were doing the demon-
ating? I asked. Why, a lot of Italian war prisoners who had just
me back from Germany. But what was the point of the protest?
Vhy, they'll probably be demanding more food. They want to show
ople they're starved. They certainly do look it," he added. But
at was the connection between that and the jailbreak? I did my best
pin him down, but got no satisfactory answer, and I decided that
did not know. "They're always having demonstrations," he said.

L

At this moment, like a scene in a play, a large British security m
entered, with a small red-faced and bewildered American maj
following in his wake. "There'll bo no demonstration," said t
chief of the Allied police, a quiet-spoken fellow of enormous gir
and menacing strong-arm aplomb. "We've been over to their hea
quarters—they're just across the square. I told 'em that if th
marched to the jail, we'd have a reception committee there, and we
extend to 'em the hospitality of A.M.G.—we had cells there emp
and ready for 'em, where we'd be glad to put 'em up. When we ca
in, they were loungin' all about, and I told 'em to stand up and sho
some courtesy. And there's not goin' to be a demonstration. Th
were buzzin' about after I talked to 'em like a lot of blue-arsed fli
It was just like when we talked to Togliatti (the leader of the Co
munist Party and Minister of Justice in the new Parri governmen
He thought he was goin' to make a speech, and then he decided n
to make one."

The security man went off to the prison—just to make sure, as
said—and the major remained behind. The high official showed m
handful of literature which announced a giant demonstration
presented as a public festivity—in celebration of Bastille Day. T
invitation to the high official had on it a curious symbol that I h
already seen on all the posters advertising this celebration with whi
the city was plastered; and it dawned on me now that this curio
thing that looked a little like the head of a bird was the Phrygi
Liberty Cap, the emblem of the French Revolution, drawn, howev
in such a way that it was not necessarily recognisable and mig
perhaps be explained away as an arbitrary decorative design. T
officers, too, had been puzzling over it and seemed to regard it wi
some suspicion, and when I suggested my explanation, the maj
perturbed and dazed, cried, "Does *that* mean the French Revol
tion?" This major presently left us. "In my opinion," said t
Jewish official, "the sooner we get out of Italy, the better for
concerned. When a baby is learning to walk, you have to let it f
down sometimes—you have to let it make its mistakes by itself."

*   *   *

I made a point of taking part in the big turn-out in celebration
the Fourteenth of July. While I was sitting on a curb in the pa
waiting for things to begin, a man came and sat down beside me a
immediately began to talk to me volubly in some patois th
was hard to understand. I made out that he wanted me to kn

at he had always been against the Fascists. He showed me his
ommunist card and told me how he and his father, who was blind,
d suffered at the hands of the regime, and how the workers had had
eir own methods of dealing with the Fascists in the factory. An
merican journalist said to me that this had several times happened
him: humble people like this think that showing their C.P. cards
Americans will give proof of their sincere anti-Fascism and
commend them to the anti-Fascist liberators.

Suddenly people, with many children, began to troop across the
ass from behind me, and I had to get up, as I was in their way,
nd move in the same direction. But as they swarmed in a thick
ass in the vicinity of the triumphal arch, where there was a plat-
rm for music and speeches, I worked my way out, and eventually
ack through the park and home to the Albergo Diana. All the way I
ad to squeeze through the solid mob pushing in the other direction.

was prodigious: I had never seen a city where the streets seemed so
led with people. There are said to have been a million of the
illion and a half that populate Milan and its environs. But they were
mply walking around—they were not particularly celebrating any-
ing. There were a prize-ring and a little circus, some pop-stands and
me ice-cream carts, and two small blimps moored above the park
ith the inscription *"Fraternità."* There was a band, and the crowd
ere and there would clear a circle around three or four dancing
ouples. But the voice from the loudspeaker sounded rasping,
etallic and grim. *"Attenzione! Attenzione!"* it would snap out again
nd again. *"Ballate!"* it would exhort the people in the tone with
hich the blood-freezing voice used to announce to the audience in
Iellzapoppin that the spiders were about to descend on them.
Questa è la notte della libertà. Gli uomini liberi sono allegri!" But
ere was little spontaneity or gaiety, and in that threatening and
idactic tone I recognised the impersonal accent—the same every-
here—of the Communist Party, as I had recognised its efficient
irection in the methods with which the demonstration had been
ublicised and engineered.

A young Public Relations man, newly arrived in Milan, who took
e around in a jeep, kindly explained the occasion—the first
ourteenth of July ever celebrated in Italy—as an attempt to make
p to France for the so-called "stab in the back" of Mussolini's
ttack upon her. "What are those things thay are wearing?" he
sked. It was the Phrygian Liberty Cap, which a large number of the
trolling citizens had pinned to their lapels or blouses.

*   *   *

Sick of contemplating mines and bombings and reading abo
Italian politics, oppressed by the feeling of being submerged in t
general wreckage and mess, I bought a new book on Stravinsky l
the Italian composer Malipiero. But what I found in it was disa
pointing. It has been written to order for a series, and, althou;
Malipiero allows that *Le Sacre du Printemps* has merit, he does not
ing but grumble and scoff at the music which Stravinsky has writt
since. The whole tone is old-fogeyish and grudging, as if Malipie
were peevish with Stravinsky for outstripping him in reputation a
engaging in musical adventures which he (Malipiero) cannot unde
stand. (The twelve-tone technique of Schönberg he says flat
"is not music.") You feel the cultural backwater of Fascism rippl
and made rather uncomfortable by the presence of live spirits ou
side.

*   *   *

But there are elements of vitality in Milan that you are not awa:
of in Rome. The young people who have worked in the undergroun
and who have helped to drive the Germans out are perhaps the on
group in Italy that is in earnest, energetic and enthusiastic. Tv
examples: A woman lawyer from somewhere near the Austria
border; she has been studying and doing political work all throug
these difficult years and now, wiry, quick-eyed and intent, con
municates a certain electricity, a certain elation of hope. Italy, sh
says, is not now a great country, but she is quite enough to devot
one's life to. A young man, a lieutenant of Parri's, who has bee
trained in high principles of conduct through his contact with tha
upright and industrious man. As a boy who had grown up under th
Fascist regime, he joined the Fascist Youth Organisation and wer
as a soldier to the Ethiopian war. But he saw then that the regim
was a "bluff." The soldiers had no food or equipment while th
officers were acquiring medals; men were bleeding to death wit
dysentery for lack of ice to stop the hæmorrhage. Later, he joined th
anti-Fascist underground and went to do secret work in Germany
pretending to be a Spaniard. If the Italians had become too sceptica
the Germans, he found, were fantastically credulous. A Germa
officer, he said, had told him that they now had a powder a pinch o
which would blow up a city block: they would dust it on the Unitec
States and the United States would disappear. The women wer
terribly stupid—especially when amorous, he added, with a
delightedly rolling eye: he got a lot of information out of them.
These people may have as little idea of what the Soviet Union ha.

been up to while Mussolini was keeping them blacked out or of what England and America are up to as Malipiero has of the aims of the later Stravinsky; but there are elements among them who count on the Russians and elements who count on the Americans. Now, dating from the expulsion of the Germans, our main American contributions to following up the "liberation" of Italy have consisted of a few U.N.R.R.A. supplies and calling one of our telephone exchanges Freedom; and, after our arming and encouragement of the Partisans through the period when they were serving our purpose, we are now taking their weapons away from them, forbidding them to make political speeches and throwing them in jail if they give any trouble. It is true that, since the departure of the Germans, the Partisans in the North have been guilty of some ruthless and probably unjustifiable bloodshed: they are supposed to have killed some twenty thousand people. But the new Italian revolution is something more than a savage vendetta, and it is hardly, I believe, a movement whose impetus can be curbed at this point. The Partisans, according to the A.M.G. estimate, have been disarmed only about sixty per cent: they have hidden a great deal of equipment, and we have no means of knowing how much, since they still had the arms that they took from the enemy as well as the ones that we gave them. And they have worked up their own methods for maintaining the strength of their organisation.

*   *   *

How they were doing this I soon came to see. I had continued to be puzzled by the problem of the Italian ex-prisoners from Germany who had had to be restrained from protesting against the local jail-break, and I had asked a number of people about it. Nobody seemed to be able to explain, and I began to get a distinct impression that there was something that the Americans hadn't grasped and that the Italians didn't want to reveal. Once when I was talking to an Italian journalist, the young man mentioned above, who seemed to know what was going on and to be just on the point of telling, we were interrupted by someone who came up, and when the other conversation was over, my friend went on smoothly and cheerfully, with the air of returning to our original subject: "And so I hope to go to America as press attaché to the Embassy." At last I found an American correspondent who had been a long time in Italy and who was exceptionally well-informed. He had been pondering on similar problems. There had occurred, he said, in the last month or so, a whole series of demonstrations that did not seem to have much relevance to their pretexts: festivities, protests, strikes. Even the undertakers had once been called out. He had finally come to the conclusion that the Left parties of the governing "federation" were systematically organising the people, who had lost the habit of mass action under Fascism, and exercising them in a series of turn-outs which would prepare them for an eventual crisis. These demonstrations, he said, were always perfectly well-conducted, and if the authorities intervened, as in the case of the protest which I had just seen nipped, they simply called them off. Neither side wanted a repetition of the disaster in Greece last winter.

I put to him another question which I had already tried on Allied officials. Was there anything in the following statement, which I had found in the English liberal weekly, the *New Statesman and Nation*, of June 16, 1945?: "In a revealing dispatch last Tuesday, a special correspondent of *The Times* stated bluntly that A.M.G. has refused to recognise decisions of the local liberation committees (in Northern Italy) which had successfully captured and taken over nearly all the industrial plants before the arrival of our armies. In the cause of 'efficiency' managing directors such as Valetta of Fiat, who collaborated actively with the Germans, are being reinstated, under the threat that the Allies will not release coal and other raw materials to factories run by workers' councils." The amiable A.M.G. official whom I had visited at the moment of the averted demonstration had told me that, whereas he couldn't say specifically about Valetta and Fiat, whose factories were in Turin, he could positively assert that this kind of thing was not being done in Milan, where it was the policy to allow the Italians to purge their Fascist officials. But the newspaperman had just come from Turin and he told me that it was perfectly true that these companies had the same old management. Valetta now sat in an office with a real-estate sign on the door, but from that office he still ran his factory. "The greatest shock I had" said my friend, "was when I found out that the Fiat stock was all owned by the original people."

*   *   *

The general impression I got from talking to people in Milan, including two of our top officials, was that the ideal our policy was aiming at was to keep Italian industry going enough to relieve unemployment and to weaken the appeal of the Left, but not to allow it to revive sufficiently—since the factories themselves are in excellent shape—seriously to compete with England. Many Italians, I found, shared this impression.

The morning before I left, I visited two sights which I had not yet seen.

The place where Mussolini's body and those of his mistress and the members of his staff were exposed after the executions is not one of the city's great squares, as the reports may have sometimes suggested, but a small crossroads in the working-class section. They were hung up by the feet, in a gas station, to the thing under which the cars stop, and the names that indicated which was which are still daubed on it in crude black letters. The station is closed and deserted, and now and then somebody comes up to stare at it.

At the other end of the city, behind a mountainous heap of rubble, is the refectory of Santa Maria delle Grazie, where Leonardo painted his *Last Supper*. It is always being said that this picture was already in bad condition and that the bombing did not do it any harm. But, after all, most of the building went down: there is nothing but a husk of four walls, which has been sketchily roofed in for shelter, and an immense amount of debris must have fallen upon the mural, which, with the fresco at the other end, also in very bad condition, is the only object surviving that is even recognisable. The *Last Supper*, at any rate, is little to-day but a grease-spot—a vague and incomplete phantom, which, however, does assert its reality in a curious and poignant way. From a distance, the three open windows in the wall behind the figure of Christ, dim though they become when you approach them, do still seem to give a vista on a landscape of peace and shining light. And the subtleties of green and blue, faded and half-effaced, the lovely modelling of an open hand where the faces can hardly be seen, introduce into the bare place that element which we pathetically like to call human because it recreates and ennobles, though it represents ¦relatively so small a part of the activity of human beings and though it appears in any intensity so rarely.

The dead tyrant and the living Christ are to-day both dishonoured in Italy.

11

GREEK DIARY : NOTES ON LIBERATED ATHENS

IT is a piquant and novel sensation to travel from Naples to Athens in an army transport plane. Our airports and planes create a world of their own, an extension of the American system, that has been superimposed on Europe and makes a dissonant contrast with it. Over the blue Ionian Sea, you are handed a neat cardboard box, which contains, carefully wrapped in oil-paper, sandwiches of three kinds, each with a small printed slip that tells what that filling is— beef-spread, melted cheese or marmalade and peanut butter—so that you will know in what order to eat them; a hardboiled egg, with pepper and salt done up picnic-fashion in paper; a cookie; a small container of cut-up peaches and pears, with a miniature paste-board spoon; a bag of fruit drops of assorted flavours; and a paste-board cup for water.

When you look down and see the first Greek islands, you are surprised by the difference from Italy, whose dense plantings of parched yellow fields you have so short a time before left behind. Here is a paler, purer, soberer country, which seems both wild and old and quite distinct from anything farther west. The sea is absolutely smooth, sometimes violet, sometimes blue, with a softness of water-colour, glistening in patches with a fine grain of silver; and the islands of all sizes in bulbous or oblong shapes—blobs and round-bottomed bottles and the contours of plump roast fowl—seem not to rise out of the water but to be plaqued on it like cuff-links on cuffs or to lie scattered like the fragments of a picture-puzzle on a table with a blue cloth cover. These islands are a dry terra-cotta—quite unlike the deep earthly clay tints to which one has been accustomed in Italy—almost the colour of too well-cooked liver, and the vegetation looks like gray lichens. The marblings on the looping beaches set up a feeling of uncanny familiarity which refers itself, as one recognises in a moment, to the patterns on the ancient Greek vases made out of this very soil. Even on the large islands and the mainland, there are visible little cultivation and few plainly cut ribbons of roads, and the country, after humanised Italy, seems grander and more mysterious. The haze of the fawn-coloured fore-ground shades farther away into blue, where the mountains stand dim and serene. These are the "shadowy mountains" of Homer.

Swooping down upon the airport at Eleusis you seem to be
moving among billows that do not really resemble hills, with their
dry green of foliage, pale grey of stone and curious pale yellow of clay.
There is a special apparent lightness of substance and absence of
strong colour which characterises Greece and sets it off from other
countries. As you descend into the hot airport, you have a general
grateful impression of simplification and gentle austerity.

The transportation truck speeds with jolts along the Sacred Way
that leads from Eleusis to the Acropolis. One is surprised and
thrilled to see from the street-signs that it is still called the Iera Odos.
The lavender mountains of Salamis make a contrast that harmonises
with the bright-blue water beneath. Above the low roofs of Athens
the Acropolis rises on its pedestal of rock: astonishing, dramatic,
divine, with at the same time the look of a phantom.

*   *   *

The Grande Bretagne Hotel, the principal hostelry of Athens,
which has been taken for a billet by the British and at which
transient Americans also stay, has an atmosphere entirely dissimilar
to the atmosphere of Italian hotels. In Italy the porters and desk-
men still think thay are giving service to tourists: they bow constantly,
show you places on street-maps. But something is wrong at the
Grande Bretagne. You are first told by a slant-eyed Greek that there
are no decent rooms left but that he will be glad to give you a room
in his house at a price only a little higher than what you would be
obliged to pay at the hotel. When you insist on seeing the sergeant in
charge of the American side, you find an insolent equally slit-eyed
fellow, quite untypical of the American Army, who also seems to be
some kind of Greek. "Dere's so many drips comin' in," he says, "so
many generals and high-rankin' officers—dat I'm full up all de time.
I have to put you in a room wit two odder beds in it." I thought he
was hoping I'd take the private room, but I insisted on staying here,
and he repeated several times, as he reluctantly got a boy for my bag,
"Dere's so many drips all de time."

The room with the three beds had been riddled by what I took to
be a machine-gun, which had sprayed bullets all around the doorway
and made several holes in the door. One of the shots had struck just
above my bed and left a scar in the plaster. Out the window I could
see blinds knocked askew, snarls of German barbed wire on the roof
and other evidence of close range fighting. The Grande Bretagne
had first been occupied by the Germans, who lived in it all through

the war; then it was put at the disposal of the British after t
Germans had been driven out. At the time of the civil war la
winter, the fatal demonstration by E.A.M. (the National Liberati
Front), at which the police fired into the crowd, took place in t
square just outside it; and when the battle to the death was on a
E.A.M. for a time had the British at bay, the Grande Bretagne w
one of the only places in Athens that the latter succeeded in holdi
The bullet-holes in my door were probably made by one of E.A.M
guns. Later, when the royalists had won, Winston Churchill, on
hasty trip to Athens, stayed at the Grande Bretagne and held
conferences there; and some of the Partisans loaded the baseme
with dynamite and planned to blow the place up—thereby wipi
out at one stroke, as a sympathiser with E.A.M. told me, the
spirer of the foreign policy which was backing the monarchy
Greece and General Scobie and Ambassador Leeper, who had be
carrying that policy out. But someone gave the play away, and t
wires were cut in time.

The employees of the Grande Bretagne, many of whom ha
worked there for years, have been through a good deal. One cann
precisely know whether they are sullen or discouraged or stunne
but, with the exception of a few of the waiters, they have neglect
to learn any English. They do not even expect tips: they disappe
without waiting a second, as soon as you have succeeded in catchi
one and inducing him to do something for you. Greek callers at
hotel complain that they are treated by the Greek employees with
utmost impoliteness.

*   *   *

One gets a sudden revelation in coming to Greece from Ita
of all that was vulgar about ancient Rome and all that was trashy
the Renaissance. There is no Renaissance art in Athens and, exc
for some Byzantine churches, nothing between ancient and mod
Greece. You have no overlay of Catholic history; the Orthod
Church, in general, is singularly unobtrusive; and I confess that
came as a relief not to find the scene incrusted with the three hund
and thirty-six churches that you meet at every turn in Rome. Y
have, instead, a clean and well-swept city of small buildings, wh
pale gray or dry yellow, that are almost never ornate in the Medit
ranean manner, but rather simple and uniform, with a dignity
classical taste; and among these, a few ancient monuments t
are perhaps the things of the kind most worth seeing in the wh
Western world. You understand for the first time that it is true th

matters of architecture, the Romans merely imitated the Greeks,
d you realise what a coarsening and deadening process this
.itation was. The Parthenon itself, the Erechtheum, the temple of
e Wingless Victory keep a vitality, a splendour and a grace that I
.ve never seen in any other ruins. They do not seem the bones of
rished ages; they still transform the world where they shine—a
orld of square houses and shops that might otherwise seem chalky
.d meagre but that, beside them, catches something of their
stinction.

* * *

It has been shown that the classical Greeks had a rather uncertain
nse of colour. They used the same word for yellow and green, and
ey seem to have confused red with purple. It was the Romans who
ought colour into European poetry with the Italian landscapes
Virgil—as well as the sense of materials, of hardness and tightness
d weight, with the marbles and bricks and bronzes that Horace and
irgil both describe in their verse and imitate by its structure. The
reeks lacked this feeling for matter, for their very mountains
em immaterial, and they worked in Pentelican marble, which
ves the effect of solidified light. As soon as one arrives in Greece,
e understands how a native of this country who had never seen
ything else might have had no conception of a world painted in
efinite colours. The olive trees, the pepper trees, the tiny firs are
determinately blue, green and gray; the yellow of the earth
a neutral tint which is always turning pink or brown, and the pinks
d browns themselves sometimes deepen or brighten to red. What
.e Greeks did have highly developed—besides the architectural
nse of proportion—was an appreciation of the light and shade that
e the main features of visible Attica. You find it in the choruses of
.e plays, where things are always darkling or gleaming, and in the
ttings of Plato's dialogues, when they take place on sunny days in
.e shade; and you find it exploited in the most masterly way in the
olonnades and porches of the temples. You still have to learn in
thens to appreciate everything in terms of light.

* * *

All the American soldiers love Athens: they infinitely prefer Greece
Italy, and I have been trying to figure out why. I remember a man
Rome who kept assuring me that Athens was "a real metropolis,"
hich it certainly is strikingly not. When you ask them why they
ke it so much, they immediately say that it is "clean," which up to a

point is true—that is, the filth of the slums is kept in the back str
as they are used to having it kept at home, instead of, as in Nap
being all over the place. But, for another thing, the Greeks, to
American, seem relatively non-foreign and normal. They are m
less theatrical than Italians. They are quieter and do not jabber. T
are more independent, have more backbone. There are few begg
in Athens and few prostitutes—a great contrast to the state of thi
in Italy. I had somehow got the impression that the Athen
women were still more or less in the harem phase, but, though t
really is the case in Italy, I did not find it true in Greece. The Gr
women seem remarkably intelligent, and they do a good deal on th
own. There are few professional sirens.

But I have finally come to the conclusion that there are oth
perhaps less admirable, qualities that recommend the Greek capi
to the Americans: a certain monotony of the streets, of which
French guidebook complains, and a certain mediocrity in Athe
It comes back to me that an American who had grown up in Gree
once told me that Athens was "a hick town," and I understand n
that it looks more like home to the exiled and wandering G.
because, compared to other places in Europe, it seems order
prosaic and new. This is unquestionably what was meant by
friend in Rome when he pronounced it "a real metropolis."

*   *   *

In any case, one realises, as one walks in the streets, that Gree
now is really the country where nobody has anything at all. In Ita
there are still many commodities that are being produced and sold
striped neckties, pink silk slips and lace brassières, new books
crisp bright covers, perfume and candy and cakes—and that revi
some of the brilliance of the shops in places like Milan and Rom
But in Greece there is not much beyond remnants of old stocks th
must predate the war, and, in clothing, a scanty supply that on
meets rudimentary needs. No woman in the streets wears make-u
and they have only rather dreary cheap dresses, mostly of t
national blue; none of the men has a necktie on, even when his shi
collar is buttoned. If you go to a better-class restaurant, you ca
get little but a slice of fish, a dish of cut-up tomatoes, a bottle
resinated wine and a slice of water-melon. The people are n
riding bicycles, as they are in Italy and England; but this fact
due, I am told, not so much to the difficulty of getting them as to th
scornful aversion that the Greeks have always felt toward bicycl

riding. They regard it, it seems, as undignified. The one thing that the Athenians have that the Romans and Neapolitans don't have is quite enough light at night. They defended their electric plant and saved it when the Germans were evacuating; and it is very cheerful, coming from cities where the streets are murky and blind, to find Athens twinkling among its hills under the dry clear summer sky.

I got the impression at first of a city depleted of life (though its actual population has been increased by the influx from towns destroyed by the Germans), as if everything that was going on were at once underpatronised and understaffed. But I was told by several foreigners who had lived there before the war that this impression was partly misleading: the Athenians had always been frugal and they had never made much of a show; and the lack of organic town-life was not wholly the result of the war, since the inhabitants of Athens had always been, as a Russian lady explained, content with "*une douce anarchie.*" But here as elsewhere in Europe the disorganisation brought by the war is generally profound. After all, out of a population of only seven million in the whole of Greece, a million have died during the last five years—six hundred thousand of these from starvation. I had not expected to find whole streets of the city as badly battered as London or Milan—full of walls nicked or speckled with bullets and of the blasted-out husks of buildings. E.L.A.S. (the Greek Popular Liberation Army, the military aspect of E.A.M.) blew up police headquarters and other strongholds of the royalist authorities, and the British retaliated with bombing raids, mortar-fire and tanks shooting-up the streets.

*　　　*　　　*

I share a bathroom with an American major, a former Standard Oil engineer now engaged in "petroleum rehabilitation," who is eager to talk about his work. He is a tall energetic Westerner who is enthusiastically intent on a purpose—a purpose which is probably typical of the American approach to Europe. There are two main points of which he is anxious to convince me and to which he usually reverts when I meet him, prefacing each step of his argument with an emphatic and cogent "*Aw right!,*" on the assumption that I have agreed with the step before. The first of these points he immediately raised when he saw that I was a war correspondent. He flourished before me a clipping that had just been sent him from home and declared with indignation that the newspapermen had been misrepresenting the situation in Greece. The editorial from his home-

town paper asserted that the present regime was a lawless and ruthless tyranny, which was arresting thousands of people on political
charges and holding them without trial, and that it ill became the
United States to countenance a government by terror that made
democratic processes impossible. I told him that this was very much
the picture that I had gotten, before I came, from American correspondents who had been in Greece, and I suggested that British
policy, in its brutal repression of a movement which is generally
admitted to have had at the time the support of eighty per cent of
the Greeks, and in its backing of the unpopular royalists, had
hardly evidenced a serious concern for the extension of the Four
Freedoms. Like most Americans, no matter how predatory, no
matter how hungry for power, he was daunted and embarrassed for a
moment by the appeal to democratic principles. But he quickly
shook off these objections. Political problems did not really exist for
him; he was interested in something else. He only wanted me to
admit that it was best that the radicals should be kept down—the
Greeks needed a period of stabilisation, didn't they?—and then to
take me up with "*Aw right!*" and expand on the subject that he had at
heart.

This subject was the favourable openings for American business in
Greece—not for "exploitation" (he always made this disclaimer);
no: that wouldn't do!—the Greeks were suspicious of us, "rightly
perhaps." What he had in mind was something quite different:
to develop Greek water power and oil wells by organising international companies for which one third of the capital and the
technical advice would be supplied by American enterprise, another
third of the money by Greek financiers, and the remaining third be
put up by the Greek employees themselves, so that they would have
some real interest in the project. "Liberal labour and capital" were
beginning to get together at home, and he didn't see why they
shouldn't in Greece. He beamed with an impersonal elation behind
his professional glasses. Volos, to which he had just made a trip,
reminded him a lot of the Yosemite; the Greeks were perfectly fine:
it wasn't hard to arouse their interest and they would work with you
in a wonderful way. When I remarked that I had been told that the
government stood in the way of technical training, he violently
reacted, assuring me that this was not necessarily true: he had, he
said, a young engineer who was a damn sight keener and more
competent that the average man at home turned out by the technical
schools.

The drive of his point of view—capitalistic and engineering-minded—in the direction of the non-political and the anti-nation-alistic was illustrated by a story he loved, about a German who had lived thirty years in Greece in the neighbourhood of Volos and whom the Germans put in charge of the oil installations when they arrived in 1941. This oil had been owned by the Shell Company, and the Shell Company manager at Volos had been also the British vice-consul. He was now put on parole by the Germans and made to report to them every day. When the Germans were getting out of Greece and blowing up all the public utilities, the German expatriate went to the military authorities and persuaded them to spare the oil installations, pointing out that the people of Volos had done the invaders no harm and that they needed the oil for their economy. Now the British vice-consul is back in charge, the German has returned to his farm, and the Greeks have refrained from bringing charges against him, as they would have with any other collabora-tionist, because he has saved their oil.

This major was a likable man and I found his excitement infectious. He referred with pride to his wife, who had been getting a college degree in some subject like sociology, and who, he said, was "a good-looking little son-of-a-bitch."

* * *

I was fortunate in having letters from a Greek lady I knew in New York. She sent me to her mother, Mrs. D., who turned out to be in touch with many strata and departments of Athenian life. Mrs. D. is one of seven sisters who came originally from the island of Samos; her father was a classical scholar, the director of a Greek school in Smyrna. She is remarkably intelligent, as well as lively and charming; fair-haired and blue-eyed, with almost the profile of an ancient statue. You do not find often, among the modern Greeks—who run to round faces and round black eyes—these types that recall the great age, but you do see a few startling examples. The women of Samos are famous for their beauty, and the pure race is represented by these blondes who have blue or glaucous eyes, and sometimes look almost English. The innumerable nephews and nieces of Mrs. D.'s whom I met were all more or less distinguished by these Greek sea-coloured eyes and these archaic foreheads and noses. They and their husbands and wives and their various family connections are active in education, in the government, in business, in archeology, in the newspaper world, in the theatre; and they include every degree of political opinion from Communism to the official conservatism.

You run into them everywhere, and if there is anything I want to see or anybody I want to meet, one simply passes me on to another. These relations and a variety of friends are always dropping in on Mrs. D. When I had remarked on one occasion that I had encountered in her family every shade of opinion except royalist, one of the nieces, at my next visit, came over and whispered to me that there were two royalist ladies present—not, she hastened to add, relatives but friends.

I have several times visited Mrs. D. in a house she has rented for the summer in a residential suburb called Philothei. It is a well-designed modern villa—a pleasant refuge from the terrific, almost tropical heat, the worst they can remember, they say: white ceilings, pale straw-coloured walls, large casements and green latticed blinds, cupboards of natural wood and green-and-white linoleum that imitates tiles. Among the barren and sun-baked mountains, Hymettus, Pentelicus and Parnes, it seems very much like southern California, with its comfortable outdoor furniture, its potted ice plants, its collection of cactus and its dry aromatic smell. There are a turbid green pool with big goldfish, a garden with dahlias, petunias and bushes of yellow roses, fig trees with ripe green figs and clusters of heavy green grapes draping the arbour that shades the back porch.

There have always been so many people, and they have all been so familiar and casual that I have had to ask questions later to identify them and straighten out their relationships, but I have pretty clear impressions of the following:

A nephew, who has qualified himself to teach physics and mathematics but who has been waiting eight years for a job, in the meantime making a meagre living by giving private lessons. I got from him for the first time a picture—which was later confirmed by other sources—of the miserable illiteracy of Greece. He told me that seventy per cent of the Greeks have had only the most rudimentary schooling or none, and that there are thirty-two hundred teachers out of work, while it is impossible, with the reactionary government, to establish a democratic educational system. There are only two good public libraries in Greece—one in Athens and one in Salonika —and it is an almost insuperable task to find anything you want in either of them. He is a sympathiser with the E.A.M. movement. He told me that before the war the Greeks had seen so much of the English that they had learned to get on with them and like them, but that, except for those Greeks who wanted the monarchy, the attitude toward the British was now bitter. After all, only seven British tanks —since E.L.A.S. had no tanks—had stood between E.A.M. and

ictory (they were American tanks, by the way); and, after all, he
hought that they, the Greeks, could say that, given their equipment
nd manpower, nobody else in Europe had done more to stand up to
he Nazis than they had and that they deserved the kind of demo-
ratic regime that most of them had thought they were fighting
or.

A little niece of twenty-two, who speaks French, studies literature
nd is preparing to be an archeologist. She is bright and well brought-
p and has, I should say, a good deal of character. She has a sister,
hom I met later, a year younger than she. This sister was out in the
nountains with the Partisans and is a passionate supporter of E.A.M.
told the older one that I got the impression that her sister was a
ttle on the Communist side. "*Pas un peu*," she answered slyly.
Assez." She herself is wholeheartedly pro-E.A.M. but her attitude
oward the Communists is critical. The nuance of difference in
olitics between these two girls is typical of the state of things in
Greece.

An old schoolmate of my friend in New York—a young woman
vho, before the war, had started to study medicine but given it up
vhen the family fortunes had broken down in the general disaster.
he had ended by marrying a lawyer and going to live in Salonika.
They had had to sell their best carpets and such other things of
alue as they possessed in order to get enough to eat. She seems to
ne an able woman who would have had a career of her own if she
ad not been grounded by the war and whose life is rather unsatis-
actory.

Two sisters, cousins of Mrs. D. One is married to a man in the
overnment: white suit, tan-and-white shoes, fine Panama hat; very
uave, speaks English well. The other sister has all of what I found
o be the typical conventional opinions of the well-to-do Greek
ourgeoisie. She was appalled by the British elections—was Attlee
s "intelligent" as Churchill? Churchill had saved them from the
Communists, who would otherwise have won and "shot everybody."
E.A.M. had been run by the Communists, and Greek Communism
vas the fanaticism of ignorant people. She had asked her maid the
ther day what she would do after the revolution—didn't she see
hat she would still have to be a maid because she didn't know how
o do anything else? The girl hadn't thought of that: she had thought
he would be a lady. That was what Greek Communism was made
f!

The two royalist ladies. They had got to know each other in jail
nd had been good friends ever since. They had been sheltering

M

British soldiers during the German occupation and had been im
prisoned in a room with eighty women and children—where one had
spent six months, the other eleven. They had not been allowed to
read and were unable to relieve themselves except when a large pail
was put in the middle of the room for everybody to use. Of the
British they had been punished for helping, they said that the New
Zealanders were nicest, the Australians somewhat "rougher," and
the English "very selfish."

Two children: a boy and a girl of about thirteen and ten, who had
been left with Mrs. D. for a visit. They were serious and quiet in a
way that I have never seen in any other children: it was evidently the
impress of the war. I tried amusing them with a jumping mouse
made out of my pocket handkerchief, with which I have usually had
great success, but it did not go over very well. The boy at any rate
seemed much more interested in listening to the political discussion.
He made two rather acute observations not intended for me to
understand but translated by his elders. "The Americans and
English," he said, "don't seem to know their own language, because
they hesitate and stammer over words," and "It's a funny thing that
the English didn't celebrate the English elections—it was the Greeks
that did all the celebrating." But when they were sent to bed, they
sat up talking and giggling, like all children and had to be hushed
and told to go to sleep.

The person I talked with most except Mrs. D. herself was her son
who was staying with her, an importer with a business in Bagdad.
Unlike most of the rest of the company, he did not belong to the
intelligentsia, and his point of view was non-political, practical and
a little cynical. He spoke English and talked about his experience in
the East with the various English-speaking peoples. You were never
able, he said, to get on any kind of terms with the English: you might
succeed in inducing them to come to your house, but they would
never ask you back, they were awfully unscrupulous in business
and his English rivals in Bagdad, finding that they could not
compete with his firm, had tried to get him and his associates
locked up as Nazi spies. The English, however, were quiet in
public, where the Americans were most obnoxious: they apparent
ly regarded themselves as miraculously invincible with women or
privileged with some sort of *droit de seigneur*, for they were always
coming up to unknown couples and insisting that the ladies should
dance with them. (I had to recognise that this was true: I had seen an
American soldier in a restaurant in Rome butt in on a party of
Americans and make an obstinate attempt to carry off the wife of

one of the men in the Embassy.) The Greeks now thought they loved the Americans, but he told them that they only liked them because they didn't know them yet. He had no confidence at all, he declared, in the disinterested pretensions of U.N.R.R.A.: it would turn out that it was being used to put over American products in Europe. He swore that an American had once asked him whether the war between Athens and Sparta was still going on in Greece. The Scotch he considered cruel on account of their treatment of the Greeks at the time of the civil war. The New Zealanders were the English-speaking people who had made the best impression abroad: they were quiet, agreeable and decent. (I asked a New Zealand girl in U.N.R.R.A. about this overwhelming popularity of the New Zealanders, and she said that they had somehow, in Greece, known how to "take the right tone." They had felt that Greece resembled New Zealand—it was a small, rural, mountainous country, mostly surrounded by water—and they approached the Greeks as people like themselves.)

Young D. had been a sailor in the Greek Navy in Egypt at the time of the mutiny of April, 1944, and I asked him to tell me about it. The incident that had set off this trouble had been the imprisonment by the puppet Greek government in Cairo of the delegates sent from Greece by the Free Greek government of the mountains. This organisation, E.A.M., represented the resistance to the Germans and consisted of a national council which had just been chosen by underground elections held all over Greece. It had sent a committee to Cairo to try to arrange a union between the Greek government in exile and itself. But the British, intent on the restoration of the monarchy and wanting nothing so far to the Left as E.A.M. was threatening to be, had the delegates sent to jail. The Greek fleet then mutinied in protest and would not continue fighting with the British. D. was at that time in training camp, and he and his companions refused to obey orders for thirty-three days. A Scotch officer who spoke Greek came and pleaded with them and told them that they were costing the British £25,000 a day because the Germans were sinking the ships that the Greeks were no longer convoying. The Greeks laughed and said that they were glad to hear this evidence that the English without the Greeks were helpless against the Germans. Finally, the British told them that they needed the training camp for something else, loaded them into lorries and took them to a prison camp, where they were kept for twenty-six days. At one point the British lined them up and offered to escort with bayonets any who wanted to leave. Out of eight hundred and nine

men, only seven accepted. The sailors on one of the ships further
infuriated the British by cutting the crown out of the Greek flag, as a
result of which the British refused to salute it. Then the word got
around among the Greeks that the mutiny had been engineered by
the Communists, and the morale of their resistance crumbled.
Sixty per cent. of them, D. included, agreed to go back to the fleet.
The British sorted them out in four categories, each of which was
dealt with in a way that was regarded as appropriate to it. Category
A consisted of sailors who from the first had not approved of the
movement; B, of men who had sympathised with it but had taken no
active part or whose sentiments it was impossible to determine
because they had been in the hospital or on leave; C, of sailors who
were definitely known to have "shouted" or done something positive
(this category included also all persons who had grown beards, since
the Partisans had had beards in the mountains and this was regarded
as a proof of Left sympathies). To D category the leaders were
condemned. D. told me about this procedure with an irony, amused
but mordant, at the expense of British system and stupidity. One
man who had written a letter expressing concern lest the people at
home were not getting enough vitamins in their diet was consigned
on that evidence to C, since it was considered by the British authorities in itself a dangerous sympton to show an interest in the welfare
of Greece. A. B and C categories were eventually all set free, but the
men in D were sent to the Sudan, where presumably they still were.
It was afterwards said that the mutiny had been provoked by the
British themselves in order to find out, among the Greek sailors, who
were and who were not Communists.

During the early part of this story, D.'s young wife, whom he had
married only five days before—a good-looking girl, gray-eyed and
tanned—listened with the decorous quietness that Greek women
usually show in the presence of males, but as he was telling of his
disaffection, when he had finally become convinced that the mutiny
was being managed by the Communists, she began to try to sabotage
his story—she was sitting on the couch beside him—by burrowing
under his arm like a setter that wants to be fed or tackling him around
the waist and making as if to throw him over. "You must let me tell
my version of the mutiny," she said when her husband had finished.
"She's a Communist sympathiser," he explained to me. "She doesn't
know what to think about anything till she gets the directive from
headquarters." At any rate, she never did give me her version. Her
husband teased her for being a Communist and also teased her for
being the niece of a prominent public man who had come to represent

for more realistic republican opinion the most obsolete political old-fogeyism. D. himself, in all this talk of politics, was a little bit aggressively a businessman, but he was not, I think, quite satisfied with business. He asked me, with Socratic irony, whether it were possible in the United States to make a lot of money and still be honest. "It's not possible over here," he said. "You can make a little money and be honest, but you can't make a lot of money without cheating or exploiting somebody."

The atmosphere of the D. household seemed to me distinctly different from anything I had ever known before. These Greeks showed profound effects of the hardships and horrors through which they had passed, but they treated them with the utmost lightness. It was as far from the crisp matter-of-factness of the British—their understatement that is almost ostentatious—as it was from the historical consciousness which never deserts the Italians and which, once having allowed them to accept Mussolini as a rein-carnation of the Cæsars, now leads them to talk about recent events in terms of the age of Justinian, when the Roman general Belisarius had had to invade Italy in order to fight the Goths, and to conceive their hopes for the future in terms of the reappearance of the great figures of the Risorgimento. In the course of my visits to the D.'s, I sometimes heard of shocking incidents of the years of German occupation. There had been a gibbet at the corner of the street where Mrs. D. lived in Athens; the Germans, on one occasion, in reprisal for the killing of a soldier, had stopped a tram full of women and children on their way to the beach for an outing and shot every human being in it; one lady, whose husband had been in hiding, spoke of her nervousness in her house at night as she waited for the doorbell to ring; someone else said it was awfully pleasant to be able to have lights in the evening—the Germans had been in the habit of firing machine-guns at lighted windows and had sometimes killed the people inside; one of the men, as he was taking his leave, remarked that he had still not got used to not having to dodge the Germans when he was going home late at night. But they usually laughed about these things, as if they were speaking of such inconveniences as cranky neighbours or torn-up roads. "One day you would have a friend," said D.'s little wife, smiling, as she told me about what the Germans had done, "and the next day you wouldn't have one." Unlike the Italians and the Southern French, the Greeks do not like to show emotion; and they give you a curious impression of having waited with perfect self-confidence till the barbarian hordes had passed. After all, as someone reminded me, there Xerxes had once been sitting on the top of one of the hills of Salamis waiting to see the Greek fleet defeated. So, one day, as I was walking along the Tritis Septemvriou with the girl who was giving me Greek lessons, and she was showing me how, during the civil war, the Greeks had been lined up on one side of the street and the British with their tanks on the other, when I said that it had all been terrible, she had mildly replied, "Oh, no: our men showed how brave they were."

Yet these people do differ in certain ways from any other similar group of people whose conversation I have ever listened to. They do not really make a social world, flourishing and complete in itself within its range of relations and interests, as such people usually do. They have good sense and good humour and poise. They joke about Kou-Kou-e's and Chites, the current nicknames for Communists and royalists, accusing one another of extremism. But they have lived through shocking deprivations; they cannot see a year ahead into the future; they do not really have the security that their kind of life ought to imply. And, as one of the ladies said in some connection that I have now forgotten, "We say that we are free, but we are not free."

                    *   *   *

The first night I spent at Philothei, I was awakened at early dawn by a loud, abrupt, strangulated cry that was evidently not human but animal. I went to the window but could see nothing, though the cry came again and again, like the choking of a dog that has swallowed a bone or the convulsive gasps of a man who is being revived from drowning. The best I could imagine was that the sound was made by some kind of monkey, though I had never heard of monkeys in Greece. Later, when the boy came out, I asked him whether he knew what it was, "He shouts like a man," said the boy. "He jumps with his two legs. He is green." I was trying to picture this bandersnatch when the boy, who could not think of the English word, explained that it was called *vatrachos*. It pleased me to think that Aristophanes' play had been due to the existence in Greece of some species of superfrog. And I was even more charmed in a moment when one of the ladies came out of the house and remarked, "He says *ko-ax ko-ax*."

                    *   *   *

I went to performances at the principal theatres: the Ethnikon and the Lyrikon. Like a good many things in Greece, they are closer to ancient Greece than you expect: the audience sits out of doors before a small and severe proscenium. At the Ethnikon, I saw Gogol's

The Inspector General, which seemed to me very well done; at the Lyrikon, which is definitely Left, J. B. Priestley's *And They Came to a City* and a play by a young Greek dramatist, Nikos Tsekouras, called *If You Work, You Will Eat*. The Priestley play is feeble enough, with its watered-down Shavian satire and its thoroughly depressing picture of a well-adjusted socialist utopia where everybody is uniformly cheerful; but the people at the theatre say that they have to produce what they can get. They have had almost nothing new from abroad, and they asked eagerly what was interesting in the theatre in England and the United States. More than Italy even, and to a degree that has been very damaging, Greece has been culturally cut off from the West since before the beginning of the war. The little Greek play was also in the nature of a socialist fable, but, in a genre which has been standardised by the Russians, it seemed to me, as relayed to me by a Greek companion, partly redeemed by its very naïveté and by a certain unstandardised folk charm. An Athenian stockbroker and his family are stranded on the island of Rhodes and have to depend on the lighthouse-keeper to put them up and give them something to eat. But the old man who attends to the light is an eccentric and a social philosopher. He will not let the city guests pay him anything, because that is the rule of Greek hospitality; but also he will not give them meals unless they agree to work. On the other hand, the arrival of the financier brings a principle of corruption to the island. He is carrying a large sum of money, which the captain of his ship has got wind of and tries to induce the lighthouse-keeper's son to steal. A conflict ensues between, on one side, the power of money and the parasitism it breeds, and on the other, honest virtue and wisdom. Of course, in the long run, the rich man is cured of his imaginary ailments by his new regime of open air and exercise, while he rather enjoys the discomfiture of his spoiled and disagreeable wife; his daughter, a charming girl, takes to the simple life with delight and shows herself thoroughly competent, converting also the city slicker who is in love with her; and the young wife of the lighthouse-keeper's son frustrates the designs of the captain by blowing up his ship so that the thieves cannot leave the island. The audience would applaud with a crash at every reference to social justice, and my companion laughed like a school girl at every crack at the bourgeoisie—a form of baiting which seems to be new in Greece and these examples of which she would explain to me with evident doubt as to whether I could grasp the joke.

But there was something both serious and important in the atmosphere of the Theatro Lyrikon when this little socialist play was

performed. The director and some of the actors were young people
who had brought to it the same kind of spirit that one used to find
back in the twenties in the Cherry Lane Theatre and the Province-
town Players; but certain of the older actors were among the best
known in Athens, and one of them, Aimilios Veakis, is the foremost
actor of Greece. Veakis had "been in the mountains"; he had lost his
daughter there when she had fallen into a ravine while riding. And a
month ago the pro-government reactionaries had rioted in three of
the Athens theatres. They had broken up *Julius Caesar* at the
Lyrikon at one of the speeches of the regicide conspirators, and *The
Merchant of Venice* at the Ethnikon during the scene in which
Shylock makes his plea for the Jews—under the impression, I was
told, that these passages had been interpolated by the Left-Wing
producers with subversive political intent; and they had attacked
Miranda Myrat, a well-known pro-E.A.M. actress. They had
shot and wounded a number of people. Miss Myrat was still in bed;
and Veakis, who had also been injured, was reappearing for the first
time that evening and had been hailed with a great ovation. The
more radical of Mrs. D.'s two nieces was engaged to the director of
the theatre and took me behind the scenes to meet Veakis. He had
been playing the lighthouse-keeper and had made him remarkably
real. Like most good European actors, he had submerged himself in
his part without exploiting his own personality, and now, with his
make-up half rubbed off, the sensitivity and intelligence of his face
were thrown into relief by contrast with the homely old-man mask I
had been watching. He made me a little speech: he said that he was
glad to meet an American because the Americans to-day were the
only people who knew what it was to be free; the Greeks had fought
for their freedom and won it, and now they had lost it again.

It was an embarrassing moment for me. It had become very plain
to me since I had been in Greece that the movement which the
British had disarmed and which the United States had allowed them
to disarm was neither a chess play directed from Moscow nor a
foray of bandits from the hills, but a genuine popular movement
which had been able to recruit almost all that was generous, courageous and enlightened in Greece, the most spirited among the young,
the clearest-sighted among the mature. This movement has been
broken: the prisons are crammed with tens of thousands of political
prisoners, and the government police have been practicing just such
methods of torture and terror as had made the Gestapo hated (they
include the same security battalion that formerly worked for the
Nazis), while the British, after calling out their tanks against E.A.M.

nd expressing indignant horror over outrages perpetrated by the
Left, have done little or nothing to curb the Right. "What *is*
E.A.M.?" I was challenged one day by a rabidly reactionary Greek
ady. "E.A.M. is not a party. It is only a state of mind!" That is
rue, no doubt, but states of mind may prove more powerful than
rganisations—especially when they are persecuted. The state of
aind of E.A.M. has been similar to that which in Northern Italy is
niting diverse elements in a formidable bloc of the Left, and it is
imilar to the state of mind which has prevailed to such an extent in
ngland that, unexpectedly to Labour itself, a Socialist government
as been voted in.

The people at the theatre told me that they had tried to get the
tory of the riots sent through to the outside world, and, like many
ther Greeks I talked to, they seemed to have the desperate feeling
aat nobody knew what was happening in Greece. The only thing I
puld say to Veakis was that I would try to write about it.

*　　　*　　　*

Overheard in the open-air café outside the King George Bar:
How were the Indians?" "Oh, they're easy meat for propaganda.
hey've begun comparing themselves to British troops—wanting to
eep with white women—that sort of thing." A pause. "How did
ou people take the elections?" "It shocked me to the roots. I
idn't know that Labour was that strong."

12

GREEK DIARY : A TRIP TO DELPHI—
NOTES ON THE BRITISH IN GREECE

I MADE a trip to Delphi from Athens with some U.N.R.R.A.
workers in August. The heat was the most stunning in decades. The
U.N.R.R.A. people made me wear a sun helmet, and the American
chocolate bars that we bought at the PX for the journey were
immediately turned to syrup. No Greek ever understood setting
out on such exploits at noon: they wanted to eat and go to sleep. So
did we, as a matter of fact. Most things are uncomfortable in Europe;
one does not often choose one's company, and even when one has
been able to choose it, the springs of good humour and charm sometimes quickly dry up in the heat. But before we had gone very far,
bumping and baking in the jeep, I felt that I had fallen by chance
into a fortunate combination.

The sanitary engineer from U.N.R.R.A. who was taking me and
who drove the car was one of those modest, soft-spoken, shrewd,
amiable and very able men that we like to imagine representing us
among the fevers and confusions of Europe, but comparatively
rarely find. His interpreter was a young Greek woman, who expressed
herself so well in both English and French that I was amazed when
she told me later that she had hardly been out of Greece. She had
seemed to me, when she joined us, the first really smart-looking
woman that I had so far seen in Athens. I had been putting down the
absence of chic—very striking when one came from Rome—to the
non-availability of attractive clothes; and I tried to figure out
whether Eleni, as she was always called by her boss—I had not
caught her married name—had somehow managed to get a few
things from Paris or whether a natural gift of style were carrying off
inferior garments. She was slim, with bare arms and legs, so burned
that they were partly purple, and she wore a simple dress of plain
yellow, flat-soled sandals and a dish-shaped straw hat. She said that
she had borrowed the hat, as she never ordinarily wore one and did
not feel natural in them—she had lovely, slight curly brown hair—
but as she held onto the hat with one hand while she laid the other
sideways in the crease of her lap to keep her dress from blowing, she
would have done as a model for *Vogue*. She was a type of good-
looking Greek woman that I was beginning to identify—I had

already seen one winsome specimen in the young actress, Stasa
latridou, at the Theatro Lyrikon. They have dark, very bright and
alive but not enormous eyes, and small, round, rather recessive
chins that do not challenge attention like Anglo-Saxon and Latin
chins and may at first suggest weakness of character, as the eyes
suggest extreme gentleness. But one soon gets a different impression
and watches them with increasing interest, and I presently decided
that Eleni was not only smarter but prettier than any other Greek
women I had seen. She had a pointed but not salient nose, and she
seemed authentically and traditionally Greek in that she resembled—
not the classical statues, which we always imagine fair—but the dark
women with long hands and feet painted in black on the red clay
Greek vases. Such a woman, however, gives a different impression
when we see her alive and in all her dimensions. To an American—
in America we have only the grin—the play of her eyes was enchanting: not the animated lifting of eyebrows that one finds in the Latin
women and that has something of a routine coquetry, nor the quick
narrowing of eyelids of the Slavs that suggests an animal wariness;
but a marvellous sympathetic sensitivity, an instinct to respond and to
please, that was always self-possessed and quiet, and a power to
fascinate that was exerted so unobtrusively, so sweetly, that one felt
it must be almost involuntary, as if it were a spirit that lived in her
and that could not help looking out.

I was disappointed, however, by Eleni's politics. We passed
through a little town that was covered with crosses and crowns,
painted in patriotic blue, and I asked her whether this really meant
that the place was predominantly royalist. She replied, with childlike confidence, that it did, and added, after a moment, that she must
tell her husband about this: it would please him because he was a
royalist. She said she was a royalist too. Thebes, also curlicued with
blue, was an abject and sordid place if one had expected a setting
for *Oedipus*. We tried to decide which was the least forbidding
restaurant—though without any invidious comment on the part of
the U.N.R.R.A. man or myself, since Eleni, quite unlike some fine
ladies in minor European countries, never apologised for accommodations or commented on the misery of the people. The glasses and
decanters were dim with dirt, and most of the tableware showed
traces of previous meals. We sidestepped the meat and got a lunch out
of sliced tomatoes, boiled potatoes, sawdusty gray bread and a
bottle of raw retsina. The tables were out of doors, and while we
were eating, some diseased little children came in from the street
begging. They were in rags and had sores on their faces. Eleni

quietly gave them a good deal of the bread. She had two children of
her own, she told me later. The principal feature of the lunch,
however, was an English U.N.R.R.A. man whom the American had
arranged to meet there. It is always a relief in Europe to find an
Englishman who is not in the Army and who is trying to do something to help the people improve their own condition instead of to
keep them from making trouble for the English. The most striking
thing about such men, in contrast with most other exiled Englishmen, is a spontaneous middle-class cheerfulness which is inspired by
the satisfaction of doing good and the excitement of seeing foreign
parts. This man was reporting on the progress of a summer camp for
Greek children in which U.N.R.R.A. had a hand. It was one of a
large number of such camps that had been organised by the Greeks
themselves in an effort to supply a ration of normal feeding and play
to the starved and scared generation which had come into the world
during the war. It was curious to hear this little man describing, with
precise matter-of-factness and a kind of schoolmasterish humour, as
if he had been talking of British Boy Scouts, the problems of such
work under conditions that must have seemed to him abysmally
uncivilised.

We did find the setting of *Oedipus* as soon as we emerged from the
town: a row of black mountains, grim and simple, not rugged, not
comparable, in the old cliché, to anything so human as the lifted
heads of giants, but looking like thin flint blades against the pale and
impoverished sky. I remembered that the Theban plague had been
attributed to the incest of Oedipus, and reflected that we now even
knew that malaria was not due to bad air but to a particular species
of mosquito, and that the purpose of our U.N.R.R.A. expedition
was to apply a scientific technique to the destruction of this mosquito. But in Greece such historical contrasts are not really felt as
dramatic. The country has remained so primitive since the period of
its great civilisation that history does not show as a pageant. You
do not look back on the landscape of *Oedipus*. You are right in it,
and it is grand and uncanny. And those poor country people who
were stricken by the plague—working with distaffs and carrying
clay jars—are still right there around you. They are nice, they are
unusually courteous, but they are not at all "picturesque," and it
seems just as natural to an American to be trying to do away with
their diseases as if they were sufferers from hookworm in Georgia.

We looped at a terrific rate along what the *Guide Bleu* for Greece
calls "*les lacets de la Voie Sacrée*"—which also presents itself not as
an historical sight but as an unsatisfactory actuality, full of danger-

us hairpin curves with no fences to stop cars going over the side,
one-rattlingly rocky with ruts and bumps, and sometimes gnawed
way in great chunks by explosions of bombs and shells. Saturated
with dust like old carpets and lame and stiff from the jeep, we stopped
at a café for a drink. It was several degrees worse than the one at
Thebes. The waiter, in honour of Americans, produced a long-
unlaundered tablecloth, stained all over with soup, egg and wine,
that was dirtier than the top of the table. We picked out, among the
people in the café the men who looked as if they must be politicos,
and tried to figure out which parties they belonged to. Eleni told us
which papers they were reading. I had been playing a game in Europe
of trying to guess from their accents where the Americans I encountered came from. I hesitated, for the U.N.N.R.A. worker,
between Missouri and Texas, but finally took a chance on Missouri.
"No, sir," he said. "I was born in Texas, but I've been living in
Missouri and I may have picked up the accent." I hoped that Eleni
was impressed by my feat, but it turned out that her ideas about
America were extremely generalised and vague. She hadn't been
able to understand why the Texan and I talked differently, and she
didn't know what Texas was. "Texas is a state," he explained to her,
"that's almost as big as the whole Balkans. It used to be a nation
self but we combined with the United States to help 'em against
the British." This was not quite historically true, as Texas did not
join the Union till almost the middle of the century, but it had
perhaps a more general truth and may have reflected a preoccupa-
tion on the part of our companion, because he presently told me a
story about a scandal in the American PX. In the earlier period in
Athens, before there were any Americans, the British had put up a
sign announcing that Canadians and Americans were excluded from
buying at the British PX. Now that the American U.N.R.R.A.
people and the airport personnel were there and the Americans had
their own PX, the British had succeeded in obtaining something like
fifty PX cards. They had been able to draw on these cards without
revealing their nationality by having the supplies sent out to the
airport; but the Americans had discovered this ruse and were
pulling in the cards. This U.N.R.R.A. man's family name was the
same as that of a famous frontiersman, and I asked him whether he
were any relation. It turned out that he was a direct descendant and
had the famous man's first name, too.

Mount Parnassus and the Castalian spring, which we reached in
the late afternoon, are gritty, gray and bleak affairs, quite unlike the

poetical properties associated with their names; the great temple o
the Delphic Apollo you cannot see at all from the road; and th
town of Delphi, caught on this road like gobs of mutton on
shashlik skewer, has its centre in a group of little inns, which hav
been turned into British billets and were crammed with soldiers o
on holiday. Only the view below of the sweep of the Delphic valle
with its limitless olive orchard, made one expect some unimaginab
mystery: all that the name of the oracle implies. No rooms, w
thought, were fit for Eleni: the best thing that we could find was
primitive kind of closet, in a house full of British officers, that wa
imperfectly screened from the room next door by a partition that di
not reach to the ceiling. So we drove on down to Itea on the wate
The monotony of ruin in Europe becomes sickening and exaspera
ing. Though one has already seen many such places, it comes as
shock to reach the Gulf of Corinth and find a quiet little seasic
town in the same condition as Anzio and Naples. While the frontier
man went to see about lodgings, Eleni and I sat down on a bench an
fighting off the malarious mosquitoes, looked out across flat an
dull water to where the hills, in the blue-grey air, were growir
blurred like a Whistler nocturne, but more massive and more sulle
She had asked me whether Italy resembled Greece, and I tried t
explain the difference. The Italian mountains were shaggy and th
Italian country was planted. In Italy, there was too much colour, to
much flesh and too much smell, too many things sprouting an
swarming; Greece was lean and bare but somehow on a high
plane. Yes, she said: it was just the difference between the Roma
and the Greek Catholic Churches. The Roman Church proliferate
madonnas and was preoccupied with sins and pardons, whereas th
Greek Church went in for doctrine and tended to turn theology int
metaphysics.

The U.N.R.R.A. man brought back a British officer: swarth
with a dark cropped moustache, shoes and leather belt well polishe
and a smart lanyard, I think green, tucked into his left breas
pocket. His first name was Demetrius, as we saw from his trur
when he took us up to his room, and Eleni, who found that he d
not speak Greek, thought that he had the look of an Egyptian; b
he had mastered the British manner and practiced it with a cor
sistency more relentless than the native English themselves. And l
established the tone for our visit. He took us, with no comment wha
ever, through a small wooden door in a wall into a yard full o
vegetables and chickens, where a mash made of tomatoes had bee
spread out to dry, and up a tiny outside flight of steps. Then, alwa

with a dazed and indifferent air of not knowing whether he were going to do anything for us or whether we ought to be there at all, he produced a basin of water and—one cannot say that he showed or invited Eleni into a bedroom: she went in because it seemed the thing indicated. He left her with the curt injunction, "You carry on in there." He was depressing: this English world of the war, with its impassivity that masked weariness and resentment, I had been glad to leave behind in London, where anyone of whom you ask a direction will tell you to turn to the right and "carry on from there." He continued to stand by detachedly while the U.N.R.R.A. man and I washed in the room across the hall. "How is it out here?" I asked. "Pretty boring?" "No: it's all right," he answered, and then, after a short pause, as if something more were demanded: "Most of the time is spent swimming." I had already had occasion to note this use of the impersonal passive as one of their curious ways—like the use of "one" where we should say "I"—of suppressing the first person. So you will find A. N. Whitehead, in a brief autobiographical sketch for a volume devoted to his work in the *Living Philosophers* series, writing, "In the autumn of 1885, the fellowship at Trinity was acquired, and with additional luck a teaching job was added. The final position as a senior lecturer was resigned in the year 1910. . . ." The trouble about this is that the effort at self-effacement is likely to become conspicuous and betray what the French call *la morgue anglaise*, of which, as a matter of fact, it is not really a corrective but a refinement. And the Lieutenant's next remark seemed to me also characteristic (you had a good deal of time to reflect, because the gaps between remarks were immense, and my commentary expands in proportion): "The works are over there, I believe"—nodding to a corner of the yard which had a primitive and precarious W.C. "I never use it myself." The natural thing to say, I thought later, would have been something like, "If you want to use the W.C., you'd better wait till we get to the mess. I don't recommend the one they've got here"; but, though really, I think, a very good fellow, he was dominated by the British principle that you should never do any-thing for anyone without indicating a slight hostility.

Later, on the way to the mess, he told us, as if to back up his assertion that the British were quite happy at Itea, that they had been up to all hours the night before, marching around the town singing, and had finally ducked in the water the padre and all the top-ranking officers. Coming into the mess from the crumbled town and the dull and stuffy darkness was startling and disorienting: it was as if one had found, in a provincial town, an unexpectedly competent revival of some vivid old period piece. With their red faces, their bright silk lanyards, their batman standing mute like a butler and vanishing in obedience to orders given without raising the voice or looking in his direction, their gin and bitters and their bottles of wine, their miraculously complete dinner, the London *Times* and the *Evening Standard* lying on the table behind them—these Englishmen had made for themselves a snug and self-sufficient little world that seemed more obviously anachronistic—because it was self-consciously historical: that is, because it represented the role of a certain nation accomplishing certain things—than the life of the olive-growing and goat-herding Greeks who were still nearly contemporary with Homer. And we did not fit into that world. I was surprised when the American told me later that he had made several trips to Itea and had already met these men. I said that they had all behaved as if they had never seen him before. "Oh, they always do that," he replied, "but I just burst right in and start talking. They always treat me all right." But though blank silence does not matter with men, it seems schoolboyish or boorish with a woman—especially so pretty a woman as Eleni (she had changed into a blue dress), who spoke English perfectly and was obviously a lady. Nobody talked to her or gave her a look; they went on with their own conversation. Only the major who was the ranking officer in the absence of the real C.O. and who had to preside at dinner felt an obligation to show some interest. "Hot drive?" he inquired. Yes. "No top on the car, I suppose? . . . Then why haven't you got a big red beak like me?" One didn't know whether this was self-depreciation, implying an indirect compliment, or whether the implication was that she had no business to look all right when the damned sun of her native Greece had so grotesquely disfigured an Englishman. Yet he was evidently the nicest of the officers: tall and lank, with long straggling moustaches, and with a touch of the Victorian innocence of Major Dobbin or the White Knight.

But it was only a question of moments before, from another quarter, the inevitable British attack on the unacceptable foreigner began. The young officer on my left and just across the table from Eleni, on learning that she was an Athenian immediately proceeded, to tell her that Athens was "an awful place," and that the people there were lazy, untrustworthy, hard to get along with, inefficient and given to quarrelling among themselves. We Americans, I am sorry to say, allowed this rudeness to continue. We were a little in the situation that Hamburger had described to me from his trip to Trieste of being treated like captured enemies, and there was always the danger,

etween Americans and British, of exacerbated political argument. I
ad one at an Anglo-American party at the Grande Bretagne Hotel
n Athens which culminated in my being asked by an aroused English
orrespondent what we Americans were doing "messing about in
Europe." But the young man who did not like Athens would not let
he subject drop and kept going on and on, while Eleni who had not,
 imagine, ever encountered anything like this before, coloured and
lid not reply. He was finally broken up by the chaplain, a sandy-
aired little man sitting on Eleni's right, who made some rapid
omment in a voice so unassertive and low that I did not catch what
e said. "Oh, the padre's off on one of his tirades!" the man sitting
ext to him said sharply. "Yes, we all know that England has its
aults, too!" But now the presiding major felt that some sort of
ntervention was needed. "We have no manners at this end of the
able," he said, with hardly a glance toward Eleni—putting an end to
he unpleasant conversation but doing nothing to stimulate a better
ne.

Soon they were talking about water polo as if they had been
lressing in a locker room. They had organised rival teams, which
eemed to have become the chief interest of their exile. The
J.N.R.R.A. man remarked that he understood that all the officers
ad been ducked the night before. "No officers were ducked," said
Major Dobbin. "Only the padre and the doctor." (The doctor, it
appeared, was Demetrius.) I asked the young man sttting next to me
vhat else they did for amusement, and this started a new complaint.
The women made things awfully difficult, he said; you couldn't get a
girl to come anywhere near you unless she brought along her mother
and her father and her grandmother and her grandfather and her
aunt. "Our chaps are livid about it!" he ended. There was, however,
o be a dance that night—arranged by a Red Cross worker to raise
unds for a local hospital—and they had thought up an ingenious
levice to detach the Greek girls from their chaperones. The parents
had always made the girls sit down with them between dances; but
or tonight the frustrated British had had built along one wall of the
lance-hall a narrow forbidding bench and had had lined up at the
end of the room several rows of more comfortable seats, and they
vere going to try getting the girls to sit down with them on the bench,
vhere there was not room for many people and where their families
night not want to join them.

After dinner, when the table was cleared and we were confronted
oy one another without the resource of food, conversation broke
lown completely. It was difficult to talk about England because the

N

officers, apparently to a man, were opposed to the Labour government; and it was difficult to talk about Greece because you could no
talk about Greece without "talking politics." "No politics!" the
major would say as soon as anyone grazed the subject. "Politics are
taboo." Demetrius, with the requisite casualness, asked the sanitary
engineer about the American public-health organisation that he had
worked for before the war and wondered uninterestedly whether
there were anything like it in England. Apropos of raising money for
the hospital, he said that the medical situation was wretched in
that part of Greece, and that it was odd that the local doctors had no
confidence whatever in themselves and had the habit—though he'd
only just been registered—of coming to him about the simplest
problems. Finally we went to the dance. It was well enough attended
and there were people gazing in through the windows, but —partly as
a result of the heat, which made everyone exude water like sponges—
it was not an exhilarating affair. The Englishmen did induce some of
the Greek girls to sit on the narrow bench, but when they had got
them there, it was very uncomfortable and did not especially promote better acquaintance. The major asked Eleni to dance. Every
time when at the end of one of the dance tunes another was immediately to follow, the bandleader—in a voice that took the heart
out of you—would order the dancers to "carry on."

*   *   *

The next morning I went up to the temple. An English soldier
drove me in a jeep. He maintained at first the same well-trained
silence as the batman waiting on table—a silence which is a feature of
their caste system but which always seems unnatural to an American.
I asked him how it was out there. "Pretty dreadful!" he replied—he
did not have to keep up face like Demetrius. It was impossible to get
anywhere with the girls, he said; but he did not blame it all on their
families. "They're scared to death," he explained, "to be seen talking
to an English soldier." I sounded him out on the elections and found
that he was all for Labour. "Before the war," he said, "the Conservatives didn't have a very good record, did they?"

I got at Delphi my first intimation of the almost complete class
line-up, on the issue of the Churchill government, between the
English officers and the English troops. I afterwards talked with a
great many English and I found no English soldier who had not
voted for Labour and only one officer who had. Class-consciousness
in the United States is likely to be sporadic or local: you do not find
any social split that runs through the whole people like a fissure; and

I was surprised by the uniformity of the class feeling of the British Army and the sharpness with which it was expressed. I had not realised how much Winston Churchill and the War Minister, Sir James Grigg, were disliked by the English soldiers. I learned that there had been some rather scandalous incidents on the occasion of Churchill's appearances among the troops, and I asked one man why the soldiers were so bitter. "Why, Grigg's probably an able administrator, as far as winning the war goes," he said, "but neither he nor Churchill ever cared anything about the troops. They've always been treated like cattle, while the officers lived in luxury." He expressed himself very strongly on the subject of Churchill's cigar.

One factor in the situation which undoubtedly has been stimulating this sentiment on the part of the English troops is the contrast they have lately been making between the American soldiers and themselves. The Americans are better fed and they have more and better clothes. They are better taken care of. An officer who had been in Crete fixing up an old barracks for the American personnel of an airport told me that he was having an awful time because it was swarming with bedbugs and crab-lice, and they weren't sure that DDT would kill those things. "The English," he said, "let their men be quartered in places like that. I've seen English soldiers living under conditions that would cause riots in the American Army. But *we* have to do something about it." The relations between officers and men are more democratic with us—and more democratic than they were in the last war. Saluting on the street, in Italy and Greece at least, has virtually disappeared. I heard complaints about arrogant officers, and Mauldin's observant cartoons make out a case against the officer who exploits his rank without taking its responsibilities. But such men are regarded as exceptional and their behaviour as an obvious violation of the normal relations of life, whereas the whole technique of the Englishman in dealing with the men in his command is a traditional part of his system. Whether he is himself an insolent or an amiable man, his tone assumes class superiority. You see the whole situation in that British phrase "other ranks," which, to an American, seems queer and offensive. We talk about "officers," "noncoms" and "enlisted men"; they talk about "officers" and "other ranks." In Athens, you see, for example, a sign on an inferior night club allotting it to "Other Ranks"—as who should say, "This is the place for the nobodies."

What is most important of all, the American soldier is paid a great deal more than the British. This difference had evidently contributed to the extraordinary, the almost complete failure of the English and

the American soldiers to have anything to do with one another
outside their military duties. The Americans can buy more drinks,
get better girls and so forth, and this has made the English sulky. In
general, they keep to themselves and have nothing to say to
Americans. Once in Italy, when I had been visiting Herculaneum
with a couple of G.I.'s and was separating from them to go back to
Naples, one of them said to me, "There'll be plenty of trucks coming
along this road, but don't bother with the British because they won't
pick you up." When I asked him why not, he explained that they
were like that. The Americans in the beginning had always picked up
the British, but when the British wouldn't reciprocate, they stopped.
I feel sure that the resentment or envy of the English troops toward
the Americans backfired in the soldier vote.*

As for the officers, many, of course, are simply Tories with all the
old ideas. There are a few of the younger men that do not belong to
the upper classes and have not been assimilated to them who tell
you stoutly that they are backing Labour. I met a few at Labour
meetings in England and was impressed by their sober air of knowing what they were about and being determined to put it through.
They had nothing in common with the atmosphere of the mess that
I visited at Itea, and they probably represent an emerging and
important element in the contemporary English world.

But there are other kinds of motivations than the old-fashioned
imperialistic ones which impel certain British officers who may once
have been liberals or socialists to support the imperialistic policy of
the continued occupation of Italy and Greece. A major whom I met
in Crete seemed to me an example of these. He was a remarkably able
man, well-educated, serious and active. He had been working in the
underground in Crete before the Germans left and was on excellent
terms with the inhabitants. He spoke Greek, and he had somehow
found time to study the Minoan ruins. All this he had accomplished
since he came, in, I think, the last year of the war, and he had become, it seemed to me, the Britisher in Crete most respected by both
Cretans and Americans. He took me one day to a modest but very
clean and decent house where we were given little glasses of ouzo
with bits of water-melon, and where he talked at some length with
the Cretan family in his exact and fluent Greek. When we were left
alone for a moment, he explained, with a shade of a smile, that "an
unfortunate thing" had happened: a car had been stolen from outside the house while they were having a party there. I assumed that he
had come as an official to investigate the theft of the car. When we

* See Appendix A.

got back into the jeep, we were accompanied by one of the men with whom he had been talking in the house. He explained that he was taking him somewhere, and he drove him almost to the top of a hill, then dropped him when the road got too bad. The man walked up to some rudimentary houses that looked as if they were built of clay and contained only two or three rooms. "He wanted me to drive him all the way," the Major explained, when we had turned around— with the usual faintly humorous attitude toward the childishness of the native—"but I didn't want to risk it any further." And he added, "People who live in the town in rather a sophisticated way like that usually come from houses like those." Then he said something I did not understand, and I twice got him to repeat a word. "Of the girl I'm going to marry," he said. "He's the brother of my fiancée." The old couple we had seen in the house were his prospective father and mother-in-law. I distinctly got the impression that, in marrying a Cretan girl, he was settling down for a career in Crete. The completeness of his acceptance of Crete and his excellent relations with the inhabitants seemed to me at first surprising for an English officer abroad; but I learned later on that he was a Scotchman, which explained, I dare say, his willingness to ally himself with people from small houses. In Scotland, the serious world, the world of authority and learning, may have the but-and-ben close behind it. But he was typical of a whole group of officers that I met in the Mediterranean who seemed to be hoping to remain there as administrators. Conditions in England, as they have heard or seen, are not now particularly inviting: inferior food and clothes, life hemmed in by ration books, housing shortage, looming unemployment and a socialist Labour government which is not likely to try to solve these problems by letting up on the ration books. In Italy or in Greece, a British officer has the best that can be had, and he occupies a position of importance that he could hardly hope to find in England. Some of the younger men, like Bob Leigh in Rome, have spent five years in the Mediterranean immediately after getting out of Oxford or Cambridge and are better fitted for their present kind of work than they would be for anything else. (With the Americans, it is just the opposite: they are worse off, instead of better, in Europe, and practically all of them are frantic to get home). As I say, these men are not all Tories. When I asked the Cretan major how he felt about the elections, he said, "It didn't surprise me. If you followed the soldier's discussion groups, it was plain that the trend was that way. It's not necessarily a bad thing. It will give them a chance to show what they can do. They've been complaining about the government.

Now they'll have to take some responsibility." But such people as
this excellent major cannot afford to admit that these countries
would be better off left to themselves.

*   *   *

I went one day to the British Army headquarters building in
Athens to arrange transportation for a trip. I was told to go to Room
47, but when I got there I found the door locked. An English soldier
stuck his head out of the door of the next office, and I explained my
situation. "It's just down the corridor," he said, and, when I looked a
little astonished, he added, with an hilarious cheerfulness, "Yes:
we'll inundate you with 'em! There's another 47!" I was so delighted
by this—there is not much of Sam Weller surviving in bombed and
rationed England—that I was still dwelling on it as I left the building.
But as I passed out into the street, I saw something that affected me
in a different way. There were two sentries guarding the entrance,
standing rigid, heads back, eyes front, legs straddled apart and a
rifle with a fixed bayonet gripped in the right hand and held out
straight from the body as if by a marionette, with the butt planted on
the pavement. Whenever an officer went in or out, these sentries,
instead of presenting arms, would convulsively lift the rifle butt and
bring it down on the ground, at the same time stamping one foot—as
if they had been mechanical contrivances controlled, like the doors
at the Pennsylvania Station, by photo-electric cells. If you watched
them, as I did, for a moment, the effect was absolutely gruesome. It
was the same thing as the goose-step, I reflected, though in a con-
siderably milder form. They changed the guard there, I learned, with
great pomp, every Sunday morning, completely stopping traffic on
the street, which is one of the most important in Athens. An American
in U.N.R.R.A. told me that he had asked an English officer why they
persisted in doing this. "We do it at Buckingham Palace," he
answered. "But in London it doesn't tie up the traffic," the American
pointed out. This made no impression on the Englishman. The
truth is, of course, that, like the bayonets, this ceremony is intended
to serve as a reminder and a threat to the Greeks. The mood of the
good-humoured fellow who talks about inundating the visitor with
rooms numbered 47 makes no connection whatever with the
automaton outside the door, nor have his feelings, his needs and his
interests as yet been able to influence the latter's acts.

13

GREEK DIARY :
COMMUNISTS, SOCIALISTS AND ROYALISTS

I HAD interviews, in Athens, with two remarkable professors who have become political figures: George Georgalas and Alexander Svolos. Both are middle-aged men of top standing in their fields, and they are typical of the Greek intellectuals who have been driven by the needs of their country to take an active part in the E.A.M. movement, the National Liberation Front, which organised the resistance to the Germans and which controlled most of the country-side of Greece before the Papandreou government, an invention of the British, took over. They present the best possible proof that that movement has not been the exclusive creation either of professional agitators or of cutthroats from the mountains. Svolos, an authority on constitutional law, was the president and spokesman of E.A.M. through the period of crisis last winter; Georgalas, formerly the head of the government geological service, is now the director of E.P.O.N., the United Panhellenic Organisation of Youth, which is the junior branch of E.A.M.

Georgalas I saw in his office, just off his geology classroom in the Polytechnic School. He showed me the statistics on Greek education with the enthusiasm and energy of a man who was fighting for reforms that were obviously needed and that inevitably had to come: the rudiments of democratic training. The state of Greek education seems really, to an American, incredible. The figures for the school year 1937-38 show how bad the situation was before the general wreck brought by the war. At the beginning of that year, out of a population of 7,500,000, there were 987,000 children attending the primary schools, and before the year was done, 80,000 had dropped out. Of 231,000 children who had entered the first grade in these schools, only 82,000 were surviving in the sixth grade, so that only about a third of the ordinary Greeks (who did not go to private schools) even completed a primary education. The teaching, too, was quite inadequate: one teacher had sometimes a hundred pupils. In 1937, 3,700 villages had no school of any kind. In the same year there were graduated from the high schools only 94,920 students. Of these high schools there were five hundred to educate the less than nine per cent of the population who practiced the liberal professions,

and only two to give agricultural training to the more than fifty-
eight per cent. engaged in agriculture. The education in the high
schools was mainly based on the reading of the ancient Greek authors
in a purely philological way and the study of the physical sciences in a
purely theoretical way and with no direct contact with nature. "Here
you Americans," Georgalas said, "are inventing an atomic bomb,
while our physicists in Greece have hardly come to grips with any
practical problem!" Among the graduates of the two universities,
Athens and Salonika, in 1937-38, forty-five per cent. had become
lawyers, thirty-three per cent. doctors, seven per cent. philologists,
five per cent. chemists, and of the remaining ten per cent., eight per
cent. had gone in for the physical sciences. The men from these
schools and colleges that equipped them with a classical education
did not want to return to the towns: they almost invariably remained
in Athens to find or look for government jobs and become "parasites
on the bourgeoisie." There had in 1937-38 been 11,140 graduates of
the regular universities, while at the two small agricultural schools
nineteen students had been graduated, of whom only two were of
working-class origin. The principal school of agriculture, founded in
1920, had been closed in 1939 by the dictator Metaxas and its
faculty obliged to become part of the University of Salonika, where
they had been working ever since with no laboratories.

What E.A.M. was aiming at was to provide instruction in
agricultural chemistry and other technical subjects which would
make it possible for the peasants to develop their barren country and
raise their meagre standard of living. The reactionaries had never
wanted this, because they did not want the common people strengthened. There would be no real education in Greece till the monarchists
were removed from power.

E.P.O.N. itself, he told me, had taken in children under fourteen
from all sorts of political backgrounds, and had once had five
hundred thousand members. It had organised two hundred stations,
where the children were fed and given playgrounds; but all this work
had been undone when E.A.M. had been outlawed by the British
and its public activities stopped.

*   *   *

With Svolos I talked mainly about politics, and I put to him
certain questions the answers to which he was in a position to know.
I had in my mind a fairly clear version of the incidents that had led
up to the civil war. The British, in their anxiety to bring back the

King and to defeat the activities of the Communists, had been alarmed by the Left tendencies of E.A.M. and by the formidable proportions it was reaching, and they had attempted to disarm E.L.A.S., its army. They had announced that they were disarming all units, of the Right as well as of the Left, in order to create a true national army; but when E.L.A.S. in good faith had laid down its arms, the royalist troops—the Mountain Brigade and the Sacred Battalion—were allowed to retain theirs. On December 3 of last year, E.A.M. held a demonstration in Constitution Square in Athens to protest against the policy of the British. They were unarmed, and many of the women had brought their small children. The British had given a permit for this meeting, but they had revoked it at three o'clock that morning in such a way that it had been impossible to call off the demonstration. I have heard the most contradictory possible accounts of how the trouble started. Having the women and children march first, as was done on this occasion, is a familiar Communist trick which makes it more difficult to use violent methods in breaking up a procession but which invites worse consequences if this occurs. The royalists, in any case, claimed that the crowd were trying to rush the guard at the government's headquarters in the Grande Bretagne Hotel. There seems, however, to be no question that the majority of the demonstrators went on quietly marching while the royalist police fired into them and killed and wounded about a hundred people. Funerals were held the next day, and a procession passed through the streets. The royalists fired on the procession from the windows of hotels and killed or wounded between a hundred and fifty and two hundred.

I asked Svolos now whether it were true, as had been said and as might seem to be indicated by the British revocation of the permit at that impossible time of night, that the whole thing had been a British provocation intended to provide them with a pretext for crushing E.A.M. before it grew stronger. He answered that he did not necessarily believe that the British role in the drama had been so simple or so conscious as this. They had perhaps not provoked the insurrection that followed these attacks by the royalists, but they "had not been sorry" to have it happen. It was an example of the familiar British practice of half-allowing, half-stimulating actions which, though carried out by other people, would be advantageous to British interests. He said that the responsibility had to be shared, in various proportions, by the royalists, the British and the Communists. Was it true, as I had been told by an American who had seen something of what was happening, that at the time of the

Lebanon conference of May, 1944, stage-managed by the British
when Svolos had wired to E.A.M. for advice as to how to proceed in
regard to a proposed programme for a "government of National
Unity," and E.A.M. had directed him to make certain reservations
the telegraphed answer from E.A.M. had been suppressed by British
Ambassador Leeper? He replied that it was impossible to say that
the telegram had been suppressed but that it had certainly been sent
and had never arrived. Was the impression I had got correct that
at the time of the crisis last winter, the Greek Communists in E.A.M.
had been acting without the approval or knowledge of Moscow—
Stalin perhaps having agreed at Yalta, in return for a free hand
elsewhere, not to interfere with the British in the Mediterranean?
Svolos said that he believed this to be true—that the Greek Communists had at that time sent a delegate to Russia but that Moscow
had refused to see him and dispatched him straight back to Athens,
and that at no time during this period had the Moscow radio made
any mention of what was going on in Greece. I asked him about the
atrocities alleged to have been committed by E.A.M.—mass executions of civilians murdered with knives and axes, men and women
hostages marched barefoot for days in the snow till many had died
of exhaustion—of which so much was made by Ambassador Leeper
in his reports to Anthony Eden. Svolos did not deny that such things
had happened, but said that they were not, as had been declared,
mere outrages by ruffians from the mountains but a part of a long
and bitter history of private revenges and political reprisals that had
begun under the Metaxas regime and gone on through the German
occupation, during both of which periods the Greek Fascists had
been committing most of the atrocities. After the liberation, the
British, who controlled the news from Greece, had succeeded in
forestalling or suppressing reports of what the reactionaries were
doing to the liberals. At present, as everybody knew, the jails were
full of political prisoners, and every day the agents of the government
were arresting more people without warrant, shooting them and
beating them up on the street and torturing them to extort information. He was worried by Bevin's speech on British policy, which had
been delivered the day before. They had been hoping for an amnesty,
but now Bevin, it seemed, had announced that this might be
difficult, since, according to him, there were "violent criminals"
mixed up with the political prisoners, and there was a problem of
sorting these out.

I asked Svolos what sort of following he thought E.A.M. could
now command if it were free to function politically. It seemed to be

generally admitted that at the time of the civil war it had been backed by about eighty per cent. of the Greeks. He replied that, since the suppression of the uprising, the Socialists had detached themselves from E.A.M., but that the Socialists and the Communists between them could still, he thought, command a following of seventy-five per cent. of the people. And he pointed out that when these Left elements asked the British to allow the Greeks to form what was described as "a representative government," they had proposed a combination which did not at all reflect these proportions but gave undue importance to the Right—the formula being one third royalist, one third democratic and centre, and only one third Socialists and Communists.

I asked him why he had split with the Communists. Because their methods were so unscrupulous, he said. No non-Communist could get on with people who made a practice of double-dealing; nor could they accomplish their own aims in that way. He himself had always been a Socialist—he had been removed by Metaxas from his university chair; and now, dissociating himself from E.A.M., he had organised last April a new Socialist Party by the fusion of three other parties. Georgalas, he told me, belonged to a small Socialist group that was still a part of E.A.M. and that he believed to consist of camouflaged Communists. During my interview with Georgalas, I had had a very definite impression that I was talking to a convinced fellow-traveller, and I was interested by Svolos' confirmation. Later I tried to put my finger on the symptoms which had made me feel this. It seemed to me that I was able to identify them in the special kind of cheerfulness and certainty with which he rose to meet every problem. The middle-class C.P. member or sympathiser is transported into a kind of sub-stratosphere, where, like the aviator who flies too high, he falls victim to a treacherous euphoria. There is no question in his mind that he has picked the winning side and is about to cash in on the stakes, and he does not need to argue about it any more than a Rosicrucian is obliged to defend his esoteric doctrine. Georgalas, no doubt by temperament a sanguine and self-confident man, had, I felt, succumbed a little to that mood of Communist blitheness which is not entirely reassuring. He had talked to me at length and with feeling about the soul-destroying pedantry with which the ancient Greek authors were taught:"Why we love Homer and Sophocles," he said, "they would never find out from their teachers! A little niece of mine was terribly proud because she had learned a verb-form which only occurs about once in the whole of Greek literature and which, as I told her, I had taught Greek for

years without ever knowing about. But that was what our education
aimed at!" I demurred that this might not be entirely the fault of the
reactionary powers in Greece, that, even in democratic America,
Shakespeare was often taught in that way—that this was a tendency
of the academic profession at all times and everywhere. But he
smilingly shook his head, brushed my interruption off and went on,
and it seemed to me that in his Marxist optimism, he was sure that
these stupidities would disappear so soon as the Communists should
come to power. This attitude, I think, dates from Lenin, whose
certainty about social developments and conviction of the rightness
of his pupose gave him a kind of ironical good humour that some
people found uncomfortable and that, in spite of his element of
utopianism, had a relation to bitter realities. It is curious to see here,
as in the sects founded by certain saints, how the faith of a man of
genius, which has first appeared as a natural force, communicate
itself to his followers as a mere drug that shields them from ex
perience and enables them to disregard common sense.

With Svolos it was quite different. You could talk to him as to
anyone else. He lived in the same world that I did, where there were
difficulties, doubts, confused issues, conflicts between expediency and
principle. He reminded me a little of Silone, engaged in a simila
task: the attempt to create, out of the Socialist tradition and the
survivors from the old Socialist groups, a movement that would be
tough enough to stand up to the Russians and avert the kind of
paralysing dictatorship which Russian Communism has everywhere
brought with it. Such people are anxious and intent; they are never
unnaturally cheerful. Just before I had left Rome in July, while the
Socialist Congress was going on, I had run into Silone in the street
and he had told me, excited and beaming, that he believed the pro
Stalinist Socialists were certain to be outvoted on the issue of a
merger with the Communists. But this was the only time I had seen
him look happy.

(Since I wrote this, I have sometimes been taxed with having
accepted too credulously the accounts of the agents of and sympathis
ers with E.A.M. I do not doubt that revolting barbarities were com
mitted on the E.A.M. side or that the Stalinists, to the best of their
opportunity, carried on their usual practice of murdering and
imprisoning Leftists who differed with them on questions of policy.
But it was not, so far as I could learn, at that time really a question of
choosing between the Soviet domination and the domination of
Downing Street. The E.A.M. movement might, I should think, have
been detached from the Communist influence—since the Com

munists, though, of course, very active, were not numerically important—if the British had supported it instead of suppressing it. The Greeks, unlike the Russians, are naturally independent and, what with Metaxas and the Nazis, they had just had a good dose of dictatorship. The radical leaders in Greece were, for the most part, I believe, sincere socialists, full of ardour for a national new deal. Even the Communists, as in Northern Italy, seemed idealists who still thought that the Kremlin was the carrier of the banner of Lenin. If England had been in the least serious about the Four Freedoms of the Atlantic Charter, she would have helped the leaders of E.A.M. to detach themselves from the Soviet entanglement and keep in order those wilder elements whose fierceness, in the days of the Resistance, the British had been only too glad to abet. But that would have meant on the part of the Greeks, as any advance in Europe must mean, definite steps in the direction of socialism, and such steps were the last thing that Churchill had any desire to back. Nor is it easy to imagine that the United States, under our present administration, will be much more intelligent in Greece.)*

*   *   *

After my return from our U.N.R.R.A. trip to Delphi, I saw something of Eleni and her family. They belonged to the well-to-do Greek bourgeoisie—that is, they had once been well-to-do, for few people in Greece have much money or can buy much with what they have. The V.'s lived in a well-furnished apartment on the Odos Vasilissis Sophias, among the palaces, the fine houses and the embassies of the fashionable quarter of Athens; but three generations and two branches of the family had been obliged to share half a dozen rooms, so that their life was rather hampered and constricted. There were Eleni and her husband, their two children, her mother-in-law, her brother-in-law and her brother-in-law's wife. And they got water only, I think, twice a week and had to save it in buckets and heat it themselves.

Yet this was, for them, a period of relative security. Eleni's husband had worked against the Germans and had had to escape to Egypt, and Eleni had had to spend a couple of years alone with the children in Athens. Their persistence through it all in the habits and the attitudes of comfortable people made rather an odd impression—especially when one remembered how completely they had been cut off from the rest of their kind in Europe. It was as if they had

* See Appendix B.

preserved in a vacuum an abstraction of the bourgeoisie, an essence which had never been troubled by the social upheavals going on in the world or by the ordeals of their native country. Their culture was at least as much French as Greek. Eleni's husband had studied law in Paris, and Eleni spoke French with her children. Her mother and her stepfather, whom I met there one day, spoke French, they told me, even between themselves. But the effect was not to place the V.s' in a larger international world: it was rather to make the French language seem like something non-conductive and insipid, a medium of intercourse that did not imply any real relation either with actual present-day Athens or with present-day distant Paris.

On the occasion of one of my calls, I found Eleni's mother-in-law reading an old back number of *Les Œuvres Libres*, and she explained that they had not been able, in Greece, to get any new French books, since the war. I walked up to the large glass-doored bookcase and looked in at the paper-backs, which seemed to exhale a peculiar staleness. They were the biographies, the novels and the poetry, including much that was second-rate, of the early nineteen-hundreds and the twenties. I had already been conscious in Italy of the extent to which the war and Mussolini had kept the Italians behind the times; but there the crop of brilliant paper covers that had come out last spring, like flowers, in the shop windows and the sidewalk newsstands had been rapidly making up for this. In Greece there was no similar revival. To go into Kauffman's bookstore, the headquarters for foreign books, was almost like exploring an attic; and in Eleutheroudakis', the Athenian Brentano's, you were shocked to see how rare and how precious modern books on technical subjects, such as medicine and engineering, had become. A look into the V.'s bookcase was a contact, from which one drew back, with a cultural day-before-yesterday that was somehow still a part of the present world. And near the bookcase hung a small oil-painting which seemed to me in key with the books, for it depicted, not a person or a landscape, but what appeared to be a room in a museum—perhaps one of the great chambers of the Vatican—with indistinct paintings on the walls and something in a case that one could not see. It was, I thought, characteristic of the household. Eleni's husband knew an extraordinary amount about an extraordinary variety of things—the history and culture of Greece and European philosophy and music, as well as his profession of law—and wrote more or less on all these subjects; but his opinions (I do not say it invidiously of so agreeable and learned a man) made sometimes as dry eating as must have been the legendary steaks supposed to have been cut by the Russians from the mammoth found frozen in Siberia. He was a royalist, and, as with all such people whose position had been thus reduced, I could not but feel that his politics were founded—however subtly he might justify them—on an identification of his remnants of property and of the social prestige he enjoyed with the cultural interests and intellectual standards which were unquestionably what he most valued. Nor do I mean to sneer at this. How many similar people in the United States, deprived of social standing and financial independence—which is what the Greek bourgeoisie seem menaced with as no group in America is—could be sure of being strong enough to uphold or defend the ideals which they have been taught to admire?

Eleni, who was younger than her husband, did not, I thought, though loyal to Church and King, quite follow all the bourgeois prejudices, for she told us that some friend of hers was taking her to meet the Soviet Ambassador. She had the special sort of elegance and fineness that is not monied or aristocratic in the usual European sense but a part of some old kind of nobility, at once primitive and civilised, that still thrives in the Greek islands. I used to go swimming with them in the afternoons, and it depressed me to contrast with the beach reserved for the military Americans the "plage" at Gliphada, which had once, I was told, been the gayest and smartest of Athens. We U.N.R.R.A. men and soldiers on leave and engineers and war correspondents had a fine row of clean little houses that seemed to have been newly built, with various kinds of service, such as a woman who splashed you with water to wash the sand off your feet and a bar where they opened your PX beer and supplied you with glasses to drink it. But at Gliphada the old casino had been completely dismantled by the Germans, and there was nothing but a sordid little place where you had to take turns in the bath-houses, rather sickening with the smell of the muddy sand with which the floors were caked and of the fish which was always being fried right next to the wet bathing suits. Eleni, against this background, in a faded pink bathing costume that brought out the tan of her arms and legs and showed her slender and sinuous body, all the more attracted one's attention by her naturalness and poise and grace; and two glimpses of her still stay in my mind as if I had brought them home engraved on Minoan seals: one of her figure going quickly up the stairs, obliquely so that I saw her in profile, pressing firmly but lightly on each of the steps with her rather long feet, showing none of the self-consciousness or vanity of a pretty woman at the beach; and the other of her standing in the water and playing with her little girl, smiling so that she made her eyes slits as she splashed with her palm tipped back at the wrist, at every splash thrusting her face forward and hissing, as if she had been some elemental creature—some siren that resembled a water snake. When I asked her what part she was playing, she answered that it wasn't anything.

*   *   *

The V.'s invited me to dinner one evening to celebrate Eleni's birthday. It was then that I met her mother and her stepfather, and I was amazed at her mother's youth, as I had been when I discovered that Eleni had children of ten and thirteen. Eleni had been married at sixteen, and her mother when she was not much older. The stepfather was very cosmopolitan and apologised with dignity for the Greeks: they had recently been led to misbehave themselves by certain lawless and alien elements, and it was regrettable that this should have given the world a poor opinion of them. We went for dinner to one of the very best night clubs: a place such as, for gaiety and glamour, I had not seen, since the war, in Europe. It was also the first full-length meal under completely clean and attractive conditions that I had had since I had been in Greece, and for the V.'s it was evidently also a treat. You got just the same dishes as elsewhere: sliced tomatoes, rice pilaff and fish, but you got enough instead of too little. The place was full of well-groomed British officers with Athenian "society" girls, some of them very pretty with their blond hair in two rolls over their temples so that their faces looked like valentines. Eleni and her mother enjoyed themselves recognising people and gossiping about them. Some of these Greek girls, they told me, were engaged to English officers.

There was with us a youngish journalist who wrote for a royalist paper: he was a tall slim man of the world, very lively and rather dapper, with moustaches in the style of George II—as Eleni said to me later, "always perfectly delighted with himself." He was an old friend of Eleni's husband, who loved to talk politics with him. I had the impression that the combinations and projects which these two were always discussing were among the least realistic of the many schools of café-table politics with which Athens so abounds; but it had to be admitted this evening that their hopes, from an unexpected quarter, were finding the most heartening encouragement. The journalist had just heard over the radio the news of Bevin's speech on British foreign policy, and he relayed it to us with unrestrained glee and much gloating over the chagrin of the Left: "He said that the Labour Government would continue to follow the policy that England had already supported, that they could see no good reason for a change in Greece before the Greek elections took place, and that they would make every effort in the meantime to see that law and order were preserved—that they would send a police mission." And he described to us a visit to England, from which he had just returned. He had been gratified unspeakably, at a party, to see a fashionable English lady recognise, by a glance at his insignia, a fellow Greek who was present as an officer of the Greek Air Force. And he went on to tell us a story about another London party, at which he had had "*un succès foudroyant avec trois compliments—trois seulement, mais très méditerranéens.*" The first compliment I cannot remember, but the second had been detonated at the time when they were playing a game of "What famous person would you most like to be?" The lady whom he hoped to impress had, in his turn, put this question to him, and he had answered, "*La ville de Hiroshima.*" " '*Pourquoi?*' *J'ai répondu, 'Je voudrais être la ville de Hiroshima, si vous étiez la bombe atomique pour me tomber dessus!'* " Later she had returned and said smiling, "*Dîtes-moi, qu'est-ce que vous voudriez être encore?*" "*Cette fois je lui ai répondu—toujours très méditerranéen:* '*Je voudrais être une cigarette.*' '*Pourquoi?*' '*Pour brûler entre vos lèvres!*' *Le prochain après-midi, à cinq heures, elle m'a téléphoné,*" etc.*

The floor-show seemed to me positively marvellous. I had forgotten how good such things could be, had hardly realised they were still going on. There were a girl who did an Oriental tumbling dance; a girl who sang in Greek and English; a couple who did a folk-dance from one of the islands, fresh and animated and gone in a flash; and the great feature: a famous woman dancer who was also a romantic legend. I learned about her from Eleni and her mother. The Germans had had her on the carpet, the elder but far-from-old lady explained to me, for her well-known association with the English. But she had stood up to them with perfect sang-froid: " *Que j'aurais eu un amant anglais—même deux, trois, quatre,*" she was supposed to have replied, "*qu'est-ce que ça fait?*" She had had German lovers, too, Eleni thought; she had run through all the nationalities and always remained herself—and Eleni added with admiration: "*Elle ment avec une facilité inouïe.*" I saw that the myth of this performer, the great dancer who is also a great courtesan, had come to mean a good deal in Athens, which had been so much without the luxuries and so much at the mercy of the war. She was the devotee of art and love who had endured through all the hardship and conflict, and she was almost a sacred figure.

* See Appendix C.

And she *was* extremely good: very beautiful, quick, sure and dashing, and able to get into everything she did a personality of enchanting insolence. Before one knew it, she would have leapt on a chair and would be bending down and kissing one of the diners, and then would hit him over the head with her tambourine. I had avoided such Black-Market places, but I succumbed to the brilliance of this night club, and, since I had been there without my long-distance glasses and since we had been sitting in a corner to the rear of the show, I decided to go again and see better. I got up another party the very next night with a man I knew in U.N.R.R.A. and two of the U.N.R.R.A. girls, and this time we had an excellent table in the middle and on the edge of the floor. The girls, who had been there before, said we were right in the spot to be kissed. This time some of the acts, seen distinctly, turned out rather disappointing; but the star dancer continued to be fascinating. Her first appearance was a ballroom number, which had its climax in a piece of business—an ecstatic start and smile as her partner, kneeling, kissed her midriff— that, for daring, style, naturalness and timing, took your breath away. When she came out for the second time, she seemed to be some sort of priestess or idol—possibly Javanese; and, exhilarated as I was by the wine—well-cooled and non-resinated—I was preparing to fall under her spell when she abruptly disappeared from the stage. The music went on playing, but she did not return. "Did you see what happened then?" the U.N.R.R.A. man asked the girls. "Yes: the thing that held her dress behind broke." "Somebody's catching hell back there!" he said.

This was two evenings before I left Athens, and the image was to remain in my mind as my last memory, and something of a symbol, of the world of the Greek bourgeoisie.

14

GREEK DIARY : VIEWS OF BULL-HEADED CRETE

THERE is an area just outside Heracleion, the principal town of Crete, which is strewn for a mile or more with the twisted and rusty shreds from what must have been some gigantic explosion. I did not find out what had happened there. This debris may be part of the remains of the German ammunition-ship which the British blew up in the harbour. So many things have been blown up in Crete that you come to take wreckage for granted; and, for that reason, when I look back on the island, this waste always recurs to my mind. It is a place which has been blasted to bits, where people are hardly yet rebuilding but only begining to pick things up.

When, in the spring of 1941, the Greek and British forces were driven out of Greece proper by the Germans, the latter landed their parachutists in Crete and encountered on the part of the inhabitants a terrific and unexpected resistance. The Cretans have an ancient tradition of pugnacity and independence. In almost every epoch of their history, the history of their last three thousand years, they have had to stand up to invaders: in succession, the Achæans, the Romans, the Saracens, the Venetians and the Turks. And they did not hesitate for a moment, imperfectly equipped though they were, determinedly to attack the Germans. They fought so courageously that they enabled the British to get half their troops away and compelled the Germans to maintain in Crete a relatively enormous garrison of sixty thousand men. The result was a series of reprisals designed finally to crush the Cretans. The Scotch major, who had worked on the island as a secret liasion man described to me the Nazi method as he had watched it, in hiding, from the hills. The Germans would come into a village at four o'clock in the morning and round up all the people in the public square. Then they would sort out and shoot all the men who seemed capable of bearing arms, give the old people, the women and the children an hour to get away with their animals, and, at the end of that time, one by one, blow up every building in the town. They thus wiped out some sixty villages and in certain cases they killed the animals, chopped down the olive groves for fuel and took away the fishing boats. They kept the people in extreme poverty by making them exchange at a ruinous rate— demanding the better part of their orange crops in return for a little

oil; and, by these means and by cutting Crete off from traffic with
the rest of the world, they destroyed the economy of the island,
which had lived mainly on its export trade. Out of a population of
four hundred and fifty thousand, the Cretans, through the fighting
and the reprisals, lost something like ten thousand men. In spite of all
this, one region boasts that, never subdued by previous aggressors,
it succeeded in keeping the Germans at bay. An indomitable Cretan
woman, who had become one of the leaders of the resistance and
who had been taken by the Germans to Athens in an attempt to
make her work for their interests, replied, when they told her they
were doing her an honour, that no one could honour a Cretan.
When finally, at the end of the war, some twelve thousand Germans
were trapped in Crete and set to work digging up mines, the Cretans,
in acts of revenge, shot down so many of them that the British took
the Germans off this job and allowed them to keep their arms, and
later shipped them to Egypt.

A trip through Crete, as the result of all this, never ceases to be the
tour of a battlefield. The sights that are pointed out are razed villages,
of which the grey stone walls have relapsed into the grey stony
mountainside till they are almost indistinguishable from it; a valley
across which the Germans and English fought one of their stiffest
battles; a pastoral little white house to which all the ablest men in
Heracleion, the officials, the lawyers and the doctors, were brought
by the Germans and in which they were shot. The drives that one
takes through Crete—there has never been a railroad on the island—
contribute to the impression of disorder and disaster. A native
driver handles a car with all the superb Cretan carelessness of
danger: he will skid around terrible curves on a narrow strip of
road that borders a precipice, while you alternate nervously between
watching to see whether he will turn sharply enough and gazing off
into giddy seascapes, ruggedly framed and of dazzling blue, where
the mountain drops away below; and he will suddenly pull up short
right on the brink of a broken-off bridge to swerve aside down a
steep rocky path and make the crossing on a few wooden boards
hardly wide enough to accommodate the car. The jeeps are always
spinning off these roads; one of the chief events during my visit was
an accident in which an U.N.R.R.A. man had his nose squashed
sideways on his cheek. And you move, almost everywhere along the
coast, in an atmosphere of scattered explosives which keeps everybody slightly keyed up. The beaches and the water inshore are still
studded with hundreds of mines, and when you swim in the small
sections that are supposed to have been cleared, you pick your way

among air bombs and unburied mines scattered about the sand. The
Cretans are not afraid of these devils and, in fact, it seems, have some
kind of taste for them. The children get hold of bits of cordite and set
them off about the streets like firecrackers; the men and boys who go
hunting for mines, being unequipped with mine-detectors, persist—
to the dismay of the Americans and British—in practicing an
intrepid technique of simply beating the ground with long sticks:
if they hit something hard, they investigate; if the mine goes off, so
much the worse. One man, on the outskirts of Heracleion, has
surrounded his house with a fence built entirely out of very large-
sized air bombs, which he has planted on their sharp ends and
bound together with wire. The British commander in Crete, hearing
about this creation, thought he had better look into the matter and
discovered that, with the hot August weather, the bombs had begun
to "bleed"—that is, that the chemicals inside had begun to leak
out through the shells—so that he could not have the fence removed:
the bombs were dangerous even to touch. In the towns, the mornings
of boiling heat and the benumbing muted noons were punctuated,
from time to time, by casual booms and bangs to which nobody
paid any attention.

*   *   *

There are no hotels open in Crete. You read in the pre-war guidebook about comfortable accommodations afforded by the Hotel
Minos, and then find the sign of the Minos hanging on a gutted wreck.
At Heracleion and at Canea, I was put up by the U.N.R.R.A.
people. I owe the U.N.R.R.A. workers a debt for their kindness both
in Greece and in Italy, and it is appropriate to pay them a tribute
here, as they are nowhere seen to better advantage than in their
efforts to do something for Crete. They have everywhere the same
complaints: that they do not get enough supplies (though Greece is
better provided than Italy) and that their organisation is a bureaucratic nightmare. It is depressing to see offices full of capable personnel in one of the larger cities supervising a trickle of food, inadequate
and intermittent, to a great hinterland of ruined towns; or trained
sanitary engineers visiting Littoria or the Gulf of Corinth only to
find that the sprayers haven't come, and restricted to inspecting the
malarial mosquitoes, establishing the fact that they are present in
hordes and going away again. But it is unexpectedly cheerful in
Europe to find representatives of the various Allies collaborating in
some sort of attempt to get normal life started again. In an American
army mess-room, everybody is disgusted with Europe and talks of

nothing but going home. But the U.N.R.R.A. people in a place like
Crete have really had to settle down to local conditions and problems,
and make themselves an existence there. There are places where the
professional social worker, with the social worker's special incapacity
for coming to grips with human beings, exercises his dampening
effect; but the U.N.R.R.A. house in which I stayed at Canea was
presided over by a Connecticut Yankee and his Middle Western
wife, who spread good will and inspired confidence. In visiting
various centres, I was struck by the differences in tone and morale
created by the ranking officials. And this was one of the good Allied
spots, where the Americans and the British got on together and where
both respected the natives. Yet the U.N.R.R.A. worker never, at best,
knows quite what he is doing in Europe. Will he ever get more
supplies? Will U.N.R.R.A. simply fade away? Will it somehow be
used as an instrument to further somebody's political designs? Is it
already being so used? The field workers for U.N.R.R.A. themselves
are instructed to be scrupulously impartial, to keep clear of local
politics. In Crete they are surrounded by the tensions of quarrels in
which they cannot intervene and which they do not always understand. It is typical of the situation that, a night or two before I
arrived, the U.N.R.R.A. people in Canea should have been waked
up by the sound of someone's being pursued and beaten up in the
street right outside their headquarters, but should never have
inquired what was going on. And the fundamental question always
looms whether it is possible, in the world to-day, for a genuinely non-
political organisation to obtain from national governments any very
large amount of money for disinterested international aid.

*   *   *

One day in Canea, in the afternoon hour when attempting to do
anything whatever becomes a ploughing through sand, I lay down
with a book I had picked up: a paper-backed copy of the text of
Arsenic and Old Lace. I had never gone to see this play, about which
I had heard so much that I had thought I should not enjoy it. But I
found that it read awfully well, and late that night, when I got back
from an evening at the two local restaurants with music, where the
foreigners did their best to generate a little gaiety, I sat up and
finished the book, and, stimulated by a good deal of retsina, was
visited by a revelation of the true meaning of this sinister farce. It
was—I saw it quite plainly—a fable about the war. Germany
appeared in it as Jonathan, the fiendish homicidal maniac, who has a

demoralised man of science to work for him. The two genteel old ladies, who are roused to compete with their nephew, having a few corpses of their own in the cellar (all quietly put away for their own good), are England and the United States (the atomic bombs had just been dropped). The policeman who wants to write plays and talks of nothing but his banal plots, while the actual crimes going on under his nose are more sensational than anything he has imagined, is contemporary literature, which is incapable of catching up with reality. And the other crazy brother, who thinks that he is Teddy Roosevelt, unconscious of the abysses of evil beneath him and always gallantly rushing upstairs under the impression that he is charging at San Juan Hill, is, of course, Winston Churchill.

I do not seriously mean to suggest that all this was really intended by the author of *Arsenic and Old Lace*, but I am sure that this curious piece—like the production of *The Duchess of Malfi* in London and like the Britten opera, *Peter Grimes*—is a work characteristic of our time that could never have become popular, that would not have been imagined, at any other time. It is the kind of thing that makes life easier by giving expression to importunate feelings which officially we are unable to admit. The war was over; our side had won. One could afford to see the whole thing now as a fantasy of crime and horror on which a curtain must finally fall. Here in Crete, where the atmosphere is still one of fury, the landscape still scarred and disfigured, my only impression that night was of a vengeful and demented humanity tearing itself to pieces.

*   *   *

My identification of Churchill with mad Teddy Brewster may shock the American reader. I learned later from an article by Rebecca West that Churchill's defeat in the elections brought him a lot of letters from America expressing extreme surprise. She explains that this unpopularity is due, in impoverished England, to the survival in him of an insolence toward the people which is inseparable from the point of view of a well-to-do Edwardian aristocrat, and to the impracticability at the present time of a Prime Minister whose domestic policy is entirely directed to perpetuating the privileges of his class. This is no doubt correct, but I believe there is another element in the eclipse of Churchill in England when he continues to arouse enthusiasm in America. Winston Churchill is half an American, and, though he has often been praised for his revival of the glories of English parliamentary oratory and for his grasp of the

great tradition of English history, the truth is that his vision and his
eloquence have been both, to a considerable degree, those of a
romantic American journalist in love with the achievements of
England and with no very realistic sense of what they amount to or
what they involve. He has always lived more or less in an historical
novel for boys just as Theodore Roosevelt did. There was a moment
when this melodrama of history coincided with current events, and
then Churchill, of course, was superb. Unlike the typical modern
politician, he had courage, he was completely incorruptible, and he
saw politics as a part of something, melodramatic though that was,
larger and nobler than the sequence of expedients of the contemporary political careerist. But, for homeless and foodless Europe,
already half-socialised and driven in the direction of equality and
international federation, Winston Churchill's old Henty story, once
the Germans have been definitely beaten, appears suddenly the
flimsiest of legends. This was especially striking in England when I
was there just before the elections: one never found an intelligent
person who trusted Churchill to handle post-war conditions. The
reversal of feeling toward him has been one of the most curious
examples of that law of historical relativity of which Michelet made
so much: the man who has functioned effectively and brilliantly in
one set of social-political conditions loses his value overnight in
another.

I heard several amusing anecdotes which illustrated Churchill's
tendency to conceive the modern world in terms of an old-fashioned
novel, and I may well include them here in connection with Greece,
which has suffered so from Churchill's policy. Young Leigh, whom
I knew in Rome, has a story about a visit that Churchill had once
paid to his mess. "How many Germans have you shot with that?"
the Prime Minister had asked in his gruff mumbling voice, nodding
toward Leigh's pistol. The latter, who had been in France and
through some of the worst of the fighting, replied that he had never
shot a German, that he had hardly even seen one; that, under
modern conditions of warfare, you only rarely met the enemy at
close range. But Churchill rumbled on: "I shot a man with one of
those at Omdurman, and I should think it would take you too long
to get your pistol out of that holster." Leigh said that he realised then
that the Prime Minister had never learned to see war in terms of
engineering operations, but was still dreaming of man-to-man
encounters of the kind that had occurred in the Sudan, where
Kitchener's lancers, with rifles and swords, had fought dervishes
armed with spears and sabres. Another story, that I had heard in

London, I found that everybody had heard in Athens. At the time of the Greek crisis last winter, when Churchill came on to Athens, he had inquired whom the British could rely on to head a new government in Greece and defend the monarchist interests. Archbishop Damaskinos had been named. "Is he a scheming, ambitious, mediaeval prelate?" Churchill is supposed to have demanded. They told him that Damaskinos more or less answered to this description. "Good!" the great man growled. "We can use him."

*   *   *

The museum at Heracleion was closed, but people thought that the curator would let me in. On my way there, I was accosted in very bad French by an officious little man, who said, when I asked him, that there was no question at all that the curator, a man named Platon, would be in his office now, and that he would be glad to show me the way, which I perfectly well knew. He rang at various doors and brought out an elderly sub-curator, who spoke much better French. My guide addressed him in Greek and, after a few moments' interchange, told me briefly that the curator was not there, and immediately disappeared. The assistant turned to me in wonder. "He said some very ugly things about M. Platon," he explained. "He said that he was *un mauvais homme*, that he wasn't attending to his business, and that he'd collaborated with the Germans. Why does he say things like that? M. Platon is a professor, a scholar!"

He took me to see M. Platon, who was certainly attending to his business. He was directing the excavations, up the coast, of what was supposed to be a Minoan priest's house. A frail and tiny man, with pale hair, pale spectacled eyes and a thin neck punctuated by a sharp Adam's apple, he stood hatless in the heat of the forenoon, directing a couple of men with spades. He showed me a cache of little clay jars that he had just unearthed in one of the walls, and said that, if I would wait till he had finished, he would come back with me and show me the museum. I wanted to stay there and watch him as, assisted by a girl student of archeology and with a plan of the place in his hand, he bent his efforts on reconstructing this building which had gone to wreck and been buried a thousand years before. But the sun had really cooked me: I was dozing as I stood, and I took shelter in the taxi that had brought us.

When he joined me, we returned to the museum. The Germans had put three bombs through the roof and smashed a good many ancient jars and stone things, of which the fragments were lying around.

They had also, M. Platon told me, destroyed one of the royal
Minoan tombs, on which a great deal of work had been spent,
taking the blocks to build something of their own. But all the most
valuable pieces in the museum had been put away underground. He
had a few things brought up for me to see, including a piece of
fresco which had been hideously warped and charred in one of the
great fires that, in ancient times, had burned down the palace of
Minos, and he showed me how difficult it was to get the layers of
earth and ashes off without scraping the painting away. He was
extremely quiet and dry and only once or twice faintly smiled; but he
went to a lot of trouble to have me see not only the museum but also
a private collection, made by a well-to-do doctor, of Greek and
Minoan objects. I don't believe that M. Platon ever thought about
anything but Minoan ruins, and when I remembered the curious
incident of the pushing little stranger who had abused him, it
occurred to me that one can feel respect for a man who has stuck to
his interests and managed to survive and pursue them through the
disasters of recent years, and no respect at all for the man who makes
a business of being politically on the right side.

*   *   *

I went alone to Knossos to see the ruins of the palace of Minos.
This great work of excavation and reconstruction, on which Sir
Arthur Evans of Oxford was engaged from 1900 till his death in 1941,
is one of the most fascinating exploits in the history of archeology.
It revealed, unexpectedly, an unknown civilisation, neither African,
Oriental nor Greek, which, in spite of the rich materials unearthed,
remains for us rather mysterious. In the houses of Herculaneum and
Pompeii, we can easily imagine the lives of people more or less like
ourselves. But the Minoans are not only more remote in time (the
great palace was probably built first about two thousand years
before Christ and destroyed some six hundred years later): though
a multitude of images and frescoes, amazingly sophisticated and
brilliant, bring us close to the Minoan world, we feel ourselves, at
Knossos, in the presence of a unique and an alien people.

The Minoans, at the height of their power, were supreme in the
eastern Mediterranean. The Greeks of the mainland were afraid of
them and probably paid them tribute—which figures in Greek legend
as the boatload of youths and maidens sent every year to Crete to be
devoured by the Minotaur. This bull-headed half-human monster
was the child of the Queen Pasiphaë and the bull of which she became

enamoured, and he was kept in a labyrinth, from which nobody ever escaped. The truth behind the legend, the archeologists have come to believe, is that the labyrinth is the palace itself, enormous and complicated, of an architecture abhorrent to the Greeks, and that the youths and maidens were killed in a peculiar kind of bull-baiting game, of which the record has been preserved by the Minoan frescoes, seals and bronzes. The Minoan toreador had to face the bull in its charge, to grasp its horns with both hands and allow himself to be tossed in such a way that he could right himself by a somersault over the back of the animal and be caught by another performer standing behind. There were naturally a great many casualties, which are sometimes depicted on Minoan seals. One of the curious features of this rodeo was that the girls wore pseudo-masculine cod-pieces, perhaps intended to impress the bull. The statue of the Minoan goddess which had the place of honour at these sports wore one of these cod-pieces, too. The great head and neck of a bull that survives from a ruined bas-relief in one of the porticoes of the northern entrance was probably still to be seen above ground when the Greeks first came to Knossos and built a village near the buried palace, and it may partly, Evans believes, have inspired the Minotaur myth. The Greeks, it seems, avoided these ruins, regarding them as haunted ground, and to the visitor they are still uncanny.

I went late in the afternoon, and it was twilight before I left. The palace is a maze indeed. You wander up and down stone steps and raised platforms and underground chambers among rows of red and black pillars and the flocks of enormous jars that, knobbed with the innumerable handles that were required to lift and move them, give the impression, in subterranean vistas, of rows of palace servants that have been waiting through the centuries for their masters. And you come suddenly here and there upon the marvellous bas-reliefs and frescoes done in the brilliant blues and reds of the Cretan sea, sky and earth: the Cretan ladies—with their curled black coiffures and their pert breasts showing through light chemises, chattering and laughing as they watch the sports—who, by the piquant simplicity of their outlines, queerly suggest drawings by Matisse (one of these women is known as "La Parisienne"); the naked priest-king with his triple-plumed diadem, walking among slim-stemmed irises with elegantly scrolling petals; the cup-bearers and saffron-gatherers, the captain with the black slaves; the bluebirds among wild roses, the blue monkeys among crocuses and ivy, the brown partridges with their vivid white throats standing above multicoloured eggs against a

background of round leaved dittany: all running to antennae-
like foliage, lily-like flower-shapes, ferny fronds and delicate sprays—
a liveliness, frivolity and charm which, in spite of some Egyptian
influence, is as far from Egyptian stiffness as it is from the chastity
of Greece. The Minoan civilization has come and gone without
leaving the key to its secrets. There survive over sixteen hundred
documents in their half-hieroglyphic script, but their language
has not been deciphered. A Czech scholar, just before the war
was supposed to have made a beginning, but since the Germans
invaded his country, M. Platon told me, nobody knows what
has happened to him. Says the former curator of Knossos, Mr.
J. D. S. Pendlebury, in his handbook to the palace: "With that
wild spring day at the beginning of the fourteenth-century B.C.
(the day when some unknown catastrophe finally destroyed the
palace), something went out of the world which the world will
never see again; something grotesque perhaps, something fantastic
and cruel, but something also very lovely." How the memory
of it lingered in the ancient world I happened, not many days
later, to have a chance to see in Pompeii in the House of the Labyrinth. This residence of some rich Pompeian is decorated with Cretan
themes: you find the design of a miniature maze, now reproduced in
shrubbery, a mosaic of the Minotaur surrounded with human bones
and a fresco—very curious to come on at the end of this war of
aircraft—illustrating another legend of Crete: Daedalus and Icarus
escaping from Minos with the wings invented by Daedalus, the father
making the flight successfully, the son fallen, wrecked, into the water.
Daedalus, the great artificer, was supposed to have come to Crete and
to have invented, under the patronage of Minos, some of his most
unholy devices: the labyrinth, the talking statues and the wooden
imitation cow in which the king's wife, Pasiphaë, bewitched by a god,
had succeeded in making an impression on the beautiful white
bull. Minos was so enraged by this last exploit that Daedalus had to
flee for his life and hastily invented his wings of wax. Yes, certainly
there was something rather strange about Crete, something insolent
and exultant, at once refined and barbaric. The Minos of Greek
mythology had a great reputation for wisdom and was famous as a
giver of laws. Evans believes, on the basis of what he can make out
from the lists and accounts on old tablets, that the regime was even
rather bureaucratic. But with this there were a recklessness and a
richness that a little recall the Italian Renaissance, a way of life
unacceptable and frightening to the more moderate and pious Greeks.
    And as I stood before the vivacious fresco of an elongated piebald

bull over whose back a team of two girls and a boy are performing their extraordinary acrobatics, I had what seemed to me a flash of insight into the symbolism and spirit of Crete. I had been studying, that afternoon, a large wall-map, and I was struck now by the resemblance of the island to the outline of the bull in the fresco. Crete itself is an elongated bull, facing the same way as the fresco, with Capes Busa and Spatha as horns, an eye just below Phalasarna and a nose and mouth at Cape Krio, genitals at Cape Littino below and a tail at Cape Sider on the eastern end. Unquestionably the Minoans were preoccupied with bulls. Not only did the Queen Pasiphaë have a love affair with a bull but the first King Minos was supposed to have been the offspring of Zeus, disguised as a bull, and Europa, whom he had carried away across the sea to Crete; not only, among Minoan antiquities, do we find the innumerable bulls of the paintings and objects of art, but there is the motif of the bull's crescent horns that stood over the Minoan doorways and that still figures in the architecture of the island. I do not know what the state of map-making may have been in Minoan days, but I imagine that it would only have been necessary to ascend the highest mountains of Crete to get a pretty good idea of its shape. The later Cretans saw the outline of Mount Ida as the profile of the sleeping Zeus, and the theory that the ancient Minoans identified their island and themselves with bulls because that was what their country looked like seems as plausible as Evan's theory, based on very slender evidence, that the Minoan obsession with bulls was connected with the periodic earthquakes, which they attributed to the heaving and roaring of a gigantic bull underground. I tried this notion on M. Platon and on several archeologists in Athens, none of whom had ever heard it suggested. M. Platon said, "*C'est une hypothèse.*" In any case, it made me feel a naturalness as well as an appropriateness in the bull that was challenged by man as an emblem for the Cretans themselves; and of the ferocious and bestial bull-man as a bugbear for the outsiders upon whom they preyed. The bull still to-day in Crete haunts one as the inevitable symbol for their stubbornness, their belligerence and their fierceness.

*   *   *

The town of Anogeia, on the top of a mountain not far from Psiloriti (Mount Ida) is the highest town in Crete, twenty-eight hundred feet above sea-level. It is known to be nine centuries old and is probably a great deal older. It was inhabited, at the beginning of the war, by something like four thousand people. When the British, during the German occupation, kidnapped one of the German generals, he was spirited away to Anogeia and the people concealed him there. In revenge, the Germans blew up the town, but they killed only thirty-three men, because the rest of them had all managed to escape and hide out for months in the mountains.

To-day, the anniversary of the destruction of the town, a memorial service is going to be held there, and the British commander, the U.N.R.R.A. heads, the Minister of Social Welfare from Athens, the son of Venizelos and the Archbishop of Crete have all been asked and have promised to be present. An English major has offered to drive me up with a Greek brigadier general he is taking. I go punctually to an appointed place at an early hour in the morning and the major is there on the dot. If we could keep to the British schedule, the whole thing would be over by noon and everybody would be back for a nap. But the British have not counted on the Greeks. All seems ready at the Greek Army headquarters. I meet the Greek brigadier, a lean, dark-eyed and gray-haired man, and his young son, an enthusiastic Boy Scout. The tall and heavy-jawed Scotch general, commander of the British troops in Crete, goes striding up the steps in his kilt and the Greek sentries salute with violence, as if he were a magnetic force that brings their arms up without their volition. The Greek officers follow him in. We wait in the car for a time, then the major disappears inside. Presently he sends somebody out to tell me to come in, too. I am informed that there will be a slight wait while the Greek general has his coffee, and am shown into a room where I am introduced to the British commander and others, who are all standing there waiting for the brigadier's breakfast. A small cup of Turkish coffee is finally brought, and the general drinks it up in the three or four sips it requires with a nonchalant air of enjoyment that is at once exasperating and engaging. Then we all go out again.

"There's half an hour wasted for no good reason," the English major says to me before the general gets into the car. I get on well with the major, a young Yorkshireman who voted for Labour. He tells me a lot of interesting stories—especially about the Germans. He had had to drive a German officer who had just been taken prisoner, and he had become aware that the man was trembling violently and green with fright: "I said, 'You may well be afraid. There are some villages burned about here.' " The man had simply been confined in a prison camp. Another German had said to the Major, "We ought to have won the war." "I asked him why he thought they ought to have won it 'Why, look at these people,' he said. 'They're inferior, they're contemptible.' I pointed out that they had been fighting not only the Greeks but the Americans and the Russians and a few other people, but he just kept saying, 'We ought to have won.' " He told me, also, a story about an English officer he knew of who had taken some Greek Boy Scouts on a hike and by mistake had passed the Bulgarian frontier. They had at once been picked up by the Russians, who had sent the boys back to Greece but kept the officer there for days, questioning him as to what he was up to. When they had finally become convinced that he had intended nothing more serious than a picnic, they had decided to let him go but had tried to make him sign a paper affirming that he had not been questioned. He refused, and they had to release him. This puzzles and troubles the Yorkshireman, and his attitude toward the Russians is typical of that of the English, which has been reflected, in a stupid way, by the policy of the Tories in Greece. The traditional English procedure of balancing power in Europe has been up against unfamiliar difficulties in the problem of balancing with Russia, which may promise one thing at Yalta about leaving the Mediterranean to the British, and apparently, through the local Communists, do something quite different in Greece. One can't ever be certain of anything. In the mind of the Major, the peculiar reception given the Scoutmaster by his Soviet allies is connected with the larger question of how far you can trust the Russians—people who find it natural to hold an Englishman as if he were an enemy and try to make him swear to a lie.

As we pass through the little villages, we are welcomed with handfuls of laurel leaves, which the young girls throw in through the windows. We go as far as we can in the car along a wrecked and precarious road, and then have to get out and walk. It is a steep path up a mountain that hardly threads through the rocks. "The brigadier," says the Major to me, "is setting a cracking pace." We presently fall behind him, as the old man, erect and lively-eyed, strides along in his polished puttees with a rapid and elastic step. These hills are great grey barren mounds where there is nothing to examine or to look at. A curious little plant with a purple stem and pale waxy perfumeless flowers turns out to be asphodel. The path disappears completely, and we have to clamber among jagged stones. But when we have got beyond this, we find men with donkeys waiting. The brigadier sees politely that we are mounted. You sit sideways and, since there are no stirrups, you hang on to a wooden handle that sticks out of the front of the saddle. You learn to keep your balance while you look along the path ahead rather than into the abysses below.

At the end of an hour of this, you arrive at the village of Anogeia
(pronounced as if it were Anóya), where you are perched in the
Cretan sky and have everything else underneath you. The difficulty
at first is to grasp what the condition of Anogeia is. The town, which
had been built out of mountain rock, is now mostly just stones like
the other stones. The aim of the Germans was not to leave a wall
standing, and where the base of a house still remains, it looks
exactly like a Minoan ruin. One thinks with a certain affection of
good old King Minos, the bureaucrat, who only threw a few maidens
and youths to bulls and gave them a sporting chance. The one
building spared is the church, not out of reverence, however, but
because it had been the German headquarters and might perhaps
still be useful as an outpost. The thin dark-eyed women meet us, all
in black, with their shawls over their heads, and shake hands with us
as we ride. We come to a halt in the public square, where we sit down
and are offered refreshments in the shape of little pieces of water-
melon and shots of a crude kind of ouzo which is known in the
mountains as raki. We shake hands with the men, who have terrific
grips and fingers that seem made of flint. Their faces are bearded,
their hands are black, and they have piercing black or hazel eyes.
The goatherds of this mountain town are the hardest-bitten people I
have ever seen. Life is so rugged up here that many of the children die
and only the toughest survive. No wonder they could stand up to the
Germans.

We have been told that the service is to take place at eleven, but
we learn now that it will have to be deferred till the Minister from
Athens arrives, and that it may not be held till six. "Isn't that like
them?" grumbles the Major. "He was invited a month ago." He
does not understand these anniversaries which the Cretans, he says,
are always having. "I suppose it makes them feel better," I suggest.
"I should think it would make them feel worse," he replies. "I should
think it would remind them of the person who was dead and bring
back a lot of things about him."

We are shown into a dining-room through a smaller room which is
strewn with the bones of what has evidently been an earlier repast,
and entertained at an Homeric banquet. First they bring on great
platters of mutton: simply roast sheep hacked into manageable
pieces. You are supposed to eat with your fingers and throw the
bones on the floor. And there are also chunks of bread, boiled
potatoes and magnificent water-melons. When the melons appear, I
assume that we have come to the end of the feast, but they are
followed by a delicacy called kokoretsi, which consists of the entrails

of the sheep chopped up, stuffed into an intestine, wound around a
long skewer and roasted. This fare is a little appalling to some of the
British and American guests, but it is very impolite in Greece not to
do justice to hospitality, and we are watched by intent eyes looking
in on two sides through the windows. "It's important to drink a lot
on these occasions," says the Major, who is sitting next to me. They
keep refilling our glasses from great pitchers of non-resinated raw
red wine, which I get to think rather pleasant. The man on my other
side is a British Red Cross worker, another Yorkshireman, who has
hardly left his county before and talks with a heavy accent. He tells
me about the local diseases: scabies, malaria, etc.: "They say that
they never had scabies before the Germans came and conditions
got so bad, but I don't know: they're certainly not very clean." A
young girl had come to him with a swelling on her neck—"a really
beautiful girl, you'd say she was a beautiful girl anywhere—with a
wonderful lot of hair. But when I lifted up her hair, it was awful—
it was all crawling underneath." We are now becoming talkative and
genial. The Greeks are extremely agreeable. There is a handsome old
man, a retired official, whose short snowy beard, subtle smile and
generous enjoyment of the banquet seem to belong to an heroic age.
The brigadier keeps offering us things with his worn but cordial air
of a man who has experienced much but has yet remained blithe in
spirit.

After the meal, I walk through the town. There are donkeys,
chickens and goats, pigs scratching themselves on the ruins, little
half-naked keen-eyed kids. I have been warned about Cretan
hospitality, but I stop to look at a litter of pigs, which are nursing in
a regular rhythm that the mother seems to be directing by an equally
rhythmical grunting, as the coxswain sets the stroke for a crew, and
I am invited at once into the house beyond, where they offer me
bread and wine, and I thus have a chance to see how poor their
common nourishment is. After that, I make a point of not looking in
the direction of any house, but while I stand gazing out at the dusty
hills, a woman in a doorway sends her daughter to give me some
water-melon. They are beginning to rebuild the town, but most of the
people are living merely between plugged-up and roofed-in ground
floor walls. A little whitewashed cell in a ruin, with grapes growing
over the door, seems an attractive and comfortable home.

But I am going to sleep on my feet and I look up the rest of the
party. They have retreated into a house to escape the sun and are all
sitting together on benches. Some are dozing, with their heads in
their hands. The Scotch commander is in this position and somebody,

N

asks him, well, how does he feel? He does not reply for a moment, and then declares, "Bloody awful!" Everybody laughs, then again becomes numb. At intervals they hand us in more water-melon. It seems that a second banquet on the same enormous scale is now taking place in the dining-room in honour of Venizelos' son.

It is not till I have been some time in the little building in which we are sitting that I recognise it as the village store. There is so little left to sell: a small bin of grain, a few tiles, a few jars, a few bony cuts of meat. There are children with bright clear eyes—some of the girls are pretty but, like everybody else in the town, as lean and fibrous and swarthy as if they had grown out of the soil like some kind of meagre mountain tree. I make a jumping mouse out of my handkerchief. This did not go over well in Athens, but in Anogeia it is a mad success. The children—what rarely happens—at once discover how the trick is done and demonstrate the principle with their fingers. Then they go and bring in other children, and keep crying, "*Pontikos! pontikos!*" But, in the presence of the severe Scotchman, I feel that once has been enough.

Of course the Minister of Welfare fails to come. They wait until six, then start. In the square there is a shaft inscribed with the names of their hundred and one men who have been killed in the fighting or reprisals. One sees on it the word *hoplitai*, which takes one back to Xenophon. Here the widows and bereaved mothers have been standing in mourning all day. They have brought most extraordinary wreaths that are wreath-shaped loaves of bread. Now young girls take their places here, in the traditional costume of the country: black blouses braided with gold, reddish snoods with gold embroidery, silver necklaces and strings of gold coins. In the background hangs the blue Greek flag between poles that are twisted with laurel. A procession marches into an enclosed space: a long row of priests in black, the Archbishop of Crete at their head, a patriarchal and impressive old man with an immense and well-cared-for beard spreading across the breast of his robe; the Scotch general and the British delegation; the U.N.R.R.A. representatives and all the rest. There are litanies, sermons, prayers; anthems by a choir. The sun is still stupefying; it is hard to remain on one's feet. We keep wondering how soon it will be over, knowing well it will last a long time. At the sound of the church-bells, a donkey brays, interrupting the reverent silence. When the dead sons and fathers are mentioned, the women raise a chanting threnody. It is a traditional song, not a wail, but it seems to make the Major nervous, for he grins faintly as if to indicate that that is not the English way to behave about men who have been lost in a war. The Mayor speaks and the school-master speaks, and the schoolmaster, who is evidently an E.A.M. man, gives them a radical exhortation, which the Major is able to follow and which makes him more nervous still. "They're going to boo him in a minute," he whispers to me, but the crowd shows every sign of sympathy. Venizelos the son makes a speech—the Venizeloses come from Crete. Then innumerable wreaths are presented. The Scotch general brings up a big wreath.

By this time the sun is going down. The Americans and the British are in a hurry to get started for home so that they will not have to drive on those roads in the dark. "Wasn't that terrific? I warned you," says the U.N.R.R.A. man from Connecticut. "It wasn't even a good show for that kind of thing." Like the Major, he doesn't understand what they get out of these sombre celebrations.

But on our way to the donkeys to carry us back, the Brigadier has to stop for civilities, and we have to drink another round of raki. When we set out in the car again, we are immediately blocked by a row of Greek trucks, which are taking people home from Anogeia but which have for some reason stopped at a small settlement, parking all over the road. No one pays any attention to our efforts to induce the trucks to move, and the Brigadier himself volunteers to get out and see what can be done. He disappears for a long time. The Major by now is frantic. When we start on, it is almost dark and our progress is impeded by the trucks, which are ahead of us and which, on the narrow road, it is impossible for us to pass. And then, just after we have finally escaped, we discover with indignant horror that we are in for another service. In a village at the foot of the moun-tain, there is a crowd around a lantern-lit catafalque, and the Arch-bishop is going into action. I am as eager to get on as the Major and I urge him to shoot right through. But he knows that the Brigadier ought to be there and that he ought to be there with him, so we park and join the group. They are standing on the edge of a grave, in which looms a large coffin with trappings. This time the wreaths are made of cake, clumsily moulded and decoratively iced. The Major whispers that a man standing near us was the head of the Resistance in that region. He has a small curled and pointed black moustache and holds his hat in his hands. He is clean-shaven and soberly dressed.

But this ceremony is brief and we have come at the end. Glancing about in the inadequate light, I see that the Archbishop's cheeks are wet and that the leader of the local Resistance has tears starting out of his eyes; nor do they seem to me to be weeping for show. For

the first time in that long day's ordeal and despite my former
impatience, the scene takes me unaware and I am suddenly, painfully
moved. Perhaps the Major, too, is moved: he does not smile and has
ceased to fume. A small band plays the Greek national anthem, and
then another, much more martial tune, which, I am told, is the
anthem of Crete.

And that is how the burning of Anogeia was commemorated by
the Allies—not very solemnly or graciously, but whatever good will
we had went into that trip up the mountain.

*　　　　*　　　　*

I lay around dozing at the airport waiting for a plane to take me
back to Athens. The American engineers there begged me to give them
some publicity. They were irked at having been stranded in Crete, in
exile from the main stream of American troops. It was hard for them,
they said, to "have any initiative," because they didn't know what
they were there for and couldn't see the point of their work. What did
we want with an airport in Crete?

This airport was at Heracleion. At Canea there is a British one. I
had flown over "British" and was going away "American." There
was as usual a striking contrast. On the British plane, the discipline
had been complete. I had been made to wear my Mae West life-
preserver by a sergeant who called me "sir" and respectfully helped
me into it. A security man questioned me politely about my purpose
in visiting Crete and made certain, when I landed there, to whom I
was going to report. All the safety restrictions were scrupulously
observed. In order to make the trip at all, I had had to get orders
from the British. But here, when an American plane came in, I
simply went to it and asked to be taken back. The lieutenant who
piloted it was sitting on the ground with his crew, his hat pushed back
on one side of his head, in the shade of the wing of the plane. He did
not ask to see my orders, but simply said, sure: come along. On the
flight nobody wore a Mae West or strapped himself to the seat; the
windows were all left open; and everybody except the pilot lay down
right away on the seats or the floor and went sound asleep. There in
our bird-body plastered with pin-ups we sailed through the afternoon—delightfully cool in the upper air—above the misty blue
summer sea.

The lieutenant had been some time in Athens, but had done nothing about the antiquities and asked me what he ought to see. Some
G.I.'s on leave, on the other hand, who drove with me in the truck

into the city, had no ideas about anything but eating. They asked whether it were really true that you could get ice-cream in Athens "just the same as they have at home," and that there were doughnuts covered with sugar and honest-to-God beer.

15

STOPOVER IN NAPLES

THOUGH Greece had been a relief after Italy, it also worked a little the other way. It was pleasant, after those arid hills, to see trees and ploughed fields below one, and to find, on the road to Caserta, hay-ricks and orchards and gardens, an earth that could be cultivated, again; to speed along a high eucalyptus drive; to smell sulphur and swamp and manure. It was gratifying at first glimpse, after the neutral colours of Athens, to see the ridiculous big pink buildings with their green blinds and their plastery statues three times life-size; the yellow-haired or dark-haired women with their red or white clogs; the queer ornaments on the collars of the horses that the Neapolitans seem to love: silver rosettes, silver bells, silver madonnas, saints and birds. I like to look even at the Bay of Naples, which resembles a coloured picture post-card.

*   *   *

But since I was here at the end of April, the Americans have set their mark on the scene. A campaign for improvement is in progress. All along the road from Caserta one is admonished by signs in English which make great play with the letter F: "FLIES FOUL FOOD," "FLIES FEED ON FAECES AND FOOD," "FLIES SPREAD DIARRHOEA," etc. And there are warnings all over Naples, thought up no doubt by some advertising man: "DRIVE CAREFULLY. DEATH IS SO PERMANENT." In the middle of the Via Roma—for no reason that one can see except that of simple refreshment—a free lemonade stand for Americans has been set up by the Red Cross.

*   *   *

Last spring I saw the bombed-out section that extends a good way in from the docks: shapeless fragments of buildings rising like sand-castle stumps out of mounds of pulverised plaster, filthy children playing in the garbage of the pavementless, lightless, policeless streets, the butcher-shops with gruesome cuts of meat, the half-obliterated shrines. I have had enough of ruins now, and I give this a wide berth. But the misery is all through the city. No matter how late one walks out, the ragged little boys are still in the streets. When they get too tired to beg or pimp, they go to sleep on the curbs along buildings or on the running-boards of parked cars. And everybody who has passed the age of puberty seems to be busy making more children: the town is full of pregnant women and of women with wretched little babies that have sores all over their faces or are covered with the pink mottlings of disease. The Neapolitans seem to me sometimes to have as little relation to people as small octopi, crabs and molluscs brought in by the marine tide.

* * *

But the life here is rank and flamboyant, and even in death it exults in the flesh. I have never seen a city in which funerals seem to figure in so important a way. Where so many human creatures are begotten many must be constantly dying, and they like to make a fête of death. The streets are always full of hearses. There are cheap black ones loaded down with flowers, cheap white ones that look like pastry, more costly ones studded with crowns that give the impression of Christmas tree ornaments. And I saw one magnificent black one, drawn by eight black horses. With its crown-shaped lamps on the corners, its quantities of spiralled columns and its elaborate jet carvings, it looked like a luxurious Renaissance bed.

* * *

Yet Count Morra told me in Rome that, when he came here at the time of the invasion, the people had shown great cleverness and courage. It had been "1848 over again." When the Germans had posted an order that all the young men were to report to help defend the city against the Allies, these young men all immediately disappeared, and the Germans could never locate them. Barricades were thrown up in the streets, and little boys went about with handgrenades strung around their waists. This was not the result of organisation, but mainly a spontaneous movement. It was, he said, as if the spirit of a common purpose had run through the city like an electric current.

I liked Morra. He is not one of the Roman nobility, but something more like a country squire. He had, I was told, never left his estate through the whole of the Fascist regime, though he had refused to pay homage to Fascism and had been penalised and ostracised. He is now, though so severely crippled that it is difficult for him to get around, extremely active as one of the editors of the liberal *Nuova Europa* and in various other ways. Though cultivated and cosmopolitan like the more detached people in Rome, I thought him a thorough patriot of the old-fashioned disinterested kind. He obviously took deep pride in this demonstration of Neapolitan solidarity.

*   *   *

My earlier visit to Naples is associated with *Lili Marlene*, which I heard being played at a great rate in the enlisted men's Red Cross canteen, where, among all those dazed boys from home crowded together in their drab army clothes and breathing the bad air, it seemed to me, in its prettiness and pathos, its banality that was never too obvious, to carry the experience of war which must so largely remain unspoken but which may sometimes be picked up by a song: the hardships, the changes of scene, the blankness, the longing for home. *Lili Marlene* was originally German, but the Allies had taken it over and the street-singers had learned it in Italy, and everybody had been singing it at the same time. It had sounded through Europe—with no conscious intent on the part of those who sang it—as one of the few human utterances that had no nationalistic animus: it told simply of a soldier's girl-friend who waited for him night after night in the rain by a lamp-post at the barracks gate. A martial step and the echo of trumpets seem to have faded in the wastes or the war-years. The lover may or may not come back: if he does, he will meet her at the lantern: if he fails to, who will wait there then? And this song was all that they had had to establish human fellowship between them while they were massacring one another and bombing one another's sweethearts! This little memorial to a faith perhaps futile was all they had had to offset the tragedy of manhood destroyed and debased!

*   *   *

There were people I knew at Sorrento, but I kept putting off going out there, because my transportation might come any moment and I might have to leave at once; so I stayed on from day to day visiting Pompeii and the Naples Museum and wandering around the city, where I knew nobody.

The Via Roma at night, in the smell-thickened hot August air, was the channel for a dense traffic of women and soldiers looking for women. I spoke one evening to a very pretty girl, almost the only really pretty one I had seen, who seemed, in fact, so well-dressed and fresh-faced that she might have been taken for respectable if she had not been walking alone at that hour in the Via Roma. She was conspicuous among the Neapolitans by her type, which was unusual there: she had yellow hair, brown eyes and fair skin: and I learned later that she was not Italian, but half-Polish and half-German. She took me straight to her place of business, which was in the forbidden zone up the hill from the Via Roma. Every cross-street on this side of the main artery had a sign barring out the troops; and, exploring this quarter for the first time, it was easy for me to understand why. The little girl—who said her name was Giannetta—piloted me by the arm through the squalidest and most sinister-looking streets that I have ever seen anywhere. By a maze of stone steps and blind alleys, a whole world that, besides being closed to the troops, seemed self-contained in its degradation and partly shut off from the rest of the town, we arrived at an old dark and stinking house, where the dank and cavernous stairwell was dripping from thrown-out slops or a permanent leak in the plumbing.

Here Giannetta and three or four other girls hired the use of two disgusting rooms from an old woman who rented a small flat there. When I entered, not without misgivings, I was somewhat reassured to find a taciturn American M.P. sitting solidly in a little waiting-room which was also dining-room and kitchen. The impression that I got then and later was that the M.P.'s, instead of keeping out the G.I.'s, were giving the girls in the barred zone protection and getting repaid in kind or by a cut out of their professional earnings; and this conclusion has been confirmed since my return by an American air-transport man who spent a good deal of time in Naples and saw how the system worked. Giannetta told me that if a customer made trouble or became obnoxious in any way, she called the M.P. at once and had the man thrown out. He could always be threatened with arrest for having been found in that quarter at all.

Giannetta first said she was seventeen, and she did not look any older; but, forgetting this, she later made it nineteen; and when one day she showed me her passport, I saw that she was down as twenty-two. She had been married and had separated from her husband. She had been unfaithful to him, she confessed—but then he had been unfaithful to her. She had recently come to Naples from Rome, giving her status—she smiled slyly when I remarked on it—as that of *casalinga;* because Naples was apparently now where the biggest money was made. She charged three hundred lire, so she was earning anywhere from sixty to a hundred and fifty dollars a day. She and the other girls were frantically working overtime to rake in as much as possible before the Americans went away; and when I called on her one afternoon to ask her to dine with me and go to the theatre, she told me that she could not do anything except for a flat rate. An evening of mere amusement would mean a loss of hundreds of lire, and I should have to pay her by the hour, if I wanted her to do things outside with me, just as if I were going to bed with her. While I was talking to her in the little anteroom, I could see, in the room beyond, a soldier, fully dressed, lying full-length on the bed. But Giannetta had still another distraction and, in the course of the conversation, would keep running out on a little balcony to watch a street-fight in progress outside. It made the whole thing seem rather childlike. She had none of the marks yet of the professional whore, but a girlish candour and gaiety: and for this reason she was much in demand by soldiers who had picked her out as I had done, and of whom I would sometimes find a whole row sitting on the bench in the anteroom.

Her price for going out was prohibitive, but I dropped in for a call once or twice. I also got to know her half-sister, who was not pretty and seemed rather sensible: she did not look like a prostitute either. It was queer to sit behind the scenes of this business which in its way dealt in glamour. For a man, at least an American, always expects of a woman—in relations however commerical—a touch of romance and passion, and the woman must try to supply it. Nothing has ever brought home to me so sharply the difference, in this connection, between the woman's and the man's point of view as seeing these girls in Naples return to the general conversation after being away in the next room with their customers, laughing about things that had happened or discussing them in a practical way as if they had been incidents of marketing. That they were sometimes half-dressed did not make them self-conscious in the least nor was it intended to appeal to my appetites. Yet they had just lit men's expectations, created a suggestion of mystery and—even in that unspeakable den—gratified them by moments of magic.

Giannetta sounded quite cute in Italian, but when she broke into American the effect was absolutely blood-curdling. She had been able to learn from her customers nothing but the toughest talk: a jargon of male idioms and obscenities that sounded horrible as it came from her good little mouth. The Americans have brought to Italy, along with their campaign to swat the fly, some of the worst features of American society. There was plenty of racketeering in the army; and that summer the Roman police had been to considerable trouble to round up a gang of American deserters who had been holding people up for months and had committed several murders. It made me uncomfortable in Naples to see shady-looking Italians in clothes that had been stolen or bought from G.I.'s. The Neapolitan and American underworlds had merged in the Via Roma and were sometimes, except for insignia, indistinguishable from one another.

16

HOMECOMING—FINAL REFLECTIONS

FLYING back to the States, I had wonderful weather and great good luck in making connections. I left Naples about 10.30 in the morning and arrived in New York at about 12.30 two mornings later (though the actual flying time had of course been some eight hours longer). The whole Atlantic was as smooth and blue as if it had been the Mediterranean: you could not even see any white-caps.

But, as usual after long flights, I suffered somewhat from shock. It took me days to adjust myself to having travelled so far so quickly. Having grown up in the age of trains and ships, I am conditioned by the old-fashioned journeys that gave you time to prepare yourself for the new continent or country you were visiting. But when you leap across the Atlantic by plane your reflexes are caught unawares, and do not tell you that you are home again. You have the illusion that the country in which you have alighted is not really the country you left, but some sort of mirage or simulacrum.

This was partly due, no doubt, to the fact that I had been thinking, all the time I was in Europe, how much better off we were at home and had created an ideal picture, based on everything most agreeable to remember from the past, which the present in its actuality could hardly justify. And this emptiness of the present was due also to the death of Roosevelt and to the general displacement of activity to Europe and the Pacific. With all this, in that outside world—where we had suddenly found ourselves engaged and exposed as we had never been before—we were still, except as a fighting machine, more or less disoriented. It was as if at one stroke we had been deprived of most of what had been in our minds—our imaginative conception of ourselves, our complex of occupations, all formerly contained in the United States; but had not yet really related ourselves to the developments of the larger arena—so that civilians moved at home in a void and Americans returning from the services found an unexpected relaxation contrasting with the tension abroad.

In any case, I felt for a while almost as if I had merely arrived in yet another foreign country. I noticed characteristics of the Americans of which I had not been conscious when I left. They were much larger than Europeans—enormous, they looked to me now; their faces were insufficiently focussed and their personalities lacking in

flavour; they were doing a good many things expertly, but in a way
which made them seem rather uninteresting. I had looked forward to
picking up my old pursuits, but was baffled and disconcerted to find
that these no longer appeared so absorbing as they had before. Then
I saw that I had to make an adjustment quite different from the kind
of adjustment that is involved in going abroad and learning your way
about. I already knew my way about at home, yet I could not find
the values I had known, the values on which I depended; and I
realised that what made the difference was that, in visiting a foreign
country, you were always in the position of a spectator for whom the
inhabitants were staging a show. This show consists of their being
foreigners and behaving in an unfamiliar way, and it provides you
with entertainment without involving you in responsibility as to
the progress and outcome of the play. But in America you are no
longer in the audience, you have to be one of the actors, and the old
drama in which you figured will not get under way for you again
unless you go back into your role. You have now to contribute,
yourself, to creating the interest and value, and, back in New York, I
found myself still in the passive state of mind of the onlooker. I had
not begun working yet.

*   *   *

The Careerists: I had, however, acquired or had had strengthened,
during my trip and in the war-years before, certain convictions and
prognostications which I shall set down here for what they may be
worth.

First of all, I have come to believe that the accepted interpreta-
tions of history have been failing to take into account one extremely
important factor, which I have never seen adequately studied. This
factor is the always unforeseen and immediately disastrous results of
democratic education and free competition for advancement. The
point is that these results have proved to be very much the same in
any modern society in which hitherto unprivileged people have been
given a chance to do any kind of work for which they can qualify
and to go as far as they can get—that is, they have proved the same
irrespective of what the Marxists call the specific class character of
the revolution that brought them about. The reformers of the
eighteenth-century were always talking about the desirability of
"the career open to the talents." We got it in America and in France
when the revolutions in those countries occurred; but we did not
get the Reign of Reason that the philosophers and statesmen had

hoped for: the career thrown open to the talents very soon turned out to mean that it was the careerists who dominated society and not at all the superior talents of the kind that a Condorcet or a Jefferson prized. In France, the political idealisms of the revolutionary period proper, whether liberal and humane or intolerant and moralistic, gave way to the mad speculation, the exploitation of official position and the general scrimmage for money that were rampant under the Directory and still going strong under the Third Republic; and the patriotism of Valmy and Jemappes that had defended the Rights of Man turned rapidly into the "*gloire*" of Napoleon, who exploited the patriotism of the French to realise his own upstart ambitions. In America, the republican idealism, with no reactionary neighbours to fear and no feudalism at home to undermine it, was preserved in more or less sincerity for longer and with less upsetting vicissitudes; but it was choked, after the Civil War, by the wild and overwhelming growth of the same impulses to self-aggrandisement and appetites for material success that had been taking possession of the French. Our Rockefellers and Goulds and Morgans were the American counterparts of the French businessmen and financiers who had sat for the protagonists of Balzac, and they had operated on the scale of Napoleon. They had just the same relation to the Declaration of Independence, the Bill of Rights and the Gettysburg Address that Napoleon did to the Oath of the Tennis Court and *Liberét, Egalité, Fraternité.*

Now the Marxists have always told us that all this was the result of the capitalist system, which instigated cut-throat competition, and of the merchant and banking class who cared about nothing but money. Marx and Engels and Lenin and Trotsky believed unquestioningly that, in spite of the fact that the rising bourgeoisie, in displacing the feudal nobility, had brought in this murderous commercial age, the overthrow of the bourgeoisie by the agricultural and industrial proletariat would inaugurate an era distinguished by honest workmanship, human brotherhood and scrupulous public conscience. The truth was that the new revolutions of the first half of the twentieth century were to produce, in their early phases, even more degrading results than what had happened in France and America. But there were reasons why Marx did not foresee them. He made two fallacies, he argued from two false analogies, in forecasting what might be expected when the process of scrapping capitalism should begin. In the first place, being a Jew, from a family that had included many rabbis, he identified the situation of the factory worker with the situation of the Jew. A Jew like Marx, escaped from the disfranchised state, had a moral authority and an intellectual training that were his by natural right because they had been bred in him by Jewish tradition. He concluded from this that the industrial worker, liberated from the capitalist's mill, would display the same qualities of leadership. Besides, had not the bourgeoisie, breaking out of the rusty shackles of feudalism, known very well how to govern and to administer their affairs in their own interest? This was the second of Marx's fallacies. The fault of the analogy lay in the fact that the bourgeoisie, before they took over officially, had been already a well-educated group, with plenty of experience of handling property and of discharging public responsibility, who produced many able and intelligent men and accomplished some permanent reforms before the rapacities they were unleashing began to gobble up everything else. The proletariat, in so far as it approximated to the impoverished and abject state to which Marx thought it would have to be reduced before it could rebel effectively, was as unfitted for the enlightened statesmanship of which the great bourgeois leaders had been capable before the era of careerism swamped them as they were for the lawgiving and vision of the great Jewish radical prophets. Marx and Engels might have been warned by the contemptuous tone into which they themselves often fell in writing to one another about working-class leaders and movements, that the proletarian dictatorship, when it came, would not be of a kind to please them.

It was true that they had been reluctant to contemplate the possibility that the proletarian revolution might first occur in Russia, because they thought the Russians irresponsible and given to overdoing things and did not consider the country industrialised enough to make a socialist economy possible. But their disciples Lenin and Trotsky dreamt of a socialist Russia and willed it and partly brought it about. What they did not foresee any more than Marx was that what happens, when you let down the bars, is that a lot of gross and ignorant people who have been condemned to mean destinies before go rushing for all they are worth after things that they can eat, drink, sleep on, ride in, preside at and amuse themselves with. It may seem that the Soviet bureaucrats who have flourished under Stalin's regime differ greatly from the American millionaires of the big post-Civil War monopolies; but the principle that has produced them is the same: in Russia, though the opportunities for money-making are limited compared with what ours have been, the relative inequalities of privilege and pay are enormous; and the arrogant official in his car, surrounded by his bodyguard, would have been as repugnant to Lenin, with his schoolmaster discipline and addiction to study and his belief that the formalities of government, which bored him, could easily be attended to in the off-moments of serious people occupied with higher things, as the publicity-inflated tycoon would have been to Jefferson, with his ideal of the cultivated country gentleman and his aversion to industrial inventions. Both are single-minded remorseless careerists who do not realise that human beings can want anything but power and possessions. The only difference is that Stalin's machine is a gang that has to work together whereas the American millionaires were usually out each for himself.

Napoleon paid lip-service to the Revolution till he no longer needed its supporters; the American Chamber of Commerce speaks with respect of the Founding Fathers; Stalin, on appropriate occasions, still invokes the name of Lenin at the same time that he is allowing himself to be glorified in the role of Ivan the Terrible. The Nazis in Germany were not the heirs of any revolutionary tradition but careerists of the lower middle class, who, due to the bankruptcy of the feudal order and the continued degradation of Germany imposed by the Treaty of Versailles, found themselves at last with a fair field and a free hand—they exploited the prestige of socialism, so largely German in origin, by appealing to the German masses in the interest of a "National Socialism." Like Napoleon, Hitler gratified the hungers of a base but brazen little man by a series of megalomaniac conquests, which—not being founded on anything better than "reeking tube and iron shard"—have not lasted any longer than Napoleon's. Like Stalin, he drove into exile, imprisoned or put to death everyone whose brains or ideals were of a higher grade than his own. It has always been a feature of the careerist regime to suppress systematically that enlightenment which the pre-revolutionary reformers have aimed to cherish and spread. The censorship of Napoleon was less complete than that of Hitler or Stalin, but in its time it was a serious enough nuisance; and though we in the United States, between, say, 1870 and 1910, did not have a literal burning of books, we had a discouragement of non-commercial and non-genteel ideas which made it difficult for unorthodox writers to get read or even printed and sometimes reduced our most important thinkers to the status of nonentities or outlaws, as well as a hostility to aesthetic interests, which drove many of our artists to Europe, where they were almost as much refugees as those who have recently come to us from there.

In England it has worked somewhat differently. Here the structure of the feudal caste system, though modified, has been long maintained by absorbing into the "governing class," that unique English institution, as many as possible of the able people who have come up from the lower strata. There are of course in England, too, a certain number of highly successful careerists who have not been influenced by the discipline and style that characterise this governing class; but they have never had quite the same sort of field-day that they have had in the Soviet Union and in the United States. As long as the Crown is at the top of the hierarchy, the rich brewer or newspaper owner may always be tempted to buy a title or have his daughter presented at court, and as long as the public schools and universities are nurseries for most places of distinction, he is likely to want to send his sons there. The British system has thus preserved certain ideals of devotion to the State and of disinterested intellectual activity that during the later part of the nineteenth century were pretty well obliterated in the United States, and the second of which, the free play of intellect, went up in a holocaust in Hitler's Germany and Stalin's Russia, while the first, the devotion to the public service, appeared in a fanatical or a sordid form which had nothing in common with the tact, the common sense and the careful study that had been brought to it through centuries in England. Yet this system, in adhering to the feudal mould, has cramped the natural development of society and delayed the democratisation—or rather equalisation—of England in such a way that when it finally arrives, it may produce merely a dreary mediocrity of groups that have been too long kept under and not allowed to find their own way to self-improvement through the scramble for money and power. This we *have* been able to do in America, and my optimistic opinion is that the United States at the present time is politically more advanced than any other part of the world, because we have been through the worst of the careerist phase and are coming out on the other side. We have seen in the last fifty years a revival of the democratic creativeness which presided at the birth of the Republic and flourished up through the Civil War. This began to assert itself strongly during the first two decades of the century, was stimulated by the depression that followed the blowing-up of the Stock Market, and culminated in the New Deal. It was accompanied by a remarkable renascence of American arts and letters.

This phase seems now to have run its course, and I do not know what is coming next; but I doubt whether it is possible to-day for us either to relapse in our traditional way into one of those periods of industrial gourmandising and speculative inflation that have usually followed reform administrations or, in an effort to meet the need for government control of industry, without which modern life is impossible, to reproduce Hitler's brutality or Stalin's bureaucratic nightmare. Our careerism will crop up again, after war service and wartime socialism; but the old kind will be curbed by the demands of labour and the rudiments of community conscience, and we may hope that the new kind, which offers its prizes to labour officials and government clerks rather than to the "captains of industry," will be redeemed by our relatively high standards of security and education.

Democratic Socialism: I do not feel, as some people do, that socialism has been discredited by what has happened in Russia or that socialism is incompatible with democracy. The only thing that can make democracy real is the ability on the part of a people to distribute responsibility; and this ability the Russians have never possessed. An American travelling in Russia a few years before the war was amazed to find in Soviet officialdom exactly the same characteristics of timidity, evasiveness and inaction that one reads about in Herzen's memoirs as prevailing in the reign of Nicholas I. One realised that in the United States the pettiest position of authority involved a sphere, however limited, in which the individual must think and act for himself. The bank teller must decide for himself whether or not your cheque is good, the ticket-seller at the railroad station must be able to proceed unfalteringly in making out however long a ticket—whereas in Russia he immediately appealed to the official just above him, and this official appealed to another. The result of this method in Russia has been that, in order to get anything done, they have had to train a new race of officials who *would* take responsibility and have thus produced the Communist Party, a special élite caste who aimed to be energetic and conscientious and to see that what was supposed to be done got done. Anyone who has ever been stranded in a Russian provincial town and rescued by the local G.P.U. man or ill in a Russian hospital and helpless to get any steps taken about anything save by going to the Communist director or the Communist head nurse, is able to understand perfectly how this state of things has come about. (The Germans, in a similar way, delivered themselves up to Hitler by their incapacity for individual action: they are more practical and systematic then the Russians, but they seem to be able to function only as units in an organisational hierarchy, with the orders coming down from the top). It is thus not merely socialism which has created Stalin or even Stalin who has created himself, but the Russians who, by default of self-dependence, have allowed him to become their tyrant. In the Soviet Union they have passed the buck till it has become the exclusive possession of a dictator and his gang, and Comrade Stalin is soon Generalissimo Stalin and the only candidate at every election, while the Soviets—which were supposed to be popular councils—soon took counsel from the only one source. You cannot expect a people who have always been used to a despotism to produce democratic institutions simply because the power has been shifted to a different class. The Russians still wanted—it had been a part of their religion—the authority of a great earthly father; and Stalin, the political careerist, with those who had a stake in his career and cared nothing about Lenin's socialism, were glad to gratify them in this department.

But we in the United States have had a training in individual self-dependence. We have got along remarkably well in balancing government control between the state and the federal authorities, and our more of less efficient public services such as the school system and the post office have comparatively rarely lent themselves to serious bureaucratic abuses. Why should not socialised American industries and socialised American institutions be handled by their own staffs in equilibrium with the central authorities instead of becoming enslaved by these? And if we don't like our socialist president, why can we not always refuse to re-elect him?

Better Human Beings: I am beginning to suspect, however, that socialism will not simply go on to its goal of making everybody healthy and happy, but will presently change its object to that of turning out better human beings. In Naples, I had been thinking that such people as the gutter-bred swarming Neapolitans should not be allowed to exist, and that the greatest crime of the Catholic Church, and one of the greatest social crimes possible, was to forbid the use of contraceptives; but, home in New York, I was forced to admit that such people as most of the New Yorkers, pale and high-pressured and under-developed, ought not to exist either. The Neapolitans had at least one advantage over them: they were cheerful and able to sing. It may be that these big modern cities are only good to be bombed and destroyed. The respect for human life in itself has, in any case, largely disappeared in the course of this last war, and I doubt whether enough now survives to inspire the organisers of socialism to try to keep everybody alive and see that everybody gets an equal chance. The ideal of equality on a low social level is probably an impossible one, anyway. The only thing, among human beings, that really arouses enthusiasm to the point of effective action

is the idea of excelling or making other people excel. Better hygiene
and better training will certainly improve the race, but we shall not
find this enough. We shall want to *breed* better people, and it is
unlikely that, in our kind of society, we shall return in any very
intensive way to the old aristocratic method of limiting sexual
selection to the members of the families. We shall rather be coming
to apply every device of physical stimulant and mental suggestion,
resorting to the techniques of biology, psychology, glandular
science and who knows what other methods, in the attempt to produce men and women who are longer-lived or taller and stronger or
more intellectual and skilful. People may at first be invited to
volunteer for such experiments, but it is certain that, once better-
equipped people have really been produced, they will take their
place at the top, and it is likely that they will discourage the reproduc-
tion of people of inferior stock. We may even eventually have
conflicts between the people of different artificial breeds or between
different countries or groups who want to breed different kinds of
people. This suggestion sometimes rouses the objection that it would
be dangerous to give powers of biological control to any mere
committee of human beings; but if we accept without question a
Board of Health, I do not see why we should refuse in time to accept
a Board of Breeding. The worst kind of thing that can happen in the
attempt to improve the breed was demonstrated by the Nazis with
their mythical Aryan race, their snuffing-out of the insane and the ill,
and their mass incinerations of kinds of people whom they regarded
as not up to themselves; but it would be just foolish to allow this to
discourage us with eugenics as it would be to give up the practice of
medicine on account of the horrible acts perpetrated by the Nazi
doctors. If we can produce, from some cousin of the jackal and the
wolf, the dachshund and the Great Dane, the Pekinese and the
poodle, what should we not be able to do with man?

The Anthropoids: I have found it strangely reassuring to read,
during the years of the war, the current books about the anthropoid
apes. The status of these animals is changing. T. H. Huxley in the
last century had already taken account of the fact that the great apes
were much closer to men than they were to any species of monkey.
Like us, they have shed their tails and, like us, they walk erect. But
the age that linked man with the apes also tended to make a sharp
distinction between what were called the "animals" and the "human
race." The creature that talked about his "soul" and considered that
soul "divine" was frightened by the idea of kinship with creatures

that could not pronounce words, that were hairer than we and that lived in trees; and even non-religious people in that period of top-hats, straight trousers, trimmed beards and rolled umbrellas, with its background of locomotives and factories, snubbed the anthropoids like country relations. Their doings did not seem compatible with the capitalised abstractions of Empire and Progress in terms of which human beings were still able to think of their own activities. But in our age of mass stultification, wholesale destruction of human works and mechanised civilian massacre, the anthropologist can no longer afford to be snobbish about the anthropoids. Doctrines like those of the American "Humanists" or of Huxley's grandson Aldous that continue to draw a definite line between human and animal kind, or between a part of our nature which is supposed to be human and a part which is supposed to be animal, seem as quaint as the medical analysis which accounted for the human passions by ascribing them to the action of four "humours." As humanity has been shedding its religions and discrediting its political myths, as it has been demonstrating its closeness to the brute and making its pretensions to divine origin ridiculous, the higher apes have been taking on an aspect more human and "civilised." The anthropoids are treated in captivity with much more consideration than formerly. The apes in old-fashioned zoos were prisoners that lived in squalor and that deteriorated like the inmates of human jails; but the anthropoids in the Yerkes laboratory are cared for and instructed and made friends with almost as if they were human children, and the result is that they display abilities hardly suspected a century ago, and our picture of them has changed completely. They use tools, we now know; they are able to talk to one another and they more or less understand what we say; they have a family and tribal life which is evidently not very much different from that of primitive human beings. They seem to penetrate situations with what we describe as "insight"; they seem to do what we call " reason"; and the most sympathetic observers believe that they have been able to discover in them the beginnings of the moral and the aesthetic senses. It has even been suggested by Gertrude Lintz, the former owner of the gorilla Gargantua, who has kept and studied apes for years, that chimpanzees—which can be taught to sew—might be trained to do the work of mechanics.

These apes help us to face in a more agreeable way than by contemplating the ruins of Europe the fact that man is himself an animal, not so very far in advance of the anthropoids, and that his problem is to recognise this and the conditions under which he may develop. It is at the same time a relief and a stimulus to read the results of the researches of the scientists who have been working on the anthropoids. These beasts are much cleverer than we realised and more like us in their social habits; but, instead of having the effect of appearing to degrade human beings, this enables us to relegate to a more rudimentary level a good deal of human activity—sexual, political, economic—that may have seemed to us to have been a part of what we call "civilisation," and to understand the relative crudity—relative, that is, in relation to the last century's godlike idea of itself—of the materials with which we have to work. "If," says Mr. Robert M. Yerkes of the Yale Institute of Psychology, one of the foremost authorities in this field, "as servant of science the chimpanzee should help to make clearer and more attractive to mankind (by exhibiting its susceptibility to training) ways for the achievement of greater social-mindedness, dependability and co-operativeness, how immeasurable our debt to it! The really important things for us at present are recognition and active acceptance of the principles of modifiability, controllability and consequent improvability of human nature."

*   *   *

One of the most fortifying experiences of my trip was a visit to Norman Kemp Smith, under whom I had sat at Princeton, where for a time he was professor of philosophy, and who afterwards held for twenty-five years the chair of logic and metaphysics at Edinburgh University. I found him living alone. His wife had died since I had seen him last, and his daughter had married and gone to India. His family were an old Scotch housekeeper, an old black spaniel and a homeless cat who had come one day to live with them. In compliance with the government's request to avoid unnecessary travelling, he had spent the whole war in Edinburgh. He greeted me with his usual impassivity, as if he had seen me that morning in class, and entertained me with his old cordiality. He was over seventy now and had reached the age of retirement; but he was still amazingly active. The night that I arrived he had just got out of bed from a fairly serious attack of grippe, but he took me out in the damp Scotch weather for a brisk and rather strenuous walk which involved a good deal of hill-climbing and clambering over stone fences, while he explained to me the topography of Edinburgh and the various historical landmarks. He had all of his old lively interest in literature, science, ideas and news—in everything men were doing. Philosophy had always meant for him everything that men had thought.

In the morning we had breakfast together, and he insisted on my eating the porridge in the traditional Scottish way: you had to take with each spoonful of porridge a spoonful of cold milk—which he said brought the flavour out better. Then we would retire to work, and the housekeeper brought tea at 11. In the afternoon people dropped in, or we would do something in the city, to which he was a wonderful guide. He seemed to know every street and took me to see a variety of people in the sombre and august old houses. I remember one man especially, who wanted to talk about nothing but Greek. He came from the country and had had few "advantages," but had made himself a formidable scholar. He now lived retired and alone, in shabby high-ceilinged rooms, and devoted himself to Plato. I had met C. M. Bowra in London and introduced his name, but Kemp Smith's friend was positively shocked at Bowra's recent interest in Russian, as it if were a treason to Greek, and said sharply that the understanding of a single Greek writer like Plato made such demands on the reader that one's whole life was not enough to exhaust him. In the evening, if there was no one to dinner, we sat and talked in front of the fire, which, on account of the shortage of coal, could only be lighted at the times when there was somebody in the room. The house would grow cold around us. He would always send me to bed with a handful of things to read, of which I particularly remember a report written down by Boswell after an interview with David Hume. Hume was a great favourite of Kemp Smith's— he had lately done a book about him; and he said that he thought this dialogue showed both Boswell and Hume at their best: Boswell in his portraiture of Hume and Hume in his dry refusal to yield anything to Boswell's almost tearful plea for the immortality of the soul. I remembered how Kemp Smith had once told us at college that if you did not believe in immortality, you ought not to allow yourself to be convinced by the death of a favourite daughter.

One day I remarked that the immediate future seemed to me extremely depressing, and he vigorously took me up, declaring that he thought it looked hopeful. When I asked him how he could possibly think this, he replied: "People's complacency's shaken." A lot of ground had been cleared, he felt; we knew what elements we had to deal with and we should have to come to grips with our problems. A constructive age might well ensue. He often made fun of the theologies and churches; but when I said that I thought it was time to get rid of the word *God*, since we had "no need of that hypothesis" to account for the life that was in us and the coherence of the universe, he said, "I don't know any better word." He was of an older generation than I and had, I suppose, in Scotland, had a more rigorous religious training. For myself, I am extremely reluctant to call anything whatever "God," for the word has too many connotations of obsolete and miraculous mythologies; and what Kemp Smith called God was, I thought, something mainly identifiable with a vigorous physical persistence, a rectitude in relation to others and to one's own work in the world, and a faith in the endurance of the human mind.

APPENDIX A

W HEN this chapter first appeared in the *New Yorker*, I received an interesting letter from Mr. W. Hawks of Worthing, Sussex, England, which throws some further light on the situation I tried to describe. He has given me permission to quote it here.

I spent ten years in America before the war and I'm half-British and half-American by birth. Like you, I deplored the lack of friendship between the U.S. and British troops. I have set down some reasons to account for this from the British point of view. Many of them apply particularly to those who were in the Mediterranean campaign. Most of them are unfair.

1. That the G.I.'s were having a whale of a time with the girls in England while the British were doing the early fighting in the desert.

2. That the Americans were playing the same game as in the last war—collect the money and capture the British trade, then come in time for the victory parade.

3. No troops like other bodies of troops, English, American or any other nationality. (If you want to enjoy yourself, it's best to be the only unit in town). "Americans no business in Greece—look what they said in the papers," etc.

4. The British troops imagined in Italy that the Americans were all "base wallahs." (A fighting division seldom sees any other division when it is in the line, and it is only when they come out for a rest that they meet other formations.) "There's a hundred men in Naples for one Yank in the line," etc.

5. It was argued that if everyone was putting everything into the pot, the Americans were using up too much war effort on their own comfort. For example, unlimited supplies of clothes and food, "a jeep for every private," particularly in the rear areas, when the British couldn't get them for use in the forward areas. This partly answers your comment *re* the lack of lifts to U.S. troops by British drivers.

6. And the old ones—that the Yanks had too much money, that they didn't know how to drink and that they made too much noise.

I'm afraid that ideas such as the above are firmly fixed in the minds of even the supposedly better-educated British soldiers. I also found that the members of an officers' mess were not interested in hearing about America, although they would condescend to read my American magazines. Of course, they cried out in scorn at those dreadful advertisements of G.I. Joes making Walt Whitman speeches on the beach just after landing, but they didn't care to be told that American soldiers also became slightly sick when they read them.

I was with a field artillery regiment. We were due for a rest after a long spell in Italy when the Greek business turned up. We went to Greece expecting an unpleasant "Black and Tan" job for the rest of the war. As far as we could gather, in the early stages, we were breaking up a riot. I saw a few examples of what the "rebels" had done. It was sufficient to make me feel, at the time, that we were on the right side. At the end of my eight months in Greece I had given up all hope of ever finding out which side was which. . . .

Entertainment in a British mess is liable to be about as gay as a church supper. One thing you must remember is that in the regular army the junior officers don't speak unless they are spoken to This goes on for years apparently, although there are occasional lapses when everyone gets stinking drunk, clothes are torn off and drink is thrown. It is talked about for some time afterwards.

You probably did something dreadful in taking a woman into that mess. If you had taken twenty, you would have been more popular.

APPENDIX B

SINCE my view of the Greek situation seems not very widely held, I am glad to be able to quote in support of it (from *Partisan Picture* by Basil Davidson) a letter to the London *Times* of February 24, 1946, by Captain Francis Noel-Baker, M.P., who, says Mr. Davidson, "had been closely associated with Greek affairs during the war and spoke from long experience of Greece."

From 1942 onwards it was difficult to detect either objectivity or consistency in British policy towards Greece, and I believe that I am not alone in thinking that that policy was one of the causes of the civil war in which it culminated. In my view, two cardinal mistakes were made. First, ignoring the popular reaction against the pre-war Fascist dictatorship and against King George for his part in installing and maintaining that dictatorship, the British Government persisted right until the eve of liberation, in "hoping" (and working) for a royal restoration. Second, in their fear of the left wing (which in Greece, as elsewhere in Europe, was the core of the resistance movement), the British authorities did nothing to encourage "moderates" to join E.A.M. in the early days when it was not yet Communist-dominated, but, on the contrary, tried to create a "counterbalance" by building up "nationalist" groups of E.A.M.'s extreme political opponents. The tragedy of this policy was that it produced precisely that situation which it sought most desperately to avoid. Baffled and exasperated by British manoeuvers, E.A.M. became more extremist, more Communist and eventually violently anti-British; whereas our "national" bulwark soon collapsed.

APPENDIX C

ANOTHER favourable Greek view of England is to be found in the following poem composed in Greek and translated by the poet.

TO MOST ADORED GREAT BRITAIN

A Hymn

How I admire and wonder thee
o! great Britain country!
as I consider thee holding
the bridles of all the world.

O respectable and glorious
and powerful England
thou art the joy of all the world
and the alone liberty.

Thou art the judge of the world
and police captain for all
and the greatest supporter
of all the weak persons.

According to thy somuch gold
thou art the richest on world
and thy paper money also
has the superior price.

But thou hast and most treasors
by much precious stones,
thou hast too and most flaming pearls
and legendary prices.

In this earth situation
thou hast the superior
and thou doest live the excellent
and much sweetest life.

Thou got many colossal ships
possessions and colonies
and abundant richness and goods
and very solid houses.

(it follows)